To parents, with love

Practical Pointers for Family Success

Darla Hanks   **Arlene Bascom**

Illustrated by Carol Jeanne Ehlers

INTERNATIONAL STANDARD BOOK NUMBER
0-88290-090-0

Printed in the
United States of America
by

**Horizon Publishers
& Distributors
P.O. Box 490
50 South 500 West
Bountiful, Utah 84010**

This book is dedicated with love

To our husbands, Gary and Lynn,

To our two special families,

And to all families who desire

to learn and progress together.

Acknowledgement

Special thanks to—

Our families who gave us the experience, motivation, support and help to make it all possible.

Mom and Dad, who gave us encouragement all along the way.

Zenda Rowley, Lou Jean and Ruth Butler, and Harold and Louise Little, who opened their homes to us when we needed a place to work without interruption.

Clyda Blackburn, Bob and Carolyn Larsen, LaDawn Jacob, Lynn Hanks, Alton and Alyse Sigman, and Lola Jensen, who read parts of the manuscript and offered helpful criticism and suggestions.

The study group, consisting of Art and Sandy Robbins, Lee and Doreen McQuivey, Larry and Barbara Lawlor, John and Michelle Green, and Willis and Lynnette Brimhall, who met and helped clarify ideas and subject matter for the book.

Shirley Begay and Karen Olsen, for their help in typing the manuscript.

Carol Jeanne Ehlers who, on short notice, willingly and capably created the illustrations to enhance this book.

All the special families we interviewed, who freely and enthusiastically shared their ideas and experiences, and all others who contributed by giving us permission to quote them.

Duane and Jean Crowther, of Horizon Publishers, who successfully used the principle of stewardship to encourage, advise and inspire us; who on small evidence believed in our ability to write this book even before we believed. Without their vision and insight this book would have remained a dream.

Introduction

This book had its beginning because of the telephone. We are two sisters who often talked on the phone about the frustrations and challenges of character-building and child-raising in an LDS setting. Basically, we knew what we "should do," but we were often uncertain about how to apply gospel principles to family life.

We talked to other parents. We studied and went to classes, looking for answers and down-to-earth ways to take the abstract ideals and shape them into solid realities. Slowly, we began to see progress, which came at first mainly from trying to follow the good examples and ideals of special parents we knew. Progress is most exciting when you share it, and since we both love to write, during our frequent phone conversations we often said "That should be in a book!"

We eventually began to recognize the real possibility of writing a book which would share the successes of many parents; but we originally thought of researching the lives of great parents in church history for most of our information. However, when we approached Duane and Jean Crowther with this idea, they suggested that contemporary parents might offer even more relevant and helpful material! That viewpoint immediately rang true with us— after all, hadn't we learned the most from our observations of other parents who were succeeding? We had often wished for a way to look inside good LDS homes to see "how other parents do it." That concept expanded into the premise of this book, and proved the motivation for nearly a hundred interviews which we conducted with progressive, and creative families who shared their ideas and real-life experiences.

Most of the "authorities" we quote are not famous names you will recognize, but parents like you, who gained their expertise from the actual experience of raising children. They did not necessarily do research or earn advanced degrees—although some parents we quote have all these qualifications. These parents shared their successes, hoping they could inspire and help others. Many of those we interviewed asked that we mention that they have their bad days too. They didn't want our readers to assume that they *always* do the things they told us about, or that their creative or "second mile" activities are easy and consistently turn out the way they are planned. Even the most conscientious parents have times when everything goes wrong! But it wouldn't be inspiring or helpful to focus only on problems or failures, so the stories we tell and the examples we give are usually about people's best days and best ideas. It does seem evident that successful parents are not those who never have problems, but ones who keep working and trying until they find solutions.

The principle of eternal progression makes it clear that we should be eternally involved in improving. Effort to improve needn't be considered grim, however, for progress itself is pleasant—it is one of life's basic satisfactions. Moving forward in the right direction (one step at a time) makes life exciting and daily efforts worthwhile. Making progress and building family strength, rather than becoming the "ideal family" will be our major concern, for we believe that family progress is family success!

No matter how well-motivated and sincere any of us may be, it is unlikely that we could (or would want to) put into practice all of the ideas presented in this book. It is our hope that each family will choose those ideas they feel are the most needed in their family situations and adapt them to fit their own personalities.

We sincerely hope this book will become a resource book— one you return to time and again for practical pointers and specific how-to's concerning the challenging job of raising a family and helping them learn to love and live the gospel.

Table of Contents

Acknowledgements vi
Introduction. vii
Table of Contents ix

1. **Especially for Fathers : Making Your Influence Felt** 17
    Making Family Time Prime Time 19
    Does the Family Come First? 21
    Show Them They Count 22
    Be a Guide and a Counselor, as Well as a Pal 24
    "How To's" for Interviewing Your Children 24
    Working and Playing Together 25
    Be Cautious of Criticism 26
    Spiritual Leadership 28
    Bless Your Family with Father's Blessings 28
    You Give What You Are. 30
    Ten Things to Try. 31

2. **Especially for Mothers** 33
    Spiritual Price of Progress 35
    Priorities for Productive Living 36
    Be Your Best to Give Your Best 37
    Keeping a Home in Its Place 40
    Love, Strengthen and Support Your Children's Father! . 41
    Perspective: the Best is Yet to Come. 42
    Ten Things to Try. 43

3. **Love, the Heart of a Happy Home** 45
    Love Can Make the Difference! 47
    Love Communication Skills 48
    Love is an Action Word 50
    Love Me because I'm Me! 55
    Legacy of Love. 56
    You Can Learn to be More Loving 57
    Ten Things to Try. 58

4. **"Your Child's Self-Esteem is Showing!"** 61
    Give Them Positive Labels for Positive Impact 62
    Tell Them Their Strong Points 64

Make Small Emergencies a "Family Affair" 65
One-To-One Time Says: "You Are Important" 65
Make Time with Each Child "Special Time" 66
Share Your Skills with Them 68
Real Life "Practices" Increase Confidence 69
Help Them See They Can Make a Difference 71
"Show and Tell Them Who They Are" 73
Ten Things to Try 74

5. Prayers and Promptings 77
"And They Shall Also Teach Their Children to Pray..." . 78
"...And They Will Not Depart from It" 81
"Behold, the Lord Hath Heard the Prayers
  of Thy Father" 82
"Pray in Your Families Unto the Father" 83
"A Sure Guide" 84
"Your Bosom Shall Burn Within You" 85
"I Will Tell You in Your Mind and in Your Heart" 86
"Thy Will Be Done" 87
"Having Been Warned of the Lord" 88
"Your Diligence, Perseverance, Patience and Works" .. 89
Ten Things to Try 90

6. Helping Children Love and Use the Scriptures 93
Medicine or a Meal? 94
Making Scripture Time Family Time 95
It's Never Too Soon to Begin 96
Make Scriptures Meaningful 97
Unexpected Blessings 98
Introduce the Scriptures Creatively! 99
The Good Samaritan Could Be Me! 100
"Our" Scriptures—Not "the" Scriptures 101
Tapes and Records Can Be Storytellers 104
Scripture Games to Liven Up Learning 105
Ten Things to Try 107

7. Family Traditions Can Teach Values 109
Cotton Candy Traditions or Lasting Memories? 110
Sundays to Look Forward to! 111
Focus on the Family Home Evening Tradition 112
Sharing the Home Evening Spotlight 114
Adapt the Program to the Need 115
Get Away Together 117

Traditions Can Make Any Day Memorable 119
Early Morning Traditions 120
Pick a Bouquet of Birthday Traditions 120
It's Never Too Late to Make Traditions 122
Ten Things to Try. 123

8. **Traditions Make Holidays Special**. 125
Adding More Thanks to Thanksgiving Traditions 126
Food Adds Flavor to Traditions. 128
Christmas: Great Time for Traditions!. 128
Family Fun and Service 130
Bringing the Married Children Home 131
Let Them Feel the Joy. 132
Countdown to Christmas 135
Now for the Fun and Action! 135
Ten Things to Try. 137

9. **"It's Time to Master Time"** 139
For Priorities Sake—Keep Track of Your Minutes. 141
Time-Use Keys from a Mother of Ten 142
Twice the Mileage from Your Minutes 145
Snatch the Value from Snatches of Time 146
Miscellaneous Time Management Tips 147
One More Tip 150
Time-Management Can Be Child's Play 151
"Work Before Play" is What We Say 151
Clock Work Can Be Fun! 151
Who's Afraid of the Big, Bad Clock?. 152
You Can Do It! 152
Ten Things to Try. 152
Epilogue 153

10. **Parents Can Be Practically Positive!** 155
The Positive Approach Defined .156
Why Be Positive? Because It's Practical!. 156
Give Your Children a "Happiness Insurance Policy" . . .157
The Leaven of Learning. 159
Experiences Are Teachers Too .161
Control the Context. 162
Harness the Horses and Hold the Reins. 164
Make it Easier for Them to Behave! 165
The Positive Approach to Children and Church. 166

Spiritual Implications 167
Ten Things to Try 167

11. Building Faith and Overcoming Discouragement 169
Teaching Moments Matter 170
Building Faith by Sharing Faith 172
Focusing our Faith 173
The Dangers of Discouragement 176
How To's for Overcoming Discouragement 177
Live the Law—Reap the Blessings 181
Nourish the Word 183
Ten Things to Try 184

12. Making Greatness the Goal 187
Heroes Children Can Follow to Heaven 188
The Greatness of Early Church Leaders 189
The Powerful Lives of Modern Prophets 190
The Good Example of Church Leaders and Teachers . . .191
Pointing Out the Path of Greatness 191
Read About Them, Walk with Them 193
Great Branches on Your Family Tree 194
Very, Very Human Heroes 196
Good Examples from Living Relatives 196
Heroes Are Homemade 197
Ten Things to Try 198

13. Preparing for a Mission: Ways Parents Can Help 201
Guiding Them to the Goal 202
Effective Missionary Work Begins at Home 203
A Diller, a Dollar 204
Healthy is Happy! 204
Social Skills Bring Security 205
"The Lord Thy God Shall Lead Thee by the Hand" 206
"For in Them Ye Have Eternal Life" 207
Miscellaneous Preparation and Motivation Ideas 208
Ten Things to Try 210

14. Teaching Chastity in a Framework of Reverence 211
The Plan 212
Putting the Plan Into Action 213
Making the "Date" 213
The Presentation 214
Build the Foundation 215
Explain the Lord's Plan 215

Demonstrate Family Love and Unity 216
The Script 217
Script for a Girl's Book 217
Script for a Boy's Book 221

15. Taking the Drudgery Out of Discipline 227
The Golden Thread of Respect 228
Clear Instructions Clear the Air 229
Thou Shalt Nots Aren't Negative .230
The Long and Short of Expectations. 231
Expect Reasonable Behavior 232
Fewer Words, Greater Influence .233
The Far-Reaching Effects of Expectations 234
Routine: One of Discipline's Best Friends 235
A New Definition of Consistency 236
Fish Swim, Birds Fly, and People Feel 236
Correct with Respect 237
"Catch Them Doing Right". 238
I Want to be Free! 239
Consider Consequences 242
Discipline and Relationships 243
Ten Things to Try. 244

16. The Chore and the Challenge 247
The Younger the Better to Make Helping a Habit 249
It's our Home—So It's our Work Too! 250
Pick a Plan to Fit Your Needs 251
Check Up on Chores with Charts. 254
Hustle Not Hassle 255
Work Has Its Own Rewards 256
Give Them a Broader View 257
More Motivations to Keep Them Moving 258
Give Children a Choice 259
To Pay or Not to Pay? 260
Ten Things to Try. 263

17. Skills for Turning Mountains Into Molehills 265
Learn to Foresee and Prevent 266
Listen, Listen! 267
Keep Them Talking 268
The Right Time for a Parent to Talk 270
How to Help Them Seek Solutions 271
Problem Solving Pointers. 272

Humor Helps 274
When Your Kids are in Conflict 274
Two Together Seeking Solutions 277
Problem Solving as a Family Affair. 277
The Spiritual Center of Problem Solving 279
Ten Things to Try. 280

18. **Happily Ever After?** 283
Making Marriage Work Takes Work! 285
Mutual Agreement to Change 285
Marriage is Not a Reform School! 286
Acquire the Acceptance Attitude 287
The Only One You Can Change is Yourself 288
Different Roles, Different Needs 289
The Need for Appreciation and Admiration 290
"Wives Submit Yourselves Unto Your Own Husbands" .291
Spiritual Leadership in Action 291
Financial Leadership 292
Get Away Together 293
Communicating and Co-operating 294
Ten Things to Try. 295

19. **Get Ready, Goal-Set and Go!** 297
We Could All Use a "Goal Rush" 298
Five Steps to Reach Your Goals 299
"The Goal Mine" 300
Getting Together to Set Goals 300
Organizing to Reach Family Goals 302
New Goals for the New Year 303
Summer Specials 303
Guide Children to Personal Goals 304
Satisfaction or Regret? 306
Ten Things to Try. 307

20. **Growing Toward Our Goals** 309
Habit Can Offer a Helping Hand 311
One Step at a Time: Where to Start 311
'Try On' Free Agency. 312
'Put Off' Procrastination. 313
Pinpoint the Need to Change. 314
Be Willing to Pay the Price. 315
Get the Point of Perspective 317
'See' a New Self 317

Set the Pattern 318
Give Creative Motivations! 319
Chart Their Progress! 320
Principles, Patience and Progress 321
Ten Things to Try 322

21. **Spiritual Signposts** 325
Signpost Number One: Create a
  Spiritual Atmosphere 326
Signpost Number Two: Maintain a Spiritual
  Attitude 328
Signpost Number Three: Put Spirituality
  Into Action 330
Summary Findings 333

THE BASCOM FAMILY:
(front, left to right) Holly, Julie, Gary, Arlene, Michael.
(back) David, Janalee, Loree, Robert.

THE HANKS FAMILY:
(left to right) Mark, Benajamin, Lynn, David, Darla, Brian.
A fifth son, Scott, was born as the book went to press.

1

Especially for Fathers: Making your Influence Felt

One January afternoon, after an absence of three-and-a-half months, daddy came home! His two sons, Brian (age one), and Mark (who was two-and-a-half), were more curious than friendly. When Lynn first held them, they both leaned way back and studied his face as if they were thinking, "Haven't I seen you somewhere before?" Later that evening, after a contented hour watching the children play, Lynn said, "Mark, it's time to pick up your toys." Mark looked at his dad with a puzzled expression. Then he said, "Mama, do I have to do what that man tells me?"

Lynn was taken completely by surprise. Did his own son think of him as "that man?" Lynn Hanks was a pilot doing oil and mineral survey work, and had been away from home a great deal. He loved flying; it was his great joy in life, and had been center stage in his training, thoughts, and ambitions since he was a teenager. Unfortunately, his employment involved traveling a majority of the time.

As Lynn thought about his son's statement, he remembered a conversation he had had with Paul H. Dunn several years before when he was faced with an employment choice. He could see the twinkle in Elder Dunn's eyes when he leaned back in his chair and said something like, "Well, Lynn, I can't tell you what to do. But I do know that in my own life the thing that becomes increasingly important to me is to be able to go home at night to my wife and kids. That's what seems to mean the most to me."

Lynn quit flying. He made the very difficult decision to leave his chosen career in order to be available to fix broken toys, help make model airplanes, wrestle with his boys every Monday after family home evening, and hear those delighted shouts when he opens the door each night—"Daddy's home! Daddy's home!"

When daddy comes home, regardless of where he has been, he comes to the place where he matters most. At home there is no substitute for father. George S. Durrant said, "When Dad leaves home, he's missed. And until he returns, there will be an empty, unfilled space in the hearts of his family. It is undeniable. A man's greatest contribution is made in his home with his family. Let us, therefore, be fathers first and everything else second."

One father of eleven children had many outside demands on his time. He was called to be bishop when his oldest son was eleven years old, and for the next seven years was gone a great deal. He said, "During those years I spent very little time with my children. When my son reached his late teens he turned against the Church, saying, 'The Church took my Dad away from me!' Our relationship was strained to the point that when we entered the same room, sparks would fly. It took long months of struggle and prayer and intense effort to rebuild our relationship. When I saw what my neglect had done to my oldest son, I began to consider time with my children as high priority time. I realized that even if I was bishop, no boy in the ward was more important to me than my own son, and he should have as much or more consideration and time from me as any other boy."

One bishop told us that he schedules family time first, then if a conflict does arise (unless it's an emergency) he says, "I'm sorry, but I have another commitment." And he keeps his commitment to his family. He says, "If *we* don't schedule my time, other people will, and I become a victim of the here and now; just taking care of the problems of the moment and never getting any time with my own family."

Elvin Christiansen tells how one of his children helped him realize he had been giving too much of his time to a good, but not central value in his life. He said, "I remember when I was the Scoutmaster and was spending a lot of time with the Scouts. (It was before my own boys were scouting age.) One day, as I was leaving to go with the Scouts, one of my children asked, 'Daddy, why is it always the Scouts?' Children have a way of asking their questions at just the right time, in such an innocent way, and I did a lot of thinking about that and decided to start spending more time with my own children. It was an important decision in my life."

Clea Burton recalls, "Many years ago, when my husband was working full-time and also trying to complete his Doctor's degree, he was extremely busy and not able to spend much time with us. One day our daughter, Ann, asked, 'Mama, when Daddy gets his Doctrine and Covenants can we have another family night?' "

There are times in every man's life when he must devote his best energies to some project outside the home. But the damage is done not in short periods, but when an "out of the home" focus becomes a life-style.

Making Family Time Prime Time

No father who loves his family wants to fail in this important role. Charles Evans, high counselor and father of four, gives some insights into the requirements of success as a father: "As with most great goals and objectives, success as a father depends upon understanding what is required and the individual commitment and willingness to pay the price. Small day-by-day efforts and consistent improvement followed by increased understanding and further resolve to follow the pattern the Lord has provided, can eventually qualify any man to be a good father."

Being a good parent requires time. It takes time to talk with children, time to encourage them, time to listen to them, time to respond to them and help them work out their problems.

Judy Richins tells of the price her busy husband has paid to become a good husband and father in spite of his many other commitments. Judy said, "Ross has been in a bishopric for six years and has been gone from home a great deal. The thing that has always saved us, is that when Ross is home, he *is* home and will do whatever we want him to. He has many other interests, but he doesn't pursue them right now, in order to be free to give himself to his family."

Sacrificing time is never easy, and some men find the price too high. But those who are willing to pay it, often observe that the rewards they receive are far greater than the effort required. The direction of a child's life can well be in the balance.

One family we will call the Smiths had twin girls. At birth one of the twins was much smaller than the other. The doctor warned them that the small one would always be slower in her coordination and development. Because of her family's love and understanding, this wasn't a big problem until she got in school and began to compare herself with the other children. "Why can't I jump the rope as well as the other kids?" she would ask. When she was in high school, she began taking Driver's Education. She desperately wanted to learn to drive a car, but her progress was slow and she was discouraged.

One afternoon her father (who was at work) kept having a nagging feeling that he should go home. He left early and was driving toward home when he saw his daughter walking by herself. When he stopped to pick her up he saw she was crying. "What's the matter, honey?" he asked. "Oh, Daddy, I'm just a failure in everything I try. It takes me so long to learn anything and I feel like I'll never be any good to anyone. I guess I never will learn to drive a car." Mr. Smith reassured her of her importance to the family and to her Heavenly Father, and promised he would go with her every night and let her practice driving until she was able to pass the test. He kept his promise, even though the learning process took *more than a year!* When his daughter passed her driving test it was a real triumph to her; a turning point in her life. It gave her a better self-image and the confidence that she could eventually succeed at most anything if she kept trying. Her mother feels strongly that if she hadn't had a dad willing to make a great sacrifice of his time (even though he had heavy church responsibilities and nine other children), that this daughter's development would have been curtailed.

Another family told of their ten-year-old boy who stole a package of batteries from a store. He was caught by the store manager who called his dad. The boy had money in his pocket, and the dad had him pay for the batteries. He also told the manager to give the boy the most disagreeable job he had in the store and he would see that his son was there for several hours after school every day for a week. The theft problem was never repeated. The mother said, "My son was lucky because he had a dad who was willing to sacrifice his time and convenience in order to teach him an important lesson at the time he needed it. There were many other things he would rather have done that week than drive his son back and forth to the store!"

Does the Family Come First?

Ironically enough, it is often the devoted, conscientious, well-meaning fathers who find themselves in a situation where there is no time or energy left over for the family. One family we know became quite desperate when the father consistently complied with the great demands and requests of work, church, neighbors, and friends, leaving the family without his companionship or help, week after week. The mother in this family wrote a letter to her husband in an effort to encourage him to find time for them. She said, in part, "We need more than anything to know by your actions and the way you choose to spend your time, that we are important to you; that we do come first as you say. Perhaps you might consider that when you say yes to every other commendable, worthwhile thing you are asked to do, then even when you are home you have little energy or strength left to give to us because you are already 'spent'. We need more of your best time, thoughts, and attention. In my heart, I feel that you are not truly doing the Lord's will (even though you may be doing his work) if you consistently leave your family without the priesthood influence and strength which you alone can give us. I feel you must decide which ball you want to carry and then say 'no' to other things which force you to drop that ball. I've been praying that you will voluntarily choose the ball labeled 'family'. When you give us the time we need, our home is blessed and strengthened."

This letter was effective in helping one priesthood holder get his responsibilities into perspective. He told his wife that he realized he had been feeling trapped by all the demands on his time, and that the only way out of the trap was a clear realization of his priorities, and the necessity of sometimes saying no.

Our peers judge us by our performance in church callings. The world judges us by our performance in our jobs, and tries to convince us that this rating scale of outside achievements is the only one that counts...and so we are inclined to shove the family aside saying, "They'll understand...they'll wait." But they don't wait.

Show Them They Count

In a survey we conducted with grade school children, we asked the question "What does your Dad do to make you feel you are special to him?" Almost every child answered with something like, "He plays with me and takes me places with him." One child said, "He takes me places and gives up what he was going to do just for me." The only replies that varied from this general idea were ones which said, "He talks to me with love," and "He helps me with my work."

Jean Orgill, an outstanding kindergarten teacher, tells what children say to her about their fathers. She hears things like, "My father is too busy to say that my work is very good." "My dad is busy doing work getting money. He doesn't have time to look at my things." "I don't like to play with my dad—he's always tired and sleepy." But she also hears, "My dad likes my work! He says if I keep working on this I will get better and better!" "I had a special day with my dad yesterday!"

"Children can feel whether or not time with them is given any priority and whether that time is more or less important to you than other things," said Margaret Johansen. "They often equate your attitude towards spending time with them with how important they are to you. It doesn't have to be a lot of time, just *some* time when they can count on having you to themselves. Of all the things we've done in our family, spending one-to-one time with each child has made more difference than anything else." Margaret's husband, Trent, feels that the most essential ingredient to help a father establish a good relationship with his children is this "one-to-one time." He believes it is just as important for small children as older ones, and that it's the best way to say, "You matter to me." His six-year-old daughter, Trina, loves to dress up and look her best when she goes on a "date" with Dad. Trina's "dates" happen at least once a month because one of Trent's goals is to spend one night a month alone with each of his children. They go window shopping, ice skating, or out to eat ...anything that is fun for both of them. The results of the one-to-one attention given to Trina are evident. When Trent was coming home from a three-day trip, she put on her best long dress, had Mom fix her hair and got all ready to greet him. She feels special to him and wants to be at her best for him. ("She's a good example for me!" commented Margaret.)

Ross Richins also believes in one-to-one time with his children. He says that one of his children usually joins him for a private little talk while he shaves in the morning. They know he's a captive audience then and they have a lot of fun just chatting. Ross says one of the problems of being gone a lot is that when he comes home, the children often get overexcited trying to tell him or ask him things. They talk as fast as they can and compete for his attention, almost as though they feel they have only so many seconds to get their message across before Dad has to leave for another bishopric meeting. He said he has arranged time alone with each child to counteract this problem. He plans a special summer "Daddy's Day" for each child where they are entitled to choose whatever activity they like and have Daddy all to themselves for that day. Ross says he has to schedule his "Daddy Days" and other special family activities on his calendar at the first of the summer; otherwise he would never have a Saturday free. But once he has family time scheduled, he tries to schedule everything else around it.

At Christmas he has given tickets or gift certificates to each child entitling them to special times out with him. The tickets also include family excursions to movies, etc., and promises to "fix" things for the children. Ross got the "ticket" idea from Glen Griffin, noted pediatrician and writer. Ross remembers Glen Griffin saying something like, "When you take more than one youngster to a ball game, they often end up fighting over the popcorn. But when you take only one, you usually have a great experience and build a relationship between you." Glen tells of a night when he had taken his nine-year-old daughter, Joan, on a one-to-one daddy-daughter date. As they drove over the hill and the temple came into view, she asked him a question about the temple. They stopped the car and talked, and more was taught about temples in those fifteen minutes than in years of prepared lessons because of the one-to-one relationship and his careful use of the teaching moment. She felt free to ask questions and they could really communicate. As they finished, Joan looked up into her dad's eyes and spontaneously said, "Dad, there's one thing I'm going to promise you—that when I get married it will be in the temple." They were a few minutes late to their date to watch a hockey game, but Dr. Griffin has reflected on that evening many times since and thought how valuable the tickets to that game were—even if they had never been used.

Be a Guide and a Counselor, as Well as a Pal

Rex Stallings, who was a bishop for nine years and is now in the stake presidency, said, "I think there's been a great emphasis put on fathers being pals to their children. But I came to the conclusion quite a long time ago that my children had all the pals they needed. What they really needed was a father and there is a difference. It didn't mean I couldn't enjoy them and play with them. But they needed more than that. They needed someone they could count on; someone steadfast who could be relied on to give wise guidance on a one-to-one basis. I think one-to-one time is the best thing a father can do. One good way to accomplish this is to interview each child on a regular basis so you can really talk about things, just the two of you. I've had a lot of really great experiences with this principle; like the time our youngest son was on the basketball team in high school. This was a time when my son and I had some really close talks about the problems of peer pressure and fathers pressuring the coach, and we were able to establish some pretty basic values."

"How To's" for Interviewing Your Children

One authority said, "Fathers often avoid a one-to-one situation because they don't know how to relate comfortably, yet they rarely realize that is what the problem is." Several fathers we talked with expressed a feeling of not knowing how to conduct a father's interview or what kind of questions to ask. We are including some suggestions other fathers made.

Delbert Eddington makes a special interview appointment with each of his children, saying something like, "I'd like to see you Sunday afternoon at 5:00 p.m." Delbert was bishop when the M.I.A. had the personal achievement books and goal-setting interviews and he follows this format with his children. He helps them set goals in different areas of their lives at the first of the year. Then in their monthly interviews he encourages them, and discusses with them the progress they are making toward their goals. His children ask for these interviews if he forgets, and even his married sons often come home for them.

Many fathers use "open-ended questions" to get their children talking and learn more about their ideas and feelings. Some suggestions for older children might be:

1. What do you think makes a happy family?
2. How do you feel about our family home evenings? How would you like to change them?
3. If we could give you anything in the world for Christmas or your birthday, what would you like?
4. What quality do you like most in a friend? What do you think makes a good friend?
5. What do you hope to be doing ten years from now?
6. What do you think makes a happy marriage?
7. Suppose our house was on fire and you could only get three things out. What would you choose?
8. What do you think it will be like after we die?
9. If you knew you only had a week to live, how would you spend your time?
10. When you can't go to sleep at night, what do you like to think about?

For younger children, you might like to try questions like:

1. What kind of an animal would you like to be and where would you like to live?
2. Who do you think are the luckiest people in the world?
3. What are your favorite TV shows, food, songs, etc.?
4. Tell me about one of your happiest days.
5. What age would you rather be if you had a choice?

Working and Playing Together

Spending group time with the children is also an important part of growing together as a family. Veldon Jones and Don Marshall have found special ways in which to accomplish this goal. Veldon, father of six grown children, was an enthusiastic scouter and made it a point to take his children camping and hiking often. He knows the names of the trees, flowers, and other plants and always takes time to explain things and answer the children's questions. Their campouts have been companionable learning experiences. He and his wife, Thelma, feel that their hiking and camping trips gave the children their best chance to get close to their father and so the trips have become one of the most important things they did.

Don Marshall got twelve chickens and a rooster and started a chicken-raising project with his boys. It was obvious from the start that the rewards were not going to be financial. But when his wife suggested they forget the project, Don said, "Barbara, we're not raising just chickens; we're raising boys, and those boys need the experience of working with their dad." Barbara hasn't objected since, and feels her husband has gotten closer to the boys and has taught them some valuable lessons about work as well. Whether working together or playing together, having Dad close at hand can make the experience more meaningful and memorable to a child.

Be Cautious of Criticism

One concerned mother said, "One thing fathers need to realize is that children do not see criticism as an indication of love and concern. Too much criticism, too many negative comments usually disguise love to the point that it might not be recognized at all. My children truly do not feel that their father loves them, although he does, very much! But he is so critical that the children feel only his disapproval and disappointment. One day I said to my son, 'Don't you understand that Daddy tells you those things because he wants you to do better so you can be happy? It's because he loves you.' His reply was, 'He doesn't love me!...not at all.' "

Another mother who has a critical husband told of the heart-break she feels when her little boy comes to her and says, "Mom, why doesn't Daddy like me?" No matter how much a father loves his children, constant criticizing gives the inner impression that he does not love. Also, negative comments often smolder and burn in a child's mind, whereas good ones, like Vitamin C, don't store well and need to be replenished constantly.

Leo R. Gifford, father of nine, said he has learned to be less critical and judgmental from scriptural fathers such as Lehi, Alma and Nephi who never condemned or gave up no matter how great their disapproval of their childrens' actions. He said, "Over the years, I have become much slower to criticize, spank and reproach, and find I want to be the kind of father my kids can sit down and talk things over with."

Bill Davies (Psychologist and Director of Pupil Services for the Salt Lake School District) said, "Usually when your teenager comes home at midnight your initial response is that of worry or fear; anger comes later because he has disobeyed you or made you feel insecure in your father's role." He indicates the wisdom of expressing the initial feelings rather than the anger, which a child discerns as critical and which makes them marshal their defenses and return anger. If we can clothe our concerns, cautions, and corrections in warm words rather than hurl them like fiery darts aimed at an enemy, our children will receive the necessary guidance they need without feeling attacked or threatened. In relation to this principle, it is wise to avoid negative labels at all costs. If you tell a child he is stupid, he will probably believe you!

One father has learned a sure-fire cure for quick criticism. He has developed the ability to "walk in the shoes of his children." One day one of his sons had mowed the lawn for him for the first time, but hadn't done a super job. The father thought, "If I was a little kid and had worked that hard to please my dad, what would it mean to hear, 'I appreciate your efforts, son. You are really learning.' Thinking it through that way kept me from pointing out what he hadn't done right—I knew there would be time enough for that later when he was more confident of what he is trying to do."

One authority has done a study that pointed out that praise is three to four times more effective in teaching better behavior than criticism. (If you can catch them doing something right just once and praise them, then they are likely to continue the right action!) Praise reinforces good behavior. Yet many children find it "necessary" to misbehave in order to get Daddy's attention. As a father, how many times do you stop reading the paper to praise your child for playing quietly? Yet what we water will likely grow!

However, authorities suggest that to be most effective, praise should be given for efforts and accomplishments, not character. When Bobby cleans up his room, comment on how good the room looks and what a fine job he did. Don't state what a good boy Bobby is. The right kind of praise helps Bobby draw his own positive conclusions about his character without making him feel obligated to live up to superlatives or prove he is not always "good".

Spiritual Leadership

Charles Evans asked in a pamphlet directed to fathers, "What does God expect of a father? What is his role in the home? The scriptures tell us the father should be the leader, the head, the priesthood bearer and the representative of the Lord to the family. To be a leader, one must lead; he must pursue a course and bring others with him...If we are to fulfill the calling, it is not enough to stand by the roadside shouting encouragement and pointing the way. We must do as the Savior did. We must follow the course, leave adequate footprints and say to our families, 'Come, follow me.'

"To be a spiritual leader, a father does not have to hold a high church position or be a scholar of the scriptures. Far more important than these is the ability to share with your children your love for your Father in Heaven. Of course, you can tell them of this love and should frequently. However, to be most effective you must live a life that shows them you really believe what the Lord has said and are anxious to keep His commandments."

Clea Burton said of her husband, "Alma was such a good leader. For instance, he helped us start our day right with prayer. We had family prayer night and morning. Our children heard us pray and thank Heavenly Father for blessings, and we taught them we could use fasting and prayer for help with our problems. And long before the church suggested family home evening on a formal basis we were holding ours, and many times we discussed the scriptures. Our children still love to come home and discuss the scriptures with their dad."

Bless Your Family with Father's Blessings

When we asked Linden Hurst (father of seven and counselor in a stake presidency) how he felt fathers could best make their priesthood influence felt in the home, he replied, "I feel that the concept of father's blessings should be used much more. I remember the finest family night we ever had. We had been having some problems in the home, and I called all the children into the living room and told them that I was going to give each of them a special blessing. As I laid my hands on each of their heads, I was so moved that the tears were rolling down my cheeks. Between blessings I saw that silent row of children on the couch being so good I couldn't believe it, and each one anxious and eager for their turn. It was really a special experience."

Every year, just before school starts, Ross Richins calls his children together and gives them a blessing for school, feeling that the challenges and temptations are so great and schooling is such a serious thing that each one needs special spiritual help to strengthen them and help them succeed. Ross said, "One time our daughter who was just tiny at the time, came and plopped herself right on the chair after I had finished blessing one of the older children. I said, 'Do you want a blessing, too?' 'Uh-huh!' she said, solemnly nodding her head yes. And so I started giving the little ones not yet in school (and my wife) blessings, too. And that has been a really close, unifying experience for our family."

Before Linda Garner left for college, her father gave her a blessing and said, "Whenever you are tempted, you will be able to remember your home and your family, and be strengthened. She says that blessing was fulfilled, and she feels there is real power in father's blessings, for she always did think of home whenever she was in a moment of decision, and the home influence helped her make the right choices.

Linda and her husband, Marshall, plan to use father's blessings even more frequently with their own children. They also have decided that another way the father's influence can inspire children is to record their blessings when they are babies. By playing the tapes later, you can remind the children of the great promises made to them through the power of the priesthood. The Garner's children have listened to their blessings in family home evenings a couple of times and even though their children are small they have been impressed by the blessings their daddy gave them.

Clea Burton said, "Alma gave the children a father's blessing whenever they had anything they needed special help with or when they were going away from home. Even now our sons come back home and ask Alma for a father's blessing when they have big decisions or problems."

Dantzelle Lewis Allen, one of the twelve children of Malin and Myreel Lewis, recalls that her father always made sure that his children had a father's blessing on special occasions such as the first day of school, when they had an important assignment, when they went away to college, or whenever they felt the need. She says, "One of the most memorable blessings was the one he gave me during a special family home evening the night before I was married. His counsel and advice, and the spiritual uplift from the blessing really helped me."

You Give What You Are

The personal life of a father will be one of the greatest influences in the lives of the family members. Marilyn Skousen said, "The thing that impresses me the most about my father, David McOmber, is his integrity and honesty. He is such a good example." The authors have this feeling about their father, Arland Larsen. His integrity is a source of strength and has had a great influence on their lives.

However, no dad is perfect, and admitting fallibility to the children usually increases their respect. But whether right or wrong, the father should be head of the house. He has the responsibility to make decisions to the best of his ability, and to influence and guide the children. When we are open and honest with our children and there is mutual respect, we can work together to solve family problems and improve the quality of life. Rex Stallings tells of an instance when this happened in his home. He said, "I've always done a lot of hard physical work, and many times the pressures of the day would build up on me. I noticed I was coming home and taking it out on the family; I was quick tempered and not very nice to be around. So I started a little project with myself. Before coming in the house, I stopped at the back door and offered a little prayer that I would be able to treat the family the way they ought to be treated instead of taking my own frustrations out on them. And some way the kids gained an understanding of my problem, too. If I did begin to respond to them in a bad way they would say, 'Are you up-tight, Dad?' 'Yes, I'm up-tight. Just give me a few minutes and I'll be all right.' And they would just kind of smile and leave me alone for a while and the combination of my prayers and their understanding just seemed to melt my problem into something of little significance and we began to have better and better times together."

Here on this home stage where we play our most private roles, our salvation and exaltation is largely determined. We are away from the eyes of others, away from the social pressure that often forces us to put our best foot forward and to wear a polite facade. In the home where we are seen as we really are and where the provocations are the worst is found our greatest test.

We teach and we give to our children what we are. And while we cannot give more than we are, we can become more than we are!

Ten Things to Try

1. Analyze how well your time commitments match your inner commitment to put your family first.

2. Try scheduling more special times with your family. When asked to do other things during that time, try saying, "I'm sorry, I already have a commitment." Then keep your commitment to your family.

3. Schedule a "date" with each daughter or son. Make it a monthly occasion if possible.

4. Give gift certificates at Christmas entitling each child to special times with you.

5. Have "Daddy Days" in the summer where you let each child plan whatever they would most like to do with you. Put "Daddy Days" on your schedule as high priority appointments.

6. Try holding a regular personal interview with each of your children. Use a goal-setting approach, or try some of the questions listed in this chapter.

7. For one week, keep a record of your positive and negative statements to your children, and try to give credit more than you criticize.

8. Pause a moment before you go into your home at night and offer a prayer that you will lead and bless, not just react.

9. Try using Father's blessings more frequently in your home. Give the children blessings before they start school, leave home, when they have problems, etc.

10 Record blessings given to your children or grandchildren in order to remind them of your promises to them through the power of the priesthood.

2

Especially for Mothers

"Is it fun to be a Mommy?" Sharlene Tyler's little girl asked her one day. "Yes, dear, it is," she answered. But Sharlene started to wonder if she *had* made being a mother look fun, or if her daughter was questioning because she had put doubts in her mind.

Most mothers have doubts themselves at times! Successful mothering like any other achievement, takes time, effort, and training. If we do not have the necessary training and skills, it may not be "fun" to be a Mommy! Any career is rewarding only to the degree we are skilled in filling its demands, and the satisfaction and enjoyment come from doing it well. Sadly enough, many modern women have been poorly prepared by society to accept the challenging role of motherhood and fill it adequately. We are living in a time when both boys and girls are receiving much the same education. This education is geared to preparing them to be successful in the world, but gives little preparation for success in the home. Girls are rarely given specific training for the career of motherhood. Only those who are fortunate enough to have mothers who compensate for these educational gaps, by thoroughly training and teaching the skills of homemaking at home, will be adequately prepared. However, this is a difficult task for a mother because girls in our society ordinarily are kept busy outside the home. When these girls marry and have children, many of them feel like a failure in their homes because they are prepared for many other things, but not for the things Phyllis McGinley (author of *"Sixpence in Her Shoe"*) calls the "day-by-day vicissitudes of being a housewife." Phyllis adds that if girls were prepared, perhaps these daily realities might seem less like the slings and arrows of outrageous fortune, and more like simple obstacles to overcome. Being unprepared for such a demanding career leads naturally to frustration and guilt feelings, especially for Latter-day Saint women who know that motherhood is a sacred responsibility. We may have had a "well-rounded" education and hold college degrees, and yet still be unhappy and frustrated in our most demanding role.

However, many women who have not had adequate preparation have demonstrated that with a strong enough desire and a dependence on the Lord, one can learn to be adequate and happy in the special and important role of a wife and mother.

"I grew up as an only child," says Carol Jeanne Ehlers (who now has twelve children of her own). "My parents had another baby when I was almost sixteen, but my mother was a perfectionist and still preferred to do all the work herself; consequently I didn't learn how. So when I got married, I was not used to doing housework, much less having it undone as fast as I could do it! And I wasn't used to being around children at all, so I had no patience. Patience is something I had to learn. The statement I hear often when people learn how many children I have is 'That's wonderful! I'd have a large family, too, if I had your patience.' Many assume that patience is something we are given, and one person is given this much and another person is given that much. I believe that is a fallacy. Patience, and all the other virtues you need to be a good mother, are things you develop through self-mastery. Some learn them in their homes as they are growing up, and some of us have to learn them after we are mothers."

Many women enter marriage well-prepared to take on the responsibility of motherhood and they enjoy it. But whether we have been prepared or not, motherhood is a challenging and demanding role to fill. How lucky we are to live where there are so many sources of help for a mother who is desirous of learning and developing qualities and skills to equip her to be a better wife, mother, and homemaker. There are classes, books, study groups, counseling and information on every subject of homemaking and motherhood which can help as we make day-by-day efforts to live satisfying, productive lives, and strive to teach our families to do the same. We have collected ideas from many of these sources which might help any mother progress toward that "ideal" she is striving for.

Spiritual Price of Progress

Each mother needs to feel a sense of progress in her life to counteract discouragement and keep up her enthusiasm level in spite of her imperfections. Many mothers we interviewed had a simple (but not easy) secret to progress—they set aside time each day for scripture reading and prayer. One mother said, "I can always tell the days when I have not taken time for my spiritual food. The results are so apparent that I wonder how I could possibly feel that anything else is more important. I am more irritable with the children, quicker to criticize, and the spirit of love which is usually easy to maintain seems to disappear." Another said, "When we take time to bring the Lord's spirit into our lives, we are actually telling Him that we will put Him first and we are greatly blessed when we do." The main blessing she felt she had received was the gift of the Holy Ghost which Parley P. Pratt said, "Quickens all the intellectual faculties, increases, enlarges, expands, and purifies all the natural passions and affections...It inspires virtue, kindness, goodness, tenderness, gentleness, and charity. It develops beauty of person, form, and features..."

This gift then is so precious and helpful to us as mothers that the price of a few minutes a day is small indeed. The mothers we talked to varied as to the time of day and the method they used for scripture study and prayer time. Some preferred to get up before the family and enjoy the "peace and quiet" of the early morning hours. Some were "night owls" and preferred the time after the children were in bed. Still others enjoyed a break immediately after the children left for school. They agreed that the time or place matters little. The important thing is to read and pray consistently so that it becomes a habit. Once formed, this habit will help us nourish our hungry spirits and be in tune, so the Lord can have moment by moment influence over us. One mother testified that when she gained the habit of scripture reading and prayer each day, she gained a new life. She said, "I gained a better understanding of the scripture which says 'feast upon the words of Christ; for behold, the words of Christ will tell you all things what ye should do' (2 Nephi 32:33). My daughter said to me, 'You don't look any different, but I know you are different. You don't yell anymore, do you, Mama?' When I learned to stop and let the spirit take over, it gave me a sensitivity to my children's needs, patience, and love that I had never experienced before. I'm still learning, and I make plenty of mistakes, but I am making the kind of progress that keeps me going."

Priorities for Productive Living

Belle S. Spafford, General President of the Relief Society for many years and author of the book *A Womans' Reach,* stated in her book, "The endless enticements and demands of life today require that we determine priorities in allocating our time and energies, if we are to live happy, poised, productive lives." All of us face this challenge to learn to evaluate our activities, analyze our interests, and weed out those activities which have the least meaning to us personally.

Each mother must fight her own battle to balance demands on her time. She must deal with filling the needs of husband and children, while still meeting outside demands and learning to use time at home in self-fulfilling ways.

Jaynann Morgan Payne, a former Mrs. Utah and runner-up to Mrs. America, in her book *To Fulfill Her Promise,* quotes Ecclesiastes 3:1: "To every thing there is a season, and a time to every purpose under heaven..." She adds that "The problems we encounter and our ability to solve them do not seem nearly so insurmountable if we zero in and ask ourselves, 'What should I become, and what should I be doing now at this time in my life?

What are the top demands on my time? How do I fit these demands into my life?' "

As you analyze your situation, take a look at what is important to you, your husband and your family. What do you value most? What does your family value most? Are you making time for these things? What makes you feel best or worst about yourself? One mother said that the thing which made her feel most inadequate as a mother was getting behind in her laundry chores, because that was what the family noticed most. However, she had not yet learned to put washing and ironing high on her priority list. And when other activities took precedence, everyone suffered because she felt inadequate and unhappy with herself.

If one of our goals is to keep our homes running smoothly and well and also to have the time to do "second mile" things with or for our families, then we must learn to arrange our time priorities to include all the activities most important to reach that goal. However, the balance is precarious, and because of this, a mother's priorities may change every day. Today it may be most important to spend time with a sick child; tomorrow perhaps we may need to spend some time playing the piano or reading to fill some of our own needs. Another day we might need to be involved with a project which will benefit the whole family (such as redoing the family room, canning the peaches, etc.). As needs change, priorities must change. A mother must learn from experience to judge which demand should receive priority at any given time. It means asking ourselves before we begin time-consuming chores if they are most important right then, or if we could use our time more advantageously some other way. Once we have made the decision, it means having the confidence that what we are doing is most important (and not worrying about what the neighbors or our best friend may think).

Be Your Best to Give Your Best

"Too often mothers think that giving their best to their families means sacrificing doing their best for themselves. They might neglect their own appearance and needs, and not put any effort into looking nice and keeping themselves up," says Carol Jeanne Ehlers. "But as the mother of many sons, I have certainly discovered that keeping up your appearance is part of giving your best to them. One experience I remember really pointed out to me how important this is to the children. When my second son was in high school, there was a function parents and sons were invited to which neither of us was really interested in, yet he kept insisting I go with him. I finally said, 'Terry, why do you want me to go tonight?' He replied, 'Well, a lot of my friends will be there who have never seen you, and I want them to know that I don't have an old wrecked-up mom!' "

Some women have felt that being a mother excludes or limits their own interests. It is delightful to discover that being a successful wife and mother can be enhanced by a well-rounded interest in life, and involvement in fulfilling activities.

"I have to see myself as a competent, intelligent person. I accomplish a great deal more for my family if I take an hour every day to develop my own interests," said Janice Burton. "I have to be determined every day not to get bogged down. Sometimes I feel I don't want to face another scheduled day, and I just want to do what I please. But if I can think of it in the long-range view and squeeze out a few minutes to improve myself each day by scheduling my time, my efforts will add up and be meaningful. I don't feel like a good mother if I am not growing myself and doing something to improve myself each day."

Janice is an outstanding organist and is presently collaborating on the writing of a basic organ course. When Janice was a young mother with small children, she felt for a time that she would need to wait until she had more free time to develop her talents, but as her family grew, she realized that she must start where she was and *make* time for herself in her daily schedule or she wouldn't be happy. She says, "I just decided to do those things in smaller doses."

Dorothy Goldberg said in her book *The Creative Woman,* "As we give of ourselves, we must reserve a little time and energy for that other life which is within each of us—that urge to make, to do, to try to create. It really amounts to putting something extra into the day—something we have seen or heard that inspired us, something we have learned or done which has added more to the quality of our day. Somehow, somewhere, there must be an island of time for ourselves."

Planning for this time is as important as planning for any other pursuit. Wise planning makes it possible for time to bring the greatest returns in good health, well-being, and renewed enthusiasm. One special lady said, "I know it is important to accept responsibility and work for the future, but I feel today is important, too. It may be all we have, and I want to enjoy life today and live it to the fullest!"

Carol Jeanne Ehlers believes that the challenge is to develop the necessary organization and discipline so that we actually use our time doing fulfilling things. She says, "I always try to have my housework done by noon. Then I can spend the afternoon on things I especially enjoy. I do some book illustrating, and the children are always very interested when I work. I think developing a special interest of your own makes you more than 'just mother' in their eyes. I don't try to shoo the children away and get them to leave me alone, but I try to include them in whatever I'm doing. I have a file of old drawings and a large supply of tracing paper. Many times, while I draw, they trace. When I sew, I give them scraps of material to drape around dolls or sew buttons onto. When I decorate cakes, they sit right up by me, and I find if I talk to them while I work they will sit quietly and watch, and we enjoy it together."

As we share with our children the excitement of our own interests, it adds a dimension to the relationship and to their experience which can be gained in no other way. It helps teach by our actions that we are individuals, with needs and interests of our own, as we want them to be. "I think one of the big things we as mothers have to do (and this is emphasized a lot in the church) is to refresh and build ourselves," commented Carol Davis, "and then we will have more to 'give' to our families. I read a lot. I have to find time for that. It is just part of my life. I also love to sew, and I do it in little snatches of time. I take time to do these kinds of things. I have to, to feel good about myself, so that I can help the children feel good about themselves. Also to keep a pleasant spirit in the home, I feel a responsibility to be pleasant myself. If I ever get grumpy, it just seems like the whole house falls apart. I have a neighbor who has been a great example to me this way. She is the most special person, and she never seems to be out of sorts. She has helped me to realize that we need to train ourselves to be that way."

Helena Evans said, "A woman can do many other fulfilling things in addition to caring for her home and family as long as it is not in preference to family or at their expense. With a mother, a family must come first. They must not be neglected."

Whatever we choose to do we must be sure that while we are developing ourselves and our individual interests, we show by the use of our time that we value our husbands and children most of all.

Keeping a Home in Its Place

Since most women do have interests besides keeping house and caring for children, to be able to develop these interests and at the same time keep an orderly, clean home is a real challenge. Homemakers we interviewed gave some good tips to help us be more efficient and effective.

1. *Have a system.* Running a home is much like running a business, and many of the same principles of organization apply. By planning your work, and learning to work effectively within the plan, it is possible to accomplish the housework and leave time for the extra activities which make life rich and rewarding for you and your family.

2. *Set some time limits on your tasks.* Remember, "work expands to fill the time available." If you set time limits and allow only a reasonable amount of time for tasks, you can accomplish far more in a given amount of time.

3. Learn to *organize parts of your day to include some uninterrupted blocks of time* for important creative work, and leave the bits and pieces of time for less important detail work.

4. *Learn the value of routine.* When an ordinary task becomes automatic, it frees our minds for creative tasks. Also having a certain time for a task, and/or a practiced way of doing it reduces effort spent on decision-making.

5. *Pick up and put away everything out of place in a room* to start your housekeeping routine each day. This makes all the other tasks easier, as well as giving a quick sense of progress.

6. *Work with your own mood swings and energy levels.* Everyone's level of performance varies from day to day, and from hour to hour. It is unreasonable to expect to accomplish the same amount when your energy is at a low, as when it is at a peak, or to expect to do as much when you don't feel well as when you feel tip-top. Observe the times of day when you have the most energy, and plan heavy tasks at those times and lighter tasks when your energy lags.

7. *Make routine work more pleasant.* Listen to educational or inspirational cassette tapes, memorize poetry, scriptures, songs or inspirational ideas while cleaning the kitchen, ironing, etc. Boredom with routine vanishes when we use our minds actively while we do these chores which take no real concentration. Some other ideas are to listen to good, uplifting music; plan next week's schedule or think through a problem as you work.

8. *Have something to look forward to.* One mother suggested keeping a list of all the things that are fulfilling to you as a person which you would like to find time to do. When you make your schedule, she suggests you plan some time for one of these activities each week. Having meaningful activities to look forward to can help you feel enthusiasm for each new day.

Love, Strengthen and Support Your Children's Father!

We've often heard the quote "the best thing a father can do for his children is to love their mother." We would like to add that the best thing a mother can do for her children is to love, strengthen, and support their father! One common denominator of the successful families we interviewed seemed to be a mother who supports the father in his role as head of the family. Shirley Andersen said, "I think it is essential that a woman support her husband. My husband has always taught our children obedience, and I tried to support him in this (even when I might not agree completely with what he did). Also I feel it is important never to argue with your husband and challenge his authority in front of the children. This is sometimes hard, (and something I had to learn) but it has made our home a happy one. Also, when the children were small and my husband had to be gone a lot, I would often mention how grateful we were for their wonderful daddy, and how hard he worked for them and I would express gratitude for him in our family prayers."

LaDawn Jacob, one of the Andersen's married daughters, recalls, "At every meal my father was served first, and my mother would always be first to greet my father when he came home, and then the children could come and greet him. Also I remember my father always conducted our family prayers and scripture reading and family home evening because he was the head of our home. I was also impressed that when there was a difference of opinion between my parents, my mother followed my father's feelings or advice even though she might not fully understand or agree. By everything she said and did, Mother always made us feel my father and his work were very important, and that we should all support him in anything he had to do. That attitude came through so strong it permeated our home. I really feel this is one reason my father has been able to write books and accomplish the things that he has."

LaDawn told how her mother had the children present special programs honoring their father on Father's Day or on his birthday. One time each child added a petal to a flower bouquet which represented the good qualities of their dad. They used a similar idea with "feathers in your hat", and "candles on your cake". Another time each child was a leaf on his family tree and they told reasons they were glad to be part of his family. LaDawn explained that these little programs (which the children had great fun planning) added to their appreciation of their father, and she is trying to do similar things with her own children. While we were in her home, LaDawn asked her children to sing a song they had learned about fathers and how much they loved their father. LaDawn's husband, Jim, just beamed, and so did the children.

When a wife builds up the father in the eyes of the children, it helps the feeling-tone of the whole family and strengthens relationships, as well as making it possible for him to fully perform in his priesthood role as patriarch in the family.

Perspective: the Best is Yet to Come

Taking pride in our divine calling as wives, mothers and homemakers, and keeping in mind long-range goals, can help us keep what one mother called an "eternal perspective". Linda Garner, mother of four small children, shared this philosophy: "I constantly remind myself that I am me, and I can't live for my neighbors or anyone else. I do what I think is most important to reach my 'forever family' goals, and don't worry about what someone else might think. This takes the pressure off, and I can feel good about spending time with the children, or doing anything else I decide is most valuable right then. I have another little philosophy which helps me, and I call it 'running away together'. If the children are getting on my nerves or I'm to the breaking point, I just leave whatever I'm doing and do something fun with the children. I forget about what the neighbors might think if they drop in and see the dishes unfinished. As long as I know I have a good reason, nothing else matters. Usually I find the children are misbehaving because they need my attention anyway, and the housework will always be there, but my children won't. I want them to remember that Mom put them first and was there when they needed her."

Other mothers also felt that at certain times there is merit in breaking time-saving rules or skipping their schedule. A mother of seven confided that sometimes she enjoys just puttering through a sinkful of dishes with her hands in hot, soapy water while she meditates, or looks out the window at a yard blazing with color and lets gratitude wash over her soul as the water washes over her hands. A simple act such as this can sometimes help us get our lives into perspective and spark up our whole attitude.

LaDawn Jacob added, "I received a philosophy from my mother which she called 'investing' in your children. Anything good you help them learn is a long-term 'investment' because it will be with them forever, increasing in value. Nothing gives me the same joy as working with live human beings, especially my own children. My real joy is to teach my children and see them learn and perform." LaDawn feels that because of the negative attitudes prevalent today about motherhood, it is essential to learn to appreciate what a truly rewarding career motherhood can be.

One mother said, "Motherhood is the greatest and most *rewarding challenge* I can *imagine.* As you see your children grow and develop, learn new skills, gain self-discipline and social awareness, the thrill must compare with creating a masterpiece."

Women whose children are raised can help us get a vision of the rewards. Colleen Pinegar, whose children are all married, says, "The real joys begin when you see them married well and raising their own families in the gospel."

Helena Evans expressed her belief that "No one can take the place of a good mother. But this is one of the rewards because it gives you the greatest feeling of accomplishment in life to have righteous children who do fine things (anything from giving a talk to building a house). There is peace and satisfaction in being able to think 'I had a part in that'."

Mary Wright adds, "Seeing the gospel principles you have taught resulting in a righteous posterity makes you realize the best is yet to come! I feel a mother's joy increases by the day when she has planted the right seeds and done her work well with a trust and dependence on the Lord."

Ten Things to Try

1. Pay the price for strength and progress in the challenging role of wife and mother by taking time for daily scripture reading and prayer.

2. Do a quick "Priorities-Check-Up." Ask yourself if you are making time in your life for the things you value most.

3. Work with your own mood swings and energy levels.

4. Have a system for accomplishing your housekeeping tasks. A plan, time-limits, and an established routine can help you use your time more effectively.

5. Make routine work pleasant by listening to tapes, memorizing, planning, or meditating while you do chores which take little concentration.

6. Schedule an "island of time" for yourself each day and watch your morale improve.

7. Share your interests with your children. If you write poetry, read and discuss it with them; if you paint, let them watch and imitate you, etc.

8. Give your best to your family by doing your best for yourself (developing your own interests and taking care of your appearance, etc.). But remember the need for balance.

9. Try new ways to show your husband love and support. Pray for him in family prayers, tell the children (in his presence) how grateful you are for their special father, or plan a special program to honor him.

10. Keep an "eternal perspective", remembering that if you trust in the Lord, do your work well, and put first things first- "the best is yet to come!"

3

Love, the Heart of a Happy Home

"What is the greatest and highest law in the gospel? The law of love. Upon this law hang all the other laws. What is the finest expression of the law of love? To accept and respect another person, in all his uniqueness, just as he is, which includes what he may become." said Stephen Covey in his book *Spiritual Roots of Human Relations.*

Lucille Johnson, a noted family counselor and lecturer, has concluded from her experiences with families that love which is made verbal and visible is the most important thing we all seek. Therefore, learning to express and demonstrate love should be a primary concern of parents—especially since parents often take for granted that their children know they are loved. Love is so much a part of a parent's motivations that we usually assume our love is apparent to our children.

Princess Grace has said, "Americans think that children automatically know they are loved. That's not true; children have to be told over and over again. Often parents say, 'It goes without saying that we love our children.' It shouldn't go without saying. It should be said frequently."

Lucille Johnson advises: "Express love to your kids. They must hear it. Children do not equate what you do and buy for them with love. They don't get the message unless it is verbalized. It would be a very unusual child that would open his drawer and say, 'Oh mother, thank you for all that clean underwear. Now I know you love me.' In their eyes that's just your 'thing', your role. Those things are expected—and not equated with love until children become parents themselves."

"The more love you can express, the better," said Helen Sharp, mother of four. "Sure you love them, or you wouldn't do so much for them, but I really think love is a verb. It's got to be spoken. If it is, they will learn to feel your love and express love back to you."

The amount of love expressed in the home has a distinct effect on the quality of parent-child relationships. Ross Richins helped on an interesting study in conjunction with some special commercials being made for television and radio. Seminary students were asked to call home and express love and appreciation to one of their parents. (The other parent had been contacted earlier for permission to record the conversation.)

One girl called her mother and said something like, "Mom, I want you to know I really appreciate all you do for me and that I really love you." "Is that all you called for?" the mother replied. When the girl hung up, she was obviously upset and said, "I would never do that again!"

Another girl called her Dad, who was principal of a school. Even though the secretary said he was busy, she asked that they please find him and get him to the phone because she had an important message for him. When he finally came, she gave him the message and he said, "Wow! You have really made my day.

That is neat and I appreciate you telling me. You know that talk we listened to last night—we can have that kind of family, can't we?" "You bet, Daddy" she replied, "but I've got to go now. Bye." She hung up feeling great about the experience.

"You could tell so much about the relationship just by listening to a few words when love was expressed," Ross commented. Expressions of love and caring are the building blocks of relationships; if they are plentiful and freely given, sturdy relationships can grow.

Love Can Make the Difference!

A teenage boy was sent to Lucille Johnson for counselling because he was in trouble with the law. He did not respond favorably to counselling and was insolent, sullen, and withdrawn. His father, a general, impressive in stature, was called in; but when he was in the same room with his son, the tension and hostility fairly crackled between them. The man was openly critical of his son and Lucille felt she had reached an impasse. In one final effort, she turned to the General and said, "Let's lay our cards on the table and tell it like it is. I guess there's nothing about this boy you like or respect. You just don't care for him at all." The father looked as though he had been struck; then bristled with anger. Then this great big general got up, pulled his skinny teenage son to his feet, and with an emotion-laden voice said, "Son, I want you to know I love you!" An electric silence filled the room, then the son dissolved in tears and threw his arms around his father's neck. "Oh, Dad, why didn't you ever tell me?" "I wanted to, son, but somehow the words wouldn't ever come out." This boy (whose problem was based on his feelings of being unloved), ceased to be a trouble-maker.

It's so easy to say "I love you" to a sweet little toddler. But many parents find it much more difficult to say it to their towering teenagers. It is even more difficult if the teenagers act as though expressions of love embarrass or displease them. But we mustn't let them fool us. Underneath that "Oh, Mom, really!" or "Dad, I *am* grown up now!" is a sensitive, vulnerable person with a real need to be assured that he is loved. None of us ever outgrow that need.

Too many negative comments, too much criticism can cover up love. No matter how much you love a child, if you are constantly criticizing, he is very apt to get the inner impression that you do not love him. One mother said she tried to explain to her child, "Don't you know that Daddy tells you all those things because he wants you to do better so you can be happy? It's because he loves you." The child's reply was, "No he doesn't love me, not at all." Negative comments often smolder and burn in the mind, whereas good ones need to be replenished constantly. Each person has a need for daily expressions of appreciation and love.

Lucille Johnson also tells of a close relative who had a rebellious son who began choosing undesirable friends when he was a young teenager. As the years progressed, he consistently made choices that broke his parents' hearts. However, he was not insensitive to the hurt he was causing them, and finally said to his parents, "Every time I come home, I just hurt you more. I can't stand it anymore so I'm leaving. We just have two different ideas about how to live, and I've got to do my own thing. I'm packing tonight and will get out of your life."

The parents watched in dismay as he prepared to leave; then as he started for the door, the father suddenly went over to him, embraced him and said, "Son, wherever you go and whatever you do, I want you to remember that I love you and that you *are* my son. Nothing can change that." The boy left, and the parents waited in vain for word of him. The whole ward fasted and prayed for him, but month followed month and they had no idea where he was. But one day he came home, and today he is a powerful, baptizing missionary. This is the story he tells:

"One night I was sitting in a dark, crowded room that really smelled of pot and booze and body odors. The air was thick with smoke which reflected the psychedelic lights. I looked around me, and suddenly could see what I had become and felt sick to think I had chosen to be there. Then, as clearly as if my father were standing right there, I heard the words, 'Son, wherever you go and whatever you do, I want you to remember that I love you, and that you are my son. Nothing can change that.' I looked at the door leading out of that place, and it was lighted up, as if a halo were all around it. I got up and went through the door out into the cool night air, determined that I was going home to change my life."

Love Communication Skills

Most parents have a very real desire to express their feelings of love to their children. Yet feelings are hard to share, possibly because sharing feelings makes us vulnerable to hurt. Many people build superficial relationships, because they fail to say what they really feel, and rarely share personal feelings or experiences. But such non-sharing on the part of parents may be the basis of the problem when children don't *feel* loved even when parents love them deeply. Most of us can probably do better than we now do at sharing feelings to assure our children of our love. The following suggestions from communication experts might be called "love-communication techniques".

1. *Learn to really listen.* If a child says, "Oh, Mom! Look at this neat rock I found on the way home", and a parent responds with "Did you get your jobs finished?" the child gets a clear message—"Mom is not listening to me."

Someone has said, "We need to have our megaphones beaten into ear drums."

To evaluate your own "Listening Quotient", try keeping track of how many times you interrupt your child when he is speaking, and the approximate time each of you spend talking. Does the child get equal time or better? Do your listening techniques encourage him to continue, open up, and get to the real issue; or do you unconsciously "turn him off" by negative or judgmental responses?

Many parents we interviewed expressed the feeling that one of the best ways to give a child the feeling of being loved is to really listen to him. Listening itself is a form of non-verbal communication, and the messages are all positive: "You are a worthwhile person." "You are important to me." "I am interested in what you have to say." "I respect your opinion." If we listen to a child in a non-judgmental way, he will be encouraged to express deep feelings and develop confidence in his ideas and his ability to communicate. Many excellent things have been written in recent years on the art of reflective or active listening and we recommend them.

Winnifred C. Jardine, a noted writer, said in the February, 1974 *Ensign*, "Just for one day: Listen to your child...with all of you. Rather than thinking of what to tell him, listen to what he is telling you. Listen patiently to the end, until he has emptied his heart. Encourage him, looking directly into his eyes, with 'I see', 'Um-hum', 'Is that right?' 'And then what?' Listen and savor the joy of having this child."

2. *Allow children the right to have their own feelings and opinions and to express them to you.* Listen without judging, even if their opinions differ a great deal from your own. Listen to feelings without thinking you should decide which feelings your

child should or should not have. "You shouldn't feel angry with your brother" doesn't sweep away the anger, but adds guilt to it, and in a very subtle way implies a condemnation of his emotions (and indirectly of him). It amounts to an unfair request for him to turn off his feelings at your demand.

Much of the richness of life is experienced through emotions, and a child who builds up defenses and covers his "bad" feelings because they are not accepted or allowed, also becomes less open to "good" feelings like love. We want to help our children learn to understand, accept and control emotions instead of feeling guilty about them or pretending they don't have them. We can help them understand in a loving way that while we are not free to choose the emotions that arise in us, we can choose how and when to express them in a way that shows respect for ourselves and others. We might say, "All of us feel angry at times, but in our home we have rules for helping us get rid of mad feelings without hurting anyone else." An understanding response to honest feelings communicates love.

3. *How many cues say "I love you?"* It is impossible not to communicate, and many "second level" communicators—tone of voice, posture, facial expressions, etc. say even more than the words. However, if touch, tone, expression *and* words communicate love, the child will more likely feel it and not misinterpret our message. Also, by being attuned to a child's non-verbal communication, we can learn to be more supportive and loving in our responses. Instead of saying, "Jimmy, you've been moping around here all morning. Why don't you try smiling?" we can say, "Jimmy, you act sad. Is something bothering you?"

4. *Use "I" statements,* rather than "you" statements, *"open-ended" inquiries* (such as "I would like to know..." "I wonder if" "I'm puzzled about this...can you explain it to me?") *and tracking or reflective statements* (such as "Seems to me you are feeling such and such." "I'm not really following you. Could you repeat that?" "O.K. got it...go on.") Good general communication between parent and child is very likely to go hand in hand with free and open expressions of love.

Love is an Action Word

As important as verbal expression is, the families we interviewed suggested many other expressions of love that are also helpful; such as:

1. *Give them time.* Thelma Jones, mother of five successful grown children, talked of ways she communicated her love as her children were growing up. "I have never lacked for love for my children. It was always so easy for me to cuddle and play and talk with them when they were small. If they were restless and needed companionship, I would sit and play games with them or help them build things. There were always other things that needed doing; but I felt that the children were my most important responsibility and the other things would wait. As I look back, I can see how the children responded to my love and attention and it was beautiful. I think I showed my children that they mattered most by giving my time. Also, I have always made it a point to be home when the children got home from school. As soon as they opened the door, they always called 'Mother!' to make sure I was there."

Leo R. Gifford, father of nine, said, "I used to think other things were more important. But now I make it a point to take time to sit and talk with my children, be close to them and express love every chance I get." "Yes," his wife, Katherine, added, "and we both try to take one of the children when we are going someplace. When we can manage, we take one child out to dinner each month, and have found the communication channels really open up in a situation like that. Then, too, we go on more picnics, outings, to the park to play, etc. We feel it is of prime importance to do things together that are memorable to the children in order to really communicate our love and caring."

"One thing I think is a great expression of love," said Joye Billings, mother of five, "is taking time to teach a child the things most important to you—like a love of the gospel, the joy of serving, etc. I really get excited about gathering my little ones around me and reading to them. I can cuddle my smallest ones on my lap, sit close to the others, and share the things with them that I love."

2. *Fill their needs.* Joye Billings also commented that she feels that scheduling and having a routine are other ways to express love to children—feeding them on time, having special times for special things so they know what to expect, making sure they get enough sleep, etc.

Darlene Gregersen said, "I really do believe that the most important thing in raising children is that the child *feels* your love. If he does, then even if you make a lot of mistakes, they won't really hurt him." We asked Darlene how she makes sure a child feels that love. She replied, "I think one way is filling their needs promptly when they are small and not putting them off in order to take care of your own needs or respond to other people all the time. If they get the concept from the time they are young that they are of utmost importance to you, then later they don't feel left out or shoved aside when you can't drop everything and fill their needs. If your relationship is 'quality' there aren't bad feelings hiding underneath. Then a child can wait when he needs to without feeling of less worth. He can accept the situation as it is, and not take things personally if he is secure in your love."

3. *Demonstrate love by touch.* "I believe touch is very important to children," said Karen Reilley, mother of eight, "and I try to make it a point to touch each of my children lovingly each day. I learned the importance of it when I was very preoccupied with a sick baby. During that time I attended a Relief Society lesson about the importance of showing love through touch. I came home and put my arm around my oldest daughter and she just came alive! I realized I had been neglecting this expression."

Another mother said that she feels that expressing love physically is so important that she tries to keep track and make it a point to spend some "loving time" with each of her six children daily.

4. *Increase love after you correct.* Elvin Christiansen feels an important aspect of showing children your love is to do something with them after you have corrected them. It assures them that your correction came because you really care. Otherwise they may doubt it. He also said that words without works have no value. But telling children you love them and then showing it by being willing to spend time with them and do things with them helps them accept correction because then they really *feel* your love for them.

5. *Encourage.* "I believe that encouragement is an expression of love," said Joye Billings. She frequently uses expressions such as "Great!" "Good, you did it right!" and "You did it before, I'm sure you can do it again" with her five children. The art of encouraging is a basic part of the gospel because it is one of the best ways we have of helping others progress, and expressions of love are the greatest encouragement of all. This is especially meaningful when we apply this idea to helping our children grow and progress. Loving implies that we want the best for the loved one, the most happiness, the most fulfillment. By learning and practicing the art of encouragement, we can show our love in a tremendously effective way.

6. *Write your expressions of love.* Many parents mentioned that they used notes in their families to communicate love. The written word can often have a great impact; maybe because it can be read over and over and savored in a way that is not possible with a verbal communication. Also, parents who find verbal expressions of love awkward can often write them easily.

Karen Reilley used this idea in a special way. She said, "I began thinking there were many good things about my children I had never told them; they are responsible, can be trusted, mind me, etc. But I could see it is all too easy to fall into the habit of telling them the bad and not the good. So, at the suggestion of a friend who had tried it, I wrote a special letter to each of my older children expressing how much I loved them and telling them every good thing I could think about each of them. I gave each child his letter privately and each one came back to me later and said something like, "Thanks for the letter, Mom. It was really nice." I feel that the letters created a warmer feeling tone between us and have helped me remember to praise more and criticize less."

Soon after the birth of her four children, Linda Garner has written a letter to them telling how she and her husband felt when they knew a baby was coming; how excited they were, and how they planned and prepared for them. She tells the child about the day of their birth and how she felt when she first saw and held them. She also tells little things they did as a newborn to show their uniqueness. She feels that these letters will be meaningful to her children as they grow older and will help them realize how much they were wanted and loved right from the start.

Another mother wrote letters to her children on each birthday and kept them in a special notebook to be presented to them on their eighth birthday. She expressed her love and confidence in them, recorded their strengths, and related little stories about them that she thought would be a source of strength or pleasure to them later. She adds a letter each year until the child leaves home, and these notebooks have become a real treasure to her children.

7. *Delight in their differences.* Janice Burton, mother of ten, says, "I believe it is a basic part of love to delight in children's differences, encourage their individuality and let them know you are glad they are who they are with all their uniqueness. This is especially true in the teen years, when they have a special need to know they are appreciated just as they are. I love my teenagers!

The most exciting thing that has happened to me in all my life is finding out that I enjoy teen-agers. I had heard they were awful and was really afraid of that time, but I find these years a lot of fun because my children are such interesting people. It has been such fun and so fascinating to watch each child develop interests and talents so different from either of their parents—to watch them become people!"

Janice also said that she believes love is the all-important ingredient of happy families and is more important than achievement. She said she encourages her children to achieve in what they are most interested in, but beyond that they relax and have fun together. Janice says, "Enjoying each other as individuals is a basic part of loving and being loved. A feeling of tension, of needing to accomplish every minute, can badly damage a loving relationship."

Ruth Heiner, an outstanding mother of six grown children, found a special way to show appreciation of her children's uniqueness. When they were small, she began a year-by-year history (to present to each one later as a token of her love). She kept many little momentos of each child's life—snapshots, birthday cards, programs with their name mentioned, special school papers, anything that showed special recognition or achievement. Ruth's daughter, Linda, recalls the sweet experience of taking her own book from the shelf many times during her growing-up years and finding that it renewed her sense of being valued and loved by her family. She says this book is now one of her most prized possessions and already influences her own children who love to learn about Mama when she was a little girl.

8. *Love, but let go.* "Part of loving is knowing when to let go," one mother commented. "I heard a quote that said, 'Love them fiercely and then let them go,' and it really made an impression on me. Love does not stifle progress or resist independence."

Beverly Nelson found a beautiful way of expressing love and "letting go" when her son, Brent, was married. She gathered pictures of Brent from the time he was a baby till his wedding day and made a picture album which she presented to her daughter-in-law, Debra. She said, "Debbie, this is for you. I thought it would help you know Brent a little better."

Love Me Because I'm Me!

"One of the most inspirational examples that the Savior and Heavenly Father set for us is their unconditional love," commented Judy Richins. "Whenever I think of them, this is what comes into my mind. Their love for us isn't decreased when we break the commandments—there is merely great sadness for us. If our children can just know that we love them like that—that we want them to do right, but will love them in spite of their actions, then they will feel loved in the way that really matters."

Stephen Covey explains why this kind of love is so important to a child: "Unconditional love frees a person from the struggle of feeling pressured to do things for the wrong reasons (like to get favor, keep love, etc.). Then they can grow and struggle with the real issues instead of struggling with you. It also frees them to choose on the basis of the real issues."

"In society we are always accepted 'because,'" said Lucille Johnson. "At home we need to be accepted 'period.' We are all children of God and real love is related to that reality and not to shortcomings. Real love also avoids letting children become extensions of the parents' ego. 'Judge not' and 'compare not' should be two primary rules for parents."

One special mother commented that the hardest thing she ever learned was to be accepting, loving and not critical when her older children made wrong choices; especially when they didn't comply with the principles she believed in. But she mentioned that the rewards for learning to love in this way had been great. Stephen Covey said, "Greater than our love of programs or principles should be our love of people. We must love our families regardless of their adherence to the principles we love."

Ross Richins, a bishop and father of five, said, "I think the security of feeling loved right from the time children are little is increased when they know you love them even when they do something wrong. They need to know that everybody, even parents, make mistakes. We have one daughter who has a very hard time admitting when she makes a mistake, and I'm sure it is part of maturity to realize that we are still loved and accepted even though we are not perfect."

"Love is communicated most effectively when we as parents are open about our own weaknesses and apologize to a child when we have been wrong," says Lucene Hougaard. "For example, my five-year-old did some little inconsequential thing one day that was the straw that broke the camel's back, and I gave him a scolding far more dramatic than he deserved. Later I explained other things that had happened to me that day and apologized, and my little boy said, 'That's all right, Mom, I feel like that sometimes too.' "

Legacy of Love

What does it do for a child to be loved in an unconditional way? Linda Garner recalls when she was four years old, the day she first recognized what a special thing it is to be really loved. She said, "Mom was making cookies, but left the kitchen for a moment. The batter looked so good and I really wanted to taste it. I was trying to get some when I knocked the bowl off the cupboard and broke it. It was Mom's favorite bowl that went to her mixing set; it made a mess, and I was afraid I had done something terrible. I ran into my bedroom and shut the door and lay on my bed crying my heart out. Mom came in, put her arms around me and said, 'Linda, don't you know that you mean a lot more to me than that bowl? I can always get another bowl, but I can't get another Linda.' I felt warm all over and remember thinking, 'Mom really loves me.' It made a definite difference in the way I felt about myself, and as my parents continued to show me their love over the years, that assurance became a great strength to me. I never rebelled against my parents as a teen-ager, even when I disagreed with them, because I always knew they loved me and wanted what was best for me. That love protected me in a lot of situations too.

"For instance, when I was in my late teens, a married man, who had been a teacher at our school, came into the theatre where I was working. We started talking and he offered to take me home after the show. It never occurred to me that his intentions were different from mine because he was so much older than I was, and I accepted his invitation. But he said, 'Are your parents still as strict with you as they used to be?' 'Oh, yes' I replied. 'Why do you think they are that way?' Without even hesitating I answered, 'Because they love me.' He looked at me in a funny, searching way as I hurried back to my duties. After the show the man approached me and said, 'Linda, I'm leaving and I won't be taking you home. But I want to tell you I know you meant it when you said your parents loved you. You are a very lucky girl to have all the right answers.' Only then did I realize what he had had in mind, and I could see that my parents' love had been just like an invisible shield protecting me from harm."

You Can Learn to be More Loving

Some parents feel they would like to give the children the strength and protection of feeling really loved, but they don't see themselves as capable of openly expressing love. Perhaps some would identify with one distraught mother who went to a counsellor (who told her that her children needed to have more love expressed in the home). This mother gave the counsellor a sad smile and said, "It's all very well for you to tell me to be more expressive and loving, but I came from a very unloving home, and I'm naturally very shy and undemonstrative. Besides, sometimes I don't feel much love inside to express anyway. Can you actually learn to be a more loving, expressive parent when you just aren't that way?"

In the April 1977 Ensign, Mollie H. Sorensen, mother of eight, gave her reply to a similar question. She said, "We all experience times when our supply of love seems to wane...how can we fill our reservoirs of love when they seem to drain out at the bottom?" Her answer was to set aside an hour a day for reading the scriptures and praying. "How can a mother of young children take that time? Well, as one of my friends put it, 'When you read the scriptures, you don't take time—you add time.'

"I think that's true, because devoting time each day for the Lord is actually saying to Him, 'I will put you first in my life—before the washing and ironing—since I know that by doing this I will be blessed to be a better mother, wife, and homemaker.' " Mollie goes on to recount some of the blessings in store for a person who does this, the most important of which is the help of the Holy Ghost in every area of life.

There is no better way to increase your stores of love or your ability to love than to sense the love the Lord has for you. The closer we get to the Lord, the more we sense our own worth and the more we have to give to others.

This approach actually touches the very heart of the problem, because as one mother said, "Our ability to love and to express love ties in with our own self-esteem. Criticism and other unloving behavior is usually an expression of inner dissatisfaction. If a parent feels good about himslf, he will usually feel loving towards his children and be able to express that love."

One authority suggests another helpful idea. He says that the way to become loving is simply to find out what a loving person does and do it, because we all become what we want to be and what we think about. Marvin J. Ashton says, "A loving person respects, responds, has concern for the welfare, progress and happiness of his loved ones. A loving person is giving and forgiving. A loving person acts on his loving feelings. He shows love through specific actions and words, in little daily things."

A loving person often has become loving through his own sincere efforts.

An incorrigible ten-year-old girl was passed from foster home to foster home because no one could handle her. Finally a lady named Marie consented to take her and try to help her. A few months later, much to the amazement of the authorities, this ten-year-old was well-adjusted in school and a happy well-behaved addition to Marie's home. They called Marie in to give a report and try to learn how she had accomplished this seemingly impossible task. She said, "I have never spent so many hours on my knees. Many times a day I would have to run to my bedroom or kneel by my sink and plead with the Lord, 'Help me to love this child.' He did, and I did!" That was the end of her report. These professional people had expected to learn some great new counselling technique; instead they heard the miracle of love.

Ten Things to Try

1. Practice expressing love verbally every day.

2. Develop your Love-Communication skills: really listen, encourage children to express their own feelings and opinions, use non-verbal communication to increase your expressions of love, and use "I" statements, open-end inquiries, and tracking.

3. Give each of your children some one-to-one time each day to help them sense their importance to you.

4. Share with your children whatever is important to you. Read to them and teach them about the things you love.

5. Remember the importance of touch. Touch each child lovingly every day.

6. Do something with a child after you have corrected him to assure him of your love.

7. Show love through encouraging words. Say "Good, you did it right!"

8. Write special letters to your children expressing love and pointing out their strengths.

9. Try keeping a special year-by-year history of your child to increase his sense of being loved and valued.

10. Increase your ability to love through daily scripture reading and prayer.

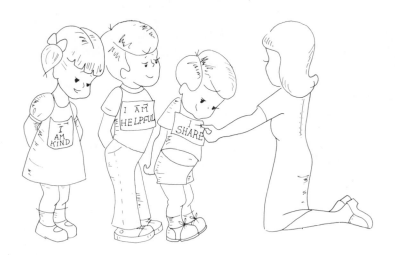

4

"Your Child's Self-Esteem is Showing!"

One day Dave said to his mother, "Do you remember those reading tests you used to give me out of the Childcraft books after we read together every night? Whenever I did one of those tests you would tell me how smart I was, and how well I was going to do in school. You know something?? I believed every word of it, and when I started school I just knew I was going to be a good student. I think that is one reason I was!"

However, his sister, Loree, laughingly recalls a different experience. She wouldn't sing for a long time because when she was young some of the family called her a "broken record." She interpreted this to mean she had a bad voice. However, one day when she thought she was alone, she began singing and her mother came in and said, "Loree, you sound beautiful." Loree's mouth dropped open and she said, "What do you mean? You know I have a terrible voice!" "Loree, that's not true, who told you that?" "Don't you remember you and dad used to tell me I was a 'broken record'?" "Oh, Loree, we only meant we were tired of hearing the same song over and over, not that you sounded bad! You have a very nice voice." After this conversation, Loree felt relieved and happy, and has been singing well, and enjoying it ever since!

Experts in the field of human behavior indicate (as Dave and Loree learned by their own experiences) that parents have a profound influence on the self-images of their children, because we are their first self-interpreters. What parents think and say of a child, he will most likely think of himself. A parent's daily reactions to a child constantly convey an image to him. If parents mirror a positive, realistic picture, the child will gain this type of self-belief, but if the parents' reflections are usually negative, the child's self-concept will likely become negative. Because a good self-image is so important to the achievement and happiness of each child, helping them think well of themselves is an important area of concern for parents and a major indication of their love.

Give Them Positive Labels for Positive Impact

"Our second son, Brian, missed the age deadline for kindergarten," Darla recalls, "and had to stay home while all his friends and his older brother, Mark, went to school. Brian was restless, irritable and uncooperative. I knew one of his problems was that he felt he wasn't as important as the 'school' kids, and I tried to think of something I could do to help him. I finally came upon the idea of a 'Self-Image Chart' which I thought would help both my older boys. I made posting charts by pasting two strips horizontally on poster paper, like this. Then I posted positive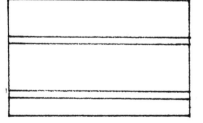

labels in the top strips. For instance, 'Brian is cheerful' and 'Mark is obedient.' During the day I watched carefully for any little action that suggested the label was true, and posted on the second strip the action I had noticed. (Under 'Brian is cheerful,' I might post 'He smiled and said 'Good morning' to his Daddy!!)

Then the chart might look like this. I honestly tried to ignore Brian's negative behavior and to look for positive things to write on the chart. As we focused on the good, Brian's negative feelings diminished, and so did his negative behavior. We could almost see his self-esteem improving each day. As Brian's

> **Brian is Cheerful!**
>
> **He smiled 😊 and said "Good morning" to his Daddy!!**

problem behavior disappeared, so did my diligence at keeping up the charts. I left two labels up for weeks. (They were: 'Brian is kind,' 'Mark is helpful.') One day Mark pushed our toddler and made him fall. I said, 'Oh, Mark, I'm disappointed! I can't imagine you being so unkind.' Mark retorted, 'But Mom, Brian is kind; I'm helpful!' Only then did I realize how much impact labels really can have!"

Since a child believes almost any label we give him, imagine the power for good which positive labels can have. If Billie is having trouble learning to ride his bike, a parent could say, "Learning to ride a bike isn't easy, but you are the kind of boy who keeps trying even when things are hard. I can remember when you were learning to walk; no matter how many times you fell down, you got right up and tried again." Stressing positive traits in a child can also encourage obedience to principles we are trying to teach. For example, when a child hears, "I was happy that you helped Susan when she got hurt. You are a kind person," or "Thank you for taking the gun back to Jimmy, I'm glad you are an honest person," he will probably be motivated to discipline himself to be true to those positive labels.

LaDawn Jacob tells of one very genuine way her mother had of raising self-esteem in her children. When someone came into their home, LaDawn's mother would always introduce the children who were in the room, and add a label to the introduction. She would say something like, "This is my daughter, LaDawn, who is such an organizer, she helps us get everything done around here," or "This is Elaine. She's our good little cook."

LaDawn said, "I always felt that my mother was sincere and consequently I wanted to live up to her compliments."

Tell Them Their Strong Points

To prepare for a family home evening lesson recently, Marshall and Linda Garner chose a character trait they considered outstanding in each of their children, wrote it on a slip of paper, and sealed it in an envelope. During the lesson they opened the envelopes and read to the children: Heather is especially good at sharing, Nathan is loving with everyone, and Heidi has a cheerful, happy temperament. The children were very impressed, and for weeks afterward four-year-old Heather said, "I 'member, Mom, I need to be good at sharing, cause my card said so." Linda began wishing she had included every virtue she could think of on their cards!

Velma Norton has always made it a practice when she was alone with one of her seven children to try to build them up by saying things like, "You have such a bright and active mind, and I can tell you are a very special spirit. The Lord has great plans for you." She would watch and become aware of the child's outstanding traits and talents so she could talk to each child about them. They loved to hear about themselves, and it seemed to build self-esteem to know someone recognized their good points. Velam feels this helped them believe in themselves, and was one reason they were never afraid to try for worthwhile accomplishments.

Carol Davis, who has six children, adds, "I really try to build my children in an honest, sincere way whenever possible. Every day I tell each child something like 'You did that job so well', or I might write them a note to tell them something good I noticed about them. I can't believe how much that helps their feelings about themselves, and about our home."

A mother whose daughter was born with coordination and learning problems, said, "I learned that I had to dwell only on accomplishments with that daughter. Criticism crushed her, and in order to give her the courage to try something hard, we had to build her up. Praise made her enthusiastic and willing to try. And, you know, I soon found that the same principle applies to all children. The best way we can help them is to tell them what they do right, and not pay so much attention to what they do wrong." A parents' attention and approval can raise a child's self-esteem measurably.

Make Small Emergencies a "Family Affair"

Another thing which families can do to help each child know he is important is to rally around him when he has a problem. Bob and Carolyn Larsen have discussed with their six children how they want to be a source of help to each other, and have made it a practice for everyone to stop what they are doing to help any member of the family who needs help immediately. For instance, if six-year-old Sandra can't find her shoes, and it is nearly time to leave for school, she will call "Family Emergency, Family Emergency." Everyone comes to her aid, and with many people looking, her problem is soon solved, and Sandra has the assurance that *her* problems are as important as anyone else's. Family emergencies, of course, could get to be a nuisance if overused, so the children are instructed that they are not to call a family emergency unless they have done everything they can to first solve the problem themselves. To help the children get the concept of working together to solve problems they often sing songs from the play "Saturday's Warrior" (by Doug Stewart), which the whole family attended together. Carolyn mentioned that the song which says, "Father, mother, sister, brother, pulling together, we can work it out" gave the children the insight that they could help each other, and they often sing this song to remind them that the family needs to cooperate and help each other.

One-To-One Time Says: "You Are Important"

Robert and Jean Porcaro believe that spending individual time with a child is one of the best ways to give a child recognition and approval and make him feel important. They have found several ways to do this. They try to spend five to ten minutes alone with each child every day, usually just before the child goes to sleep at night. One or the other of them (and sometimes both) visit with each child at their bedside about the happenings of the day. Robert also has some questions he likes to use which help him get to know the children better. Questions such as:

1. If you wanted to do something in secret for a friend, what would you do?

2. If you could go on any vacation you choose, where would you like to go?

3. If you could give your family any gift in the world, what would you give?

4. What famous person do you admire most? If you could be one of them who would you like to be?
5. When you see the word "beautiful," what is the first thing you think of?
6. What do you think we need to change about our family?
7. Do you have a dream that you are trying to make come true? Would you like to tell me about it?
8. If you had a month off from school, what would you do with it?
9. What talent do you admire and wish you could develop?
10. What do you like to do the very most when you have some spare time?
11. If you had a million dollars what would you do with it?
12. How would you finish the sentence, "What the world needs now is...?"
13. If you could choose anyone in the world for your parents, who would you choose?
14. What are the most important things in your life?
15. What things are you most thankful for?

Another special way Jean and Robert have used to spend time with one child alone is to make an outing of the grocery shopping twice a month. They use a "Whose Turn Wheel" to keep track of which child may go with them to enjoy helping pick out the groceries, and have Mom and Dad to themselves for one whole evening. To make it special for the child they usually go out for a hamburger, or buy a treat as part of the evening's activities. Also, Jean is a genealogy enthusiast, and often takes one child with her to the genealogy library and lets them copy names for her. The child learns from the experience, and Jean and the child share some time together away from the rest of the family.

Make Time with Each Child "Special Time"

Arranging time to be alone with each child, and making that time special is an excellent way to help children feel good about themselves. Children know how much we value our time, and when we choose to spend some of it with them we communicate love and 'worth' to them.

Bob and Carolyn Larsen have a creative way to spend "special time" with each child daily. Since it would take a good part of the evening for one person to give individual time to each of six children, they divide the responsibility and each night Bob visits with three of the children and Carolyn talks to the other three.

Thus, each child gets some special attention and time to talk with one of his parents nightly.

When the children were younger, Carolyn sometimes made a list of things she noticed each child doing which pleased her, and then mentioned them when she had her "special time" visit with that child. As the children have grown and are able to read she has begun to write them complimentary letters or notes to put on their pillows or in their lunch boxes, to give them recognition for the special things she notices about them.

"One of the best things I've done with my children," says Lucene Hougaard, "is to carry out Daryl Hoole's suggestion to talk with each child alone at bedtime. I always ask them what their happiest time was, and what my wish is for them. One night my little boy asked in return, 'What is my wish for you, Mom?' 'What?' I asked, 'Just that you'll always be my Mom!' I assured him he would get his wish!" Lucene has another plan for spending one-to-one time which she and her children look forward to. In the summer, one afternoon a week, she takes one child wherever they would like to go for the afternoon. The next week she takes another child, until they have all had their turn. When he was four years old, her son, Derik, wanted to go to the railroad yard, and they had a marvelous time. A very old train was there that day, and they were able to look through it, and even have their picture taken by it. Derik was thrilled that his mother would take time to share his great interest in trains. They stopped for ice cream on the way home, and for weeks afterwards Derik talked about this outing. "Anytime we show interest in a child and his interests, his self-esteem rises." Lucene said.

One of the basic benefits of spending one-to-one time with a child is that it gives parents an opportunity to listen to the child with fewer distractions. When a child feels "listened to" he feels important.

Walter and Julia Moore have eight children and a Lamanite foster son, and every Friday night (when possible) they take one child out with them on a date. They make it a special night for the child by putting him in the front seat with them, including him in the conversation, etc. They may go to dinner, the movies, a sporting event, or just for a treat (depending on the age of the child). Their six-year-old, Paula, still remembers and talks about one big night over a year ago when they went to an ice cream parlor which had a singing guitarist. She was thrilled with the experience of having her Mom and Dad all to herself while the entertainer sang songs they requested.

Colleen Pinegar, mother of five grown children, said that her children have let her know they appreciated the time she spent alone with each of them. She said, "Sometimes I had to make this time by taking one child out to get a root beer, or to the park for a few minutes. This was especially important because my children are close together in age and time alone was hard to come by. I had to learn how to make fifteen minutes stretch to accomplish whatever the child needed."

"One day I was in the Junior Sunday School," said Gayla Wise, "when a member of the stake presidency told the children about his family's 'special time box'. It is a box which contains the names of each family member on separate slips of paper. Every family home evening they draw a name from the box and during the week they do something special with the person whose name they draw. We thought that sounded like a great idea, so we tried it! Our "special times" differ widely, usually cost nothing, and work best when planned to fit the person chosen. Some child-child activities we have used are coloring together, playing tetherball, and going fishing at a nearby lake. Some parent-child activities we've enjoyed are bike-riding, feeding ducks at the pond and getting the weekly groceries. Everybody looks forward to their special time. I have seen children improve their relationship because they shared a happy special time together. Individual needs are met, precious parent-child time is provided, and love grows between each family member. And...sometimes mom and dad even get a date!"

Share Your Skills with Them

Claudia Black feels that the best way to help her children improve their self-image is to spend time with them. Each morning while the other children are in school she spends time with her pre-schooler. On weekends Claudia prepares materials for projects and puts them in large manila envelopes (such as everything needed to make a scrapbook or a collage). Each morning she keeps one pre-schooler busy with one of these projects while she spends time alone with the other one. Claudia also tries to spend a half hour every day with each of her older children, allowing them to choose what they will do together. Claudia finds that they often choose to learn skills such as tieing a quilt, knitting, or sewing. She says, "There is a basic satisfaction that comes from being able to do something by ourselves. Children need that feeling for true self-esteem. The most positive assurance we can give a child of his worth is to help him learn skills that make him a more capable person. I like to do this by spending one-to-one time with my children, sharing my skills or learning new ones with them."

Real Life "Practices" Increase Confidence

One bishop says, "I've noticed that young people who get into trouble, especially girls who are taken advantage of, all have the problem of low self-esteem. You just don't see a lot of problems with teenagers who feel confident and good about themselves. We have no idea how important it is to young people to think well of themselves, and to know that others think well of them."

Poor self-esteem is a vicious circle. Those who have low self-esteem function poorly, and this in turn lowers the self-image even more, which can cause them to function even less favorably. But this vicious cycle can be broken and a new success cycle begun by experiences which increase the self-esteem. As parents give a child experiences which help his self-image become more positive, behavior and performance usually improves.

Audra Call Moss, (mother of six, author, lecturer and dramatist) suggests that we can give children specific experiences to fill a need and to build their self-confidence and self-image. She calls these experiences "enabling experiences." These enabling experiences are experiences with the physical, emotional, social, spiritual or intellectual environment which can aid the child's development. When these experiences occur in a loving, creative atmosphere they enable the learner to grow in a specific area of adjustment in a way that builds (instead of damages) his self-esteem. The experiences facilitate learning by providing the learner with opportunities to "try-on" appropriate ideas, values, techniques and behaviorisms until he feels comfortable with them.

An "enabling experience" may be as simple as giving three-year-old Johnny a "jumpbed" to jump on when he begins to want to jump on the furniture. The jumpbed is an old springs and mattress placed in the corner of the garage, basement or porch. It is given to the child with the stipulation that he can jump on it as much as he wishes as long as he stays off the furniture. But if he jumps on the furniture, his jumpbed privileges will be taken away for a period of time.

Another example of an enabling experience might be instigating "late night" privileges when an eleven-year-old will not go to bed without protest. If he goes to bed on time all week (without reminders), he is allowed to choose his own bedtime on Friday night and plan some special activities at home for that evening. This plan gives the child the responsibility for self-discipline.

Audra says, "As a dramatist, I found it logical to look for ways to structure "rehearsals of life situations." She suggests some questions for parents to ask themselves when using enabling experiences: "What feelings are causing the child to behave in this way?" "What does he really need?" "How can I create a situation that will help him find a better way to handle his feelings?"

This creative approach to helping children make adjustments to their environment utilizes the same principles for personal growth that Christ taught:

1. *Creative atmosphere.* A creative atmosphere is characterized by unconditional love, freedom within limits, curiosity about life, time to develop and use creative approaches to problems, and non-critical, non-judgmental, supportive responsiveness.

2. *Guides.* Parents act as models and confidants to the child in adjusting to his environment.

3. *Guidelines.* The parent helps the child set the rules himself, and the logical consequences of the act become the restricting influence, so that the parent is not merely a disciplinarian.

4. *Opportunity to learn by doing.* 90% of what a child experiences is retained, but only 10% *of what they are told.*

5. *Evaluation.* A child internalizes better if each experience can be talked through and evaluated with a confidant.

Audra's book *Releasing Creative Potential: A Guide for Parents and Teachers* explains specific enabling experiences for different age groups which can help a child grow in any of the five areas of personality development.

An enabling experience may be complex and may become a long-range project with many steps involved. For example, one mother realized her daughter was having difficulty adjusting socially following a family move to a new location. The girl was a junior in high school, and seemed very unsure of herself. The mother realized her daughter lacked confidence and began her project to help her daughter gain confidence by having long talks with her. She gave her daughter encouragement, reminding her that she was a special part of a family who loved her, and a child of God with a special mission to perform. She then structured many experiences for the girl which would give her practice in handling new situations, such as entertaining friends in many new ways. Over a period of weeks they watched her self-esteem grow as she learned to approach new situations with more confidence. Now, three years later, she is happily enrolled in college and is such a great leader that her father calls her his "little top sergeant."

Rachel McOmber is another example of a mother who believes the best way to help a child's self-esteem is to provide opportunities for positive experiences. Her philosophy is evident in the nursery school she runs in her home. The youngest of her six children is now in high school, but she said "Sometimes you have to *give* them the experiences they need. We had one girl who was quite shy. She would just as soon sit on the back row in a class, and just listen. I was her Sunday School teacher at one time, and had given an assignment to do scrapbooks illustrating ideas in the lessons. I helped her work on her scrapbook, and we included things she could share with the whole group (like recipes, patterns and different ideas). She brought the scrapbook and presented it to the class. She just came alive when she had a visual aid in her hand and was presenting something she felt confident about. After that she felt more comfortable, more confident and happier in the group."

Help Them See They Can Make a Difference

Terah and Joye Billings believe that opportunities for service help develop a healthy self-esteem. "A child involved in helping someone else always feels great about himself," Joye commented. "Service helps self-esteem like nothing else I know of. Meeting people, talking to them and learning to relate to them from an early age is one of the aspects of service that gives a child confidence in human relationships, and helps him think more highly of himself." Joye and her five children like to visit retired people, the very elderly, the sick and the widows. In nice weather they go on their bikes and deliver food and notes to uplift or thank someone. The children also help her make baked goods to give away.

Joella Wolfgramm says that one of the things she really enjoys as the children get a little older is seeing them begin to take the initiative and suggest things to do for other people. Last February when Louie was just three, he suggested making Valentine cookies for all the neighbors. They did, and Louie enjoyed it twice as much because it was his own idea.

Lucene Hougaard tells of taking her little boy with her to deliver a package to a needy family. She had him take it up to the door and leave it on the doorstep. He was thrilled and said, "That was so much fun, Mom. I'm really good at that, huh? Be sure and tell me when you want me to do it again."

It is a great feeling to know that we can make a difference in someone else's life by our service to them. Carol Jeanne Ehlers tells the story of her little girl, Collette, who learned through experience that one person can make a difference in the atmosphere of a home. Collette has five older brothers and one night everyone was cross and she was being teased by all these big brothers. Carol Jeanne suggested to her that they try an experiment to see if by being extra kind and helpful she could help change everyone else's attitude. Collette took her brothers' dishes to the sink for them, did several other things to be helpful and was amazed when they stopped teasing her and started acting pleasant. Carol Jeanne said, "Collette has learned that she can really make a difference and *that* makes a person feel important. Children who don't feel this in a positive way, often resort to making a difference in a negative way."

One mother believes that a child's sense of importance can be increased when we show evidence of trust in their ability to help. She often lets her son, who is thirteen, go on his bike to take his father's check to the bank. He senses his responsibility, takes it seriously and feels very grown-up, important and trusted.

Serving at home is just as important to a child's feelings of self-worth as learning to serve others outside the home. One mother said, "We give the children work responsibilities and opportunities to be in charge of family home evening and other family projects because we feel this can add to their sense of importance as much as anything." Lynn Scoresby has said that giving children opportunities for work and service, so they know they can cause good things, are important ways we add to their self-esteem. Our interviews indicated that parents sense the importance of giving responsibility as a means of helping their children gain self-esteem. Mary Wright always felt it was not only a necessity for her fifteen children to help her and to help each other, but the best way they had to get a good feeling about themselves. She told the children she didn't have enough hands to constantly reach every child, so they would all need to help her make everyone feel loved and important. She would often assign an older child to be responsible for a younger one. The result was a great feeling of mutual cooperation and love, as well as increased self-esteem for the children as they served each other.

Real accomplishment and productive use of time also produce self-esteem, but inevitably they require self-mastery. We might say self-mastery increases self-esteem. For example, when one teen decided she needed to get some exercise, she didn't deliberately set out to increase her self-esteem; but when she developed the self-discipline to stay with an exercise program, it enhanced her feelings about herself, and she benefited doubly from her exercise program.

"Show and Tell Them Who They Are"

To help their children appreciate the fact that they are individuals who have individual likes and dislikes and talents (which is part of having a good self-image), Robert and Jean Porcaro (parents of ten children) held a family home evening and talked about this concept and then had every family member create a collage representing themselves. They helped each other outline their whole bodies on butcher paper, and then drew pictures or cut out magazine pictures which they felt described their likes, dislikes, talents or abilities, and pasted them on their own outline. Jean said, 'We hung these collages in the hall, and it was interesting to see how much time the children spent looking at them. We learned a lot about each other from this activity, but better still, we learned a lot about ourselves."

A record book which belongs to a child, in which are placed his photos, certificates, his family tree, his sayings, and perhaps his parent's comments about him, is one way to "show and tell" a child how important he is. A book which puts together all the separate pieces of his life into one easy-to-look-at place gives a child a feeling of identity and a sense of belonging.

Karen Reilley is carrying out an idea with her eight children which her mother did for her. She has made a sturdy book for each child by covering squares of heavy cardboard with fabric and putting it together with large metal binder rings. The book is filled with a combination of regular lined notebook paper and unlined type paper. This book becomes the child's special scrapbook and year-by-year history. She records her observations about the child—his strengths, accomplishments, and little successes. Report cards, pictures, and programs are pasted on the plain white sheets. This book becomes a source of pride and uplift for each child, and helps him form a positive picture of who he is.

Many mothers accomplish the same goal with a more formal Book of Remembrance for each child (which is filled with his picture history, genealogy and special keepsakes). One mother writes a yearly letter to each of her children which is kept in a notebook and presented to them on their eighth birthday, and then still added to each year afterwards. The letters include the mother's observations of the child's good points, her wise counsel, and her testimony. Shirley Andersen keeps a record of the activities of her family in a large looseleaf binder. As part of their home evening each week they talk about what has happened during the past week, and Shirley writes down the events they decide are important, then adds programs, letters, newspaper clippings or other momentos which are connected with the events. Shirley says, "This is one way to help children feel they are an important member of the family, and that the things they do are worth remembering."

There are numerous additional things which could be written about self-esteem. Improving our self-image and helping our children improve their self-image is a lifelong process. Our task is to help ourselves and our children experience pleasure and happiness in doing what is right and living the principles of the gospel, since this will build true self-esteem. A belief and understanding that we are children of God is basic, and building righteousness is the greatest way to build self-esteem.

Ten Things to Try

1. Try using a "self-image" chart for young children which lets them know that you recognize their good points.

2. Verbalize the good things you notice in your child's behavior. Give them positive labels, and build up each child by giving them credit for things they do which you approve of, and consciously try to pay less attention to the irritating things the child does.

3. Hold a family home evening in which each child is given recognition for his good qualities, talents or abilities.

4. Try a "whose turn wheel" to help you remember whose turn it is to go with you on little excursions (shopping trips, etc.) Also try taking turns spending individual time with the children.

5. Begin a "family emergency" plan to show every child that his problems are important enough for the family to come to his aid when he really needs them.

6. Try setting aside a regular time to spend with each child teaching him skills which will enhance his self-image.

7. Consider using "enabling experiences" to help your child gain confidence in some area of adjustment.

8. Involve children in service to others as a visible evidence to them that they are worthwhile people who can make a difference.

9. Help the children make collages of themselves which encourage them to think about their own likes, dislikes, talents and abilities.

10. Use record books, scrapbooks, Books of Remembrance or personal letters to help each child know who he is, and how important he is.

Prayers
and
Promptings

"My family lived in the Mormon colonies in Mexico for some time," Helena Evans recalls. "When we first moved over the border into the states we didn't have any money and my parents were having a hard time feeding their large brood. A neighbor loaned us a cow and said we could have the milk if we would take good care of her. I was about nine at the time, and Mother and Dad gave me the responsibility of taking care of the cow, letting her graze during the day and bringing her home at night for milking. Usually the cow was gentle and I had no trouble keeping track of her. But one day she went on a rampage, wildly chasing one way and then the other; then charging off in the direction of the Mexican border. I was barefooted and there were burrs and thorns on the dry ground, but I ran after her, desperately trying to close the ever-increasing distance between us. Soon my feet were full of thorns and every step was misery, but I kept going. The cow was getting close to the border and if she went over, she was lost because we couldn't cross the border to go after her. I couldn't stop because I knew my folks were depending on that cow, and depending on me to keep her safe. As we neared the border, two border guards saw my dilemma and rushed out to help me try to turn the cow around. But she was really wild, pawing and snorting and bunting at them, and they failed to change her direction. They said, 'Little girl, there's not a thing you can do about that cow. Just go home and forget her and tell your parents what happened.' My feet were so sore I could hardly take another step; yet I felt I just couldn't leave the cow. I was desperate. I saw a mesquite bush nearby and went over and knelt behind it and prayed for help. I told Heavenly Father how badly we needed that cow and that there was no way I could get her home by myself. I pleaded for His help, said Amen and when I got up our cow had turned around and was trotting docilely toward home. I followed after her with wide eyes, but because of my sore feet the cow reached home before I did. She went the shortest way home (acting as though someone were driving her). Mother opened the gate so the cow could go in the corral. Then mother came out and met me and said, 'Helena, why did you bring the cow home so early?' I soberly told her the whole story; and when I looked up at Mama, tears were running down her cheeks, although she was smiling. She picked me up and said, "Honey, I'm so glad this happened to you. Now when Mother isn't there, you will always know that you can turn to Heavenly Father for help and He will always be there.' She carried me tenderly into the house and she and my sister washed my feet and picked the thorns out of them."

"And They Shall Also Teach Their Children to Pray..."

JoLyn Christiansen's missionary brother, Norman, sent her an adorable rag doll for Christmas. JoLyn loved the doll and played with it constantly. Then one day she couldn't find it. She hunted; her mother hunted; everyone turned the house upside down looking for the doll, but it could not be found. Elaine heard her daughter crying in her room, and went in and asked, "Have you prayed about this, JoLyn?" "Yes, I've prayed three times." "Did you tell Heavenly Father how special this doll is to you, and that your brother, Norman, sent it and you love it very much?" "No, I didn't tell Him that." "You tell Him, and ask Him again to help you find your doll." In a few minutes, Elaine heard squeals of delight, "I found it, I found it! It was right in my room all the time, Mom, and Heavenly Father showed me where it was. It really works to pray!"

Teaching a child when and how to pray, and then offering gentle reminders at times when they have a need, as JoLyn's mother did; and helping them feel Heavenly Father will always be there, as Helena's mother did, are a few of the ways we can help children begin to understand the power of prayer. Helen Sharp said, "I think it is important that children have prayer experiences while they are growing up, so they will learn to automatically turn to the Lord." Prayer is such a personal thing and an essential part of the kind of life we desire for our children; and yet, like a testimony, the value of it can only be sensed through experiencing it.

"We taught our children to pray faithfully every day," said Rachel McOmber. "When my son was about nine years old, he decided to put his prayers 'to the test' and see if it really made any difference whether or not he prayed. So one morning he went to school without having his prayer. He told me later he had a terrible day! A bee stung him, he fell and hurt himself, and he got a low grade on his spelling (for the first time!). When he got home he said, 'I'm never going to be caught dead going to school again without saying my prayers!' "

Linden Hurst expressed his feelings about teaching children to pray: "Many times we start teaching children to pray by teaching them certain words, but I feel it is better to help them get the concept of putting their feelings into their own words. I think we can help the most by giving them suggestions before they start their prayer, and directing their thinking by saying things like, 'What are you really thankful for today? Did you do something special? Would you like to thank Heavenly Father for what you were able to do today? What do you really need? How's Mom? Would you like the Lord to bless her?' That way they can learn to say what is in their hearts rather than just saying memorized prayers."

Many parents agreed that when we are teaching children to pray it is the sincerity and not the words that should be stressed. Even repetition is not necessarily bad, if it is a sincere request. George Pace tells the story of the swimmer who began sinking and called for help each time before he went under. George said, "Do you think his buddy on the bank would say each time he came up, 'You are so repetitious! I don't think I want to help you. If you'll think of some new or unusual way to say it, maybe I'll rescue you.' " It is the feelings of the heart and the faith behind the prayer, and not the words alone that make prayer effective.

One father said, "My favorite scripture for teaching children about prayer is:"

Behold, I stand at the door, and knock; if any man hear my voice, and open the door, I will come in to him, and will sup with him, and he with me.

(Revelations 3:20)

He said, "I explain to my children that this promise is made to all of us; the Lord does not discriminate. But He has only promised to knock, not crash the door. If we do not listen to the knock and open the door, He will not come in and answer prayers. However, He is always there, knocking. He never leaves us alone, and if we feel our prayers aren't being heard, we can always be sure we are the ones who have moved and not the Lord. I also tell them that to pray and ask the Lord for answers, then not listen to His reply, is like calling a friend, explaining a problem and asking for advice; then hanging up on him when he is about ready to give it!"

Karen Reilley believes we should share our own prayer experiences with our children. She has a special notebook where she records experiences she considers answers to her prayers. She often shares these stories with her children and feels they help teach the children what kinds of answers to expect and what to look for. They have also helped her teach that the secret of effective prayer is to be humble and sense your need strongly. Karen feels their faith in prayer has been strengthened by knowing of times her own prayers have been answered.

Prayer can be taught by example from the time children are very young. Faye McFarland said, "We had a two-year-old girl that had never talked. She just let her older sister talk for her. Then one day she decided it was her turn to say the prayer. That was her first real effort to talk and for several weeks afterwards, the prayer was still about the only thing she would say!"

"...And They Will Not Depart from It"

One day Helen Sharp's little girl, Shelley, was tending children. One small boy disappeared while she was busy with another child. Shelley went on her bicycle searching for him, but when she couldn't find him, she came home twice and prayed that the boy would be found safe. Helen said, "After Shelley left the second time, I went into the bedroom and I prayed too. I said, 'Heavenly Father, please answer this little girl's prayer. She needs to know she's got a Heavenly Father. She's really trying to do the right thing, and she is such a good girl. You know what a good girl she is.' I had hardly finished my prayer when the phone rang, and he had been found. When Shelley found out, she broke into tears and said, 'Heavenly Father helped him get back to us safely, didn't he?' " As Helen said, our children need to learn through experience that they have a Heavenly Father who can and will help them.

Marilyn Ursenbach was scheduled for an operation when she was fourteen years old. It was one in a long series of operations that she had endured. She was worried, and her mother was concerned. The morning of the operation she got up early, came out into the kitchen where her mother, Bernice, was working and started chatting with her. Her mother was surprised at how calm and unruffled she seemed.

"Did you sleep well, Marilyn?" her mother asked.

"All night!" replied Marilyn.

Bernice expressed surprise, and Marilyn said, "I was afraid, but I prayed really hard all week that I wouldn't be afraid today and that everything would be all right, and my prayers were answered."

Rachel McOmber said, "Mark, our missionary son in Germany, wrote of riding a huge transit bus. After he got off the bus he noticed his wallet missing, with his visa, addresses needed for tracting, credentials, plus rent and spending money for the month. He took the next bus and went to the end of the line and he and his companion searched; then checked with the agent. The agent laughed and said, 'Count on it being lost forever!' Mark was desperate and contacted the mission president, who said, 'Money and wallets lost in this mission field are seldom recovered; you will have to work it out the best you can.' Mark went home and stayed up all night praying for help. He told the Lord, 'I'm on a mission for you and I can't be an efficient servant without my billfold. I have dedicated myself to you and now I need your help as I rededicate my service, etc.' Four days later the wallet was returned in the mail, intact; an unheard of thing in Germany. Then Mark spent more time on his knees thanking our Heavenly Father."

"Behold, the Lord Hath Heard the Prayers of Thy Father"

Carol Jeanne Ehlers, mother of twelve, said, "Having as many children as I do and with the challenges I face each day, if I didn't begin my day with prayer it would be worse than a teacher going into a classroom without preparing—pure confusion! Prayer just has to be the greatest way to begin each day and to prepare us to help our children."

Betty Ellsworth feels they have learned through the years as parents that prayer is the most important thing you can do to understand your children, to know how to relate to them and to know their problems and how to help them. "Years ago I started using early morning hours as praying time. I would start praying, and it would come to my mind who needed help this time, and even what I should pray about. I found if I continued praying long enough, the Lord would tell me these things in my mind and give me ideas of how I could solve problems or help a child who was having a problem. When our son was on a mission we were forewarned through prayer of a problem he would be facing. About the day after Christmas I was praying and had this feeling he was going to be experiencing a real low. He had been singing in a chorus with a group of missionaries (which had proven to be a special kind of missionary tool). Now this experience was over, I felt he was going to hit rock bottom. My husband and I prayed for him, and the Lord gave us the feeling we should write and encourage him. About the time our letters got to him he was going through a very bad time. He let us know later that our letters were the thing that helped him through, and made the difference. I think if we will get in tune, the Lord will help us help our children!"

One family had a problem with a teenaged son who was growing rebellious and avoiding contact with his family. He was resisting all efforts to include him in the family circle and there seemed to be no way to reach him. They knew he was at a crossroads in his life, and his mother and father began making it a matter of earnest prayer to know what to do to help him. His dad said, "We prayed with real intent because we really felt that we needed an answer. We got the strong impression that what we needed to do was help our son feel our love in every way possible, including touch. So we began making it a point to ruffle his hair, pat his shoulder, and give him love taps. His mother said, "It was exciting how many small things we found to express love because we were looking for ways. We sent him notes and his favorite foods in his lunches, expressed our love and appreciation to him verbally and made it a point to fix foods he especially liked when he was home, along with the things my husband mentioned. Within the period of about a year, we sensed a complete turn-about in his attitude. There was no more rebellion, no more distance, and he was participating, interacting and enjoying the family influence once more."

Stephen Covey said, "There is no greater way to bless another person than to pray with him and for him in a believing attitude. It can help open up the powers of Heaven in that person's life." Parents can and should take advantage of this great principle.

"Pray in Your Families Unto the Father"

"Praying for each other in family prayers can make prayer a 'build-up' time," said Betty Ellsworth. "We gain strength by really praying for help for each other. For instance, if one of the children is going out on a date and you have prayed for them vocally with the family that they might be safe, make the right choices and do the right things, I believe it gives them strength and a desire that they might not have otherwise."

Ross and Judy Richins believe you can teach children many things by the way you pray in family prayers. Judy said, "What you pray for and how real prayer is to you makes a great impression on them. It can also do much to set the mood in the home, and encourage love and support between family members. If you are praying that all will be kind to each other; that all will help Dad to be a good bishop, etc., you then start those positive thoughts in their minds and 'program' them for the kind of behavior you most desire."

Don and Barbara Marshall feel their family has really been strengthened by the increased closeness they get through praying together. The Marshalls have one son who has set an especially good example of meaningful prayer from the time he was a tiny child learning to talk. He has always prayed as though he were talking with Heavenly Father and prayed for his real concerns rather than just repeating words. Hearing him pray has helped each family member to pray more sincerely.

"The best prayers we have had in our family have been from our children," said Rachel McOmber. "They have been very special. Prayer time is a time of drawing our family close together. I think it is the most special time we have."

"A Sure Guide"

"I think the little prayers that I say all day long are the things that really help me through," said Helen Sharp. "In and of myself I can't accomplish a thing, but with the Lord's help I can do anything. When I don't know how to handle a situation, I say 'Heavenly Father, help me to know what to do.' It may sound silly, but when the children are having any kind of a problem, I find it so much easier to help *them* if I first ask God to help *me.* For example, if my daughter is at the piano and is frustrated because she can't play what she wants to, she may say, 'I'm not going to play this anymore.' If I say a little prayer first, then go to her, it makes all the difference and I am able to do and say the right things to help her. Heavenly Father doesn't send us here to fail; He wants us to succeed, and He is there to help us. The scriptures say He will lead us by the hand and give us answers to our prayers, and I firmly believe that."

One mother who was the Spiritual Living lesson leader in her ward learned this when she had to teach the lesson called "Poise under Provocation" which stressed the contrast between living by the guidance of the spirit and just "re-acting" to the provocations of the moment. She said, "The month before that lesson I decided I had to change my life. My real weakness was responding sharply and impatiently to the irritations of raising a family and I felt I couldn't teach a lesson I was not living. Changing was one of the hardest things I've ever tried to do, but I committed to myself that each time I was about to lose my temper or respond in an unkind way (if I couldn't get control by stopping a second and saying a silent prayer) I would leave, go to my bedroom and pray as long as I needed to in order to get the right spirit back. I soon learned that if the toast needs to be buttered or a diaper needs to be changed—they can wait; but the harm I do by reacting without the spirit is much more serious than neglecting other things for a short time." In her lesson she was able to relate some success experiences she had in learning to live this principle. "One night my son didn't want to go to bed. He fumed and fretted but finally went downstairs to his room. He hadn't been there two minutes until he was yelling for me. I felt put out, but went down. He was propped up in bed and said 'I can't sleep.' Previously I would have said, 'You lay down and go to sleep this minute! I don't want to hear another word!' But I stopped, let the spirit take over, then sat on his bed and said, 'What's the matter, David?' He confided a problem to me that night that was very serious to him, and doors were opened; feelings shared. I was able to influence him and help him. But that opportunity never would have come if I hadn't been listening to the spirit.

"Another night my daughter Sharel wouldn't say the prayer in family home evening. Before, I might have said, 'You straighten up and say that prayer immediately!' but I stopped, put my arms around her and said, 'Sharel, we really would like you to help us in this way. Is something bothering you?' I had no more trouble with Sharel.

"When I forgot and reverted back to old ways, I tried to learn from it. One morning, my little boy wouldn't go to Nursery School. He wouldn't give me any reason and finally I grabbed his arm, shook him, and said, 'Why don't you want to go, why, why?' But he was angry and noncommittal. Later, in a different spirit, we discussed it and he said, 'Well, Mama, I didn't want to brush my teeth. The toothpaste stings my tongue and I didn't think you'd let me go with dirty teeth!' It was a little thing, yet in his mind, a big thing, and children often cannot tell us the small but important things when we are impatient with them."

This mother concluded by saying, "I'm a changed woman; even my small children have commented on the difference and I'm so grateful for the change."

"...Your Bosom Shall Burn Within You"

Joye Billings teaches her children the song, "The Still, Small Voice" (from *Sing With Me,* page B-92) to help them understand the concept of the promptings of the Holy Ghost. She also has the children memorize key scriptures about prayer and the many promptings of the spirit. She believes that if you talk about these principles, diligently teach them and express your own faith in them, that the children will be led to try them and to learn from experiencing the great power there.

One of the most important things we could do is teach our children to seek and to recognize the special promptings of the

Holy Ghost. That understanding can give them the key to overcome temptations, make right choices, and ultimately fulfill their missions on the earth. Learning to listen and obey promptings gives us the 'edge' over the forces of evil.

Ross Richins, bishop and father of five, believes that the best way children can know good from bad is through the gift of the Holy Ghost. He tries to help his children recognize how the Holy Ghost affects their feelings to give them guidance. For instance, he said, "In the matter of music, I have to select my music by the way it makes me feel—and I'm trying to teach my children to do the same. I have a great concern to try to teach them to govern themselves and learn to act on and recognize the promptings—and when they feel bad about something avoid it." He said that rather than making hard and fast rules, like "no rock music," he feels he should leave it to the children to judge and educate them to recognize evil when it is there. The same thing applies with TV shows. They ask the children to evaluate what they are watching and ask themselves, "Is it a good show? Does it make me feel good inside? If not, turn it off." He also mentioned that at times, adults may see and interpret "bad" that children are totally unaware of because of their lack of understanding, so perhaps we should not always impose our interpretations on them.

"I Will Tell You in Your Mind and in Your Heart"

One father said, "We can help children know how to identify the promptings of the Holy Ghost by describing our own promptings to them. I often tell my children that the "ear" of the spirit is the heart, and the Holy Ghost speaks to us through the feelings of the heart—our consciences. This simple process is what we sometimes refer to as 'personal revelation'. It isn't mystical or dramatic, although it is sometimes accompanied by definite thoughts that come into our minds along with a peaceful, warm, comfortable feeling. I also point out that learning to recognize these feelings can help us solve all our problems, and make our prayers really effective. But we need to prepare ourselves to be able to receive promptings by doing the things we know are right."

Ross Richins said that some of their best opportunities for teaching about the Holy Ghost have been in conjunction with family home evenings; times when they have told the children things like "We are so grateful that Heavenly Father sent you to us and that you are in our family." Ross said, "There's usually been tears, and a feeling of the Holy Ghost present and we've been able to point this out to the children and it has really been special.

"The first time when we had that kind of experience when Christy was five, I went in after she was in bed, and she was crying. I said, 'What's wrong, honey?' 'I don't know,' she said. 'But I just love you and I love Mommy, and I don't know why I'm crying.' 'Do you feel happy inside?' 'Oh, yes, Daddy!' And so I explained that sometimes when the Holy Ghost is with us we feel so happy that we cry, and it is a sweet experience, and one that we shouldn't be embarrassed about. That was her first experience of really feeling the spirit of the Lord with her."

Helen Sharp said, "I had an experience soon after I was married when my life was spared because I listened to a prompting and followed it even though it was very hard for me to do. It was a real testimony to me that if we listen to the promptings and try to do what is right we will be helped and protected. I have told my children this story, and every other experience I can think of in my life that shows the promptings of the spirit because I want so much to teach them we have a loving Heavenly Father who is there to help us. I have such a testimony of prayers and promptings, and I don't think any child is too young to hear about those things!"

"Thy Will Be Done"

Vital principles concerning prayers and promptings can be taught by our personal experiences, such as the one Gayla Wise shared with us: "My story begins with a prayer. I had been Junior Sunday School chorister for a long time and was 'dried out' of ideas. I prayed and told the Lord I felt I was ready for a new challenge, one with opportunity for spiritual growth (but that if He wanted me to stay where I was I would accept that as the challenge).

"The Sunday School presidency had been reorganized, and I had not been called back into my old job, so I began to wonder if the bishop might have something else in mind for me. I prayed hard one night and I don't know when it came to me, but I knew my next job was to be Relief Society President. Over and over I said, 'That's ridiculous!' And every time the words came back, calmly and definitely, 'But that's what it is.' All night long I wrestled with it. I was overwhelmed with the seeming enormity of the position and the impossibility of carrying out such a thing with my five young children to care for.

"The emotional struggle was only the beginning. I didn't dare tell the Lord I wouldn't do it, and I didn't dare tell Him I would. In one prayer as I poured my heart out, it came to me how very much the Lord had done for me, and I was greatly humbled. By comparison, anything I might do was as nothing. So I committed to the Lord that if he really wanted me to be Relief Society president I would do it. Two weeks later the Bishop called me in and told me I was the one the Lord wanted for that job. Because of my experiences, I believed him!

"It was exciting to be an instrument of the Lord, and see His work happen through my hands. Nearly every day I could see little ways He stretched out to touch the life of one individual sister at a time.

"Four months later, a new bishopric was sustained. I went home that day eager to work with the new bishop. But as the day wore on, the spirit of the Lord gave me the message I would be released from my position. I struggled. I guess I argued with the Lord, at least I gave Him a detailed explanation of why I wasn't ready to be released. But the message was definite, "You've done a good job, but your time is up." I knew the Lord had already released me. I knew that, as hard as it was, I must accept this as the will of the Lord. Whether or not I understood was insignificant, but that I obey was vital. Here was a spiritual challenge, opposite to the commitment needed when I was put into the position (and to anything I had experienced before). Yes, it was even a sacrifice.

"I had felt from the first that I would not be in the position for long. I just hadn't expected my time to be quite that short! Many times I told the children, 'I may not have this job very long. It's important that you help me so that I can do the very best job I can while I have it.' We talked about the promptings, (and the great help they were in helping me to adjust) after I was released and I helped them understand the workings of the spirit through my experience."

"Having Been Warned of the Lord"

Arlene Barnes believes we are often given promptings for our safety and the safety of our loved ones. One day, when her baby was 3½ months old, she was prompted to check him. When she did he was turning blue! She followed her inner promptings and somehow knew what to do. The doctors called him their "miracle baby". He had "crib-death syndrome" and would have died if Arlene hadn't helped him immediately and followed all the correct procedures. She uses this story to help teach her children to recognize help and promptings when they come; also as a warning never to ignore promptings. She said they also talk a lot about similar experiences that have happened to other people they are close to and the children are deeply impressed with the concept.

Mary Lou Burgoyne tells of an experience with promptings which she will never forget. When her youngest boy had just learned to walk, Mary Lou was in the bedroom getting ready for Relief Society when she felt a distinct prompting to check on her baby. She ignored it at first because she had just left him. But when the feeling kept coming back, she hurried out to the kitchen. Mary Lou said, "I caught my breath when I saw my teetering toddler walking along holding a large butcher knife by the blade and looking down at the point. I could have panicked, cried out or moved towards him too suddenly, causing him to fall on the knife; but I was led to stay calm, walk up to him slowly, talk softly, and so I rescued him from danger. I felt weak afterwards just thinking of what could have happened if I had not listened to the prompting I received."

"Your Diligence, Perseverance, Patience and Works"

Life is not meant to be easy, and we have many problems to solve and dangers to face. But we have been given the companionship and guidance of the Holy Ghost to give us the help and protection we need. George Pace, outstanding church leader and speaker said, "Some of us find ourselves running to and fro, trying to figure out ways and means by which we might find peace, by which we might free ourselves from some habits which are plaguing us, trying to figure out ways that we can have greater self-esteem, trying to figure out how we can really become happy individuals. We try a lot of approaches, and yet the Lord is implicit and emphatic; in effect He says: 'If you want to become a mighty man or woman, you must obtain and keep the power of the Holy Ghost in your life, and every quality and characteristic of a godly personality will be yours.' " He added, "The greatest single thing we can accomplish on the face of the earth is to live by the spirit of revelation; to learn to recognize and follow the promptings of the Holy Ghost. And since it is the greatest thing, we can rest assured that it will be a mighty struggle to master the flesh, to humble ourselves and to recognize our dependency upon the Lord." John A. Widtsoe explains it this way, "But remember, when irrigation began in Utah, it was a struggle with the earth, it required toil. The water didn't flow down from these canyon streams to the farms just by asking it to do so. But men dug and drilled, and shoveled and made canals. And so, to get that spiritual stream of communication, it must be fought for. It must be labored for. It will come, but we must ask for it, and seek for it and labor for it; then comes the great change—an everlasting change. It changes men to a godlike phase of life and living."

Ten Things to Try

1. Teach a child when and how to pray; then offer gentle reminders at times when they have a need. Lead children to prayer experiences as a natural part of living so they will automatically turn to the Lord.

2. When teaching children to pray, help them put feelings into words by asking them questions which direct their thinking.

3. Share prayer experiences with your children. Try recording (in a special notebook) experiences you consider answers to your prayers and read them to the children occasionally.

4. Use prayer as a constant help in understanding, and helping your children with their problems.

5. Pray for each other in family prayer. Use family prayer to set the mood in your home, strengthen your family and "program" the behavior you most desire.

6. Teach your children key scriptures about prayer and the promptings of the spirit.

7. Learn and teach the song, "The Still, Small Voice". (*Sing With Me,* page B-92.)

8. Help them identify their own promptings by describing your feelings when the Holy Ghost influences you and pointing out the sweetness of your shared experiences with the Holy Ghost.

9. Help children appreciate the importance of a "sure guide" to help us know right from wrong, protect us from danger, and testify of truth. Share stories concerning these things.

10. Have the children help you list the many blessings that can come from having the guidance of the Holy Ghost; then

analyze the effort required to gain these blessings. Point out that this blessing like all others, is predicated on law and requires effort.

Helping Children Love and Use the Scriptures

My soul delighteth in the scriptures, and my heart pon-dereth them, and writeth them for the learning and profit of my children. (2 Nephi 4:15)

Scriptures are divine books full of the Lord's blueprints for building happy lives. They are relevant! They apply to us! They give answers and insights and specific guidance! Like charity, scripture reading should begin at home, seasoned with love and brightened with companionship.

There are three basic ways to read scriptures together: from beginning to end, by topic, and at random. Regardless of the way we choose, the important thing is that our children feel the spirit and get the messages within.

Medicine or a Meal?

Sometimes we offer scriptures to children as though they were medicine, instead of a delicious and nourishing meal. Suppose Dad says, "Johnny and Sue, come here. I am going to read the scriptures to you. Now sit still and listen. Scriptures are good for you, and you need to know them." In contrast we might use the approach of the Roy Despain family:

Just before bedtime on Sunday, Roy goes into the living room and lights a fire in the fireplace or lights two or three candles which he sets on the raised hearth. Then all lights are turned out and the pajama-clad family is drawn to him by the magic of flickering flames. In a calm and expressive voice he begins to read from the Book of Mormon. A peacefulness settles over the house as the children feel the warmth of the moment and sense that Daddy is reading something important. Two-year-old Melissa gets restless and wanders around the living room, but no one scolds; she feels part of this special time and that's enough for now. Brandon and Brenda whisper; they are not hushed, but Dad pauses a moment before continuing. The session lasts no more than fifteen minutes, and afterwards they kneel in family prayer.

Another family has a starlight scripture-reading tradition. On selected evenings when the stars are bright and the night air refreshing, the family gathers in the back yard, where the father reads some of his favorite passages by flashlight! How impressive to hear this scripture while looking at stars:

> When I consider thy heavens, the work of thy fingers, the moon and the stars, which thou has ordained;
> What is man, that thou art mindful of him? and the son of man, that thou visitest him?
> For thou hast made him a little lower than the angels, and hast crowned him with glory and honour.
>
> (Psalms 8:3-5)

Surely this would be one of those unforgettable moments in a child's life, and could help him equate scriptures with beauty and family closeness.

Making Scripture Time Family Time

When their stake president challenged parents to read the scriptures with their children regularly, Judy and Ross Richins decided to try making dinnertime their regular scripture-reading time. They take turns choosing and reading the scriptures, and the person in charge of the scripture also says the family prayer. Sometimes the children bring a special scripture home from Primary or Sunday School which they want to share at scripture time. Sometimes they read only one verse; other times they read a whole story. Judy said, "The children have really enjoyed scripture reading time and look forward to it. It has also helped the spirit of our family prayers."

Robert C. and Janice Burton (who have ten children) told us with a smile that they serve their scriptures with dessert. Janice said, "Dessert is the spoonful of sugar that makes scripture reading more fun for our children, but we probably have the messiest Books of Mormon anywhere! Each of us has his own copy and they are all decorated with dabs of everything we've had for dessert for the past ten years! But we have been through the Book of Mormon three times and we've all enjoyed it." Each child old enough takes his turn reading. After the older ones finish and leave the table, the little ones stay and go through the same scriptures in an illustrated Book of Mormon stories and Janice explains them. "When scriptures are heard by little children regularly, they become as natural as nursery rhymes," Janice says. "Once when David was three years old, he sat down to 'read a story to his little sister. He opened the book and started the fairy tale, 'And it came to pass.' "

Over the years, the Ruth and Calvin Heiner family have tried various times of the day for family scripture reading. One year they read every evening before family prayer (just before the youngest were tucked in for the night.) Their married daughter, Linda, remembers this as the best year of all for scripture-reading. They had a Venezuelan exchange student living with them and felt a great incentive to be a good example to him. He good-naturedly joined in their evening scripture-reading time; even taking his turn reading in his broken English. They were reading the Book of Mormon at the time, and he often said,

"Splain me this!" and very good family discussions resulted from his desire to understand.

Some parents mentioned that as family members grow older and begin to have varied and conflicting schedules, getting everyone together often appears impossible. Charles and Mary Lou Burgoyne have three children at home, and with Charles and all three children on completely different schedules, they had concluded there was no way to read scriptures together daily. However, when their son, Bob, received a mission call recently he said, "One thing I'd really like to do to feel prepared is to read the Book of Mormon clear through with the family." They talked it over and decided that with a change of morning routine, and some sacrifice of sleep they could get together early. They began to read ten pages daily, and will finish before Bob leaves on his mission. Mary Lou said, "Carrying out this decision has made a beautiful difference in our home. We used to all get up at different times, each grabbing a bite of breakfast and going his separate way. Now, we read scriptures first, have family prayer, eat a companionable breakfast (often discussing the things we've read) and then each one finishes getting ready at his own pace. The increased feeling of love and unity carries through the whole day!"

Of course the home picture is not always blissful just because we try to put a scripture-reading program (or any other program) into action! Annette Capener said, "We really try to have scripture reading and songs with our six children in the morning. But I have to sigh comparing the scene in our home with the idyllic picture that is so often painted. My little ones are wiggly and noisy and might be wanting breakfast, fighting over mother's lap or trying to get attention. The older ones might be fighting over who got to read the longest scripture, and sometimes they act perfectly bored. But over a period of time, we can really see the teachings and the spirit of the scriptures influencing the children, and we begin to get the vision of what can be accomplished if you just persevere, even when it is hard!"

It's Never Too Soon to Begin

We may feel it is not helpful to begin reading scriptures with small children until they can comprehend the messages. But this true story was told in a Relief Society testimony meeting: "When my children were all tiny, I began reading a few verses of the Doctrine and Covenants to them every evening at bedtime. I really felt the children were too little to understand or remember, but it was the only time I could seem to find for *me* to read, so I continued because of the spiritual uplift it gave me. Years later, my teenage daughter came home from Seminary one day and said, 'Mom, the strangest thing is happening. We are reading the Doctrine and Covenants and I know I've never read it before. Yet, so much of it seems so familiar that it's as though it were already in my mind.' I was overcome with emotion and tears filled my eyes, as I realized the value of all those little bedtime sessions."

When Linda Garner (mother of four tiny children) heard this, she began to read to her children from the scriptures. She reads one verse at a time, then explains it. The children ask for this daily session and look forward to it. They often ask questions that give Linda a good chance to explain and clarify important concepts. One night when they had read a scripture that mentioned death, three-year-old Heather said, "Tell me again why we have to die, and where Grandma went when she died."

Even very young minds are hungry for spiritual understanding. We have talked with parents who say their little ones cry if they think they are going to miss a nightly scripture-reading session.

Make Scriptures Meaningful

In a recent Stake Conference, S. Dilworth Young said we should explain scriptures, describe them and bring them down to the level of a child's experience; not just *read* them. Let's look in on a typical morning scripture-reading time in the Delbert and Vera Eddington home for an example of how this can be done.

David (the Eddington's ten-year-old son) is reading the story of Jesus's trial. He reads a verse, then stops while Dad explains it to the younger children. For instance, Mark 15:10 "For he knew that the chief priests had delivered him for envy" might be explained as "Pilate knew the chief priests had brought Jesus because they were jealous of his power and how much the people loved him." This morning as Jesus's trial becomes a reality and as they feel the spirit of that sad night, some of the children have tears running down their cheeks. Children have tender feelings, and are usually receptive to the spirit's warm touch which can be felt through the scriptures.

One morning, seven-year-old Kenneth slept through scripture reading and repeatedly quizzed his brothers and sisters to learn what had happened. He didn't want to feel left out!

We asked Vera Eddington if they have always had daily scripture reading with their eleven children. "Many times we haven't,"
she replied, "but we find that absolute consistency isn't the most
important thing. If you just keep trying and read most of the time,
it does wonders! Our missionary son wrote home and said to the
other children, 'Be sure and read scriptures with Mom and Dad!
What a great help those morning study times have been to me.
Many of the other missionaries come to me to get explanations of
scriptures they don't understand.'"

Unexpected Blessings

Reading scriptures together can bring about unforseen
benefits as well as the ones we seek and expect. One mother
said, "Not long after we began reading scriptures together at
breakfast time, my son told me he was concerned about the
interview he had just had with the Bishop. He confessed that
some time back he had been looking at questionable magazines
at a friend's house. He said he had never thought much about it
until the family started reading the scriptures. Then he realized it
was wrong and quit doing it, making certain he never went to this
boy's house if they were going to be alone. But although he had
repented, he wondered if he should have discussed it with the
Bishop." This mother was grateful for her son's concern and sensitivity, and she was impressed that by being obedient and doing
what the Prophet said about scripture reading they had solved a
completely non-related problem. She chuckled and said, "I don't
remember reading a single scripture that said, "Thou shalt not
read bad magazines," but the spirit of the scriptures got through
to my son to make him more aware of the difference between
good and evil."

Another benefit that often comes when little children become familiar with scripture stories is that the people in the
scriptures become more real to them. Matthew Johansen, who is
three, hears Book of Mormon stories every morning, and his
mother, Margaret, finds it exciting to see him act them out in his
play. His knowledge has become a good missionary tool, too!
Matthew plays with some neighbor children who are non-
members, and the parents have come to ask Margaret "Who are
the Lamanites and the Nephites?"

Another unexpected bonus of family scripture reading is the
humorous way scriptural terminology tends to creep into everyday situations. Malin Lewis and his wife, Myreel, have had early

morning scripture reading with their twelve children for many years. One night they left the children with a baby sitter, and when they got home, she could hardly wait to tell them this story: "When it was bedtime, I sent the two boys to the bedroom to get their pajamas on. They had been gone quite a while and I thought I'd better check on them. I knocked on the door and asked what they were doing. One boy called out, "Oh, Sister McKeeby, don't come in! I haven't girded my loins yet!"

Introduce the Scriptures Creatively!

There are many things a parent can do to make children more receptive to the scriptures. At Roy and Deanne Despain's house on a Monday morning about three years ago, you would have seen four-year-old Brenda adjusting the shawl over her head while Mom tied a sash around the bathrobe costume two-year-old Brandon was wearing.

"Tonight in family home evening we are going to talk about the Bible," Mother explained. "All day today we are going to pretend we are living in Bible days. We are going to dress like Bible people dressed, talk about the way they talked and I am even going to let you help make some of the kinds of food they ate."

"Oh, Mommy, this is fun!" exclaimed Brenda. "Can I be Mary?"

It was a special day as many Bible stories were told or acted out while Deanne went about her work. Roy felt the spirit of it when he came home from work and immediately joined in. (He didn't even complain when Deanne dressed him up too!) Later in the evening two little robed figures listened intently as their parents gave a lesson about the Bible.

The dramatic approach to introducing scriptures often creates enthusiasm and helps children understand their importance. Simple props and costumes can make ideas more fun and more effective.

Darla has used analogies to stress the importance of scriptures to her children. She said, "In a recent family home evening, I explained to my two oldest boys that we were going to do some play-acting and they were going to be the stars of the production. I told them, "Mark and Brian, you are going to be sent on a long, long journey far from home. Everything will be new and unfamiliar; but we will give you two things to help you. Here are letters of instructions (including stories of people who have made this journey before), and here is a lantern with a bright light and plenty of fuel. Instructions for lighting the lanterns are in the letters. It will be very dark where you are going, but you will always have a light to guide you if you will read the instructions and do as they say. Mark, how anxious do you think you would be to read those instructions?"

"I'd want to read them all—right now!" Mark replied.

"Brian, do you think you would go along carrying your lantern in the dark, or would you try to light it?"

"I'd try to light it—I don't like the dark!"

"This life is a journey and all the experiences we have here are new to us. It could be like walking in the dark, but Heavenly Father gave us the scriptures as instructions, and the Holy Ghost which is like a light to guide us." Mark and Brian really enjoyed this lesson and we talked about it for days afterwards.

Another analogy we thought would be fun is: "You are the captain of a great ocean liner and must get your crew, passengers and cargo safely across the ocean. You have a compass, charts of ocean currents, weather information from the radio and stars in the sky to help you chart your course. As captain of your life, the Lord has given you the scriptures to help you chart your course."

Other possibilities might be: "You are an astronaut, or a pilot of a jet plane, or a builder, or an electronics man with diagram and instruction books, etc."

Each parent can develop his own analogies, and explain in the way he feels most effective how the analogy applies to our possession of the scriptures and how important it is that we use them. When our children are young, if we can vividly illustrate the value of scriptures to them, they will learn to automatically turn to them later when they need help and guidance.

The Good Samaritan Could Be Me!

One mother told us she often compares scripture characters and situations with the everyday problems of the children and the people they know. Substituting familiar names for scriptural ones helps bring the scriptures to life and helps the children identify scriptural situations with their daily experiences. For example, her son came home one day and said, "That boy that lives on the corner isn't very nice, Mom! None of the other kids want to play with him, and I don't either!"

"Do you know what a Samaritan is, dear?" she asked. "In the land where Jesus lived, the people didn't like them either. They lived in a country bordering Jesus's country."

"I remember the Good Samaritan story, Mom."

"Why don't you tell it to me pretending you are the man who is hurt and the boy is the good Samaritan who stops to help."

He told the story, and then they talked about who would stop to help the boy if he were hurt. "I'm not sure I would want to stop, Mom," he admitted, obviously worried. He was very thoughtful after their conversation and talked about how hard it would be to be a good Samaritan.

Another example of applying the scriptures to an everyday situation was shared by Connie Evans, who said, "The story of Daniel has become especially significant to our family. One day our oldest daughter, Holly, came home from school frustrated and upset. She said, 'Oh Mom, what am I going to do? A lot of the most popular kids are planning to sluff tomorrow and they've asked me to go with them. I don't want to hurt anyone's feelings or make them think I'm out of it, but I need to be in school tomorrow. I have a test and everything. Besides, it's just wrong to sluff.'

"I said, 'Holly, Grandma Evans taught us a poem a long time ago that might help you. Do you remember the one about Daniel?'

'Sure, sure,' Holly replied. Then she recited in a sing-song voice:

> Dare to be a Daniel
> Dare to stand alone
> Dare to have a purpose
> Dare to make it known.

'I'll bet Daniel never went to a junior high like mine, Mom!'

'Well, Holly, it's easy to do things right when our friends back us up and support us; it's when we have to stand alone that it gets hard.' 'I don't feel much like a Daniel, Mom, but I'll try!'"

If your children feel preached to when you suggest scriptural solutions to problems, you might try Vera Eddington's solution and suggest to older children that *they* look for the scriptural answers themselves.

"Our" Scriptures—Not "the" Scriptures

Before we can use scriptures we must know them, and the better we know them the more likely we are to use them. Memorizing meaningful verses is the best way to equip our minds to think in scriptural terms.

In the Hanks' kitchen, on either side of a picture of the Savior are bulletin boards with the headings, "Scripture of the Week" and "Prophet of the Week."

To help the children memorize the scripture of the week, they say it several times together at breakfast every morning. (One family says their scripture of the week before every prayer of the day.) Children are quick to learn and often have the scripture down pat by Tuesday while mom and dad may take the whole week to learn it!

Darla says, "Our oldest son, Mark, listened to conference last October, and I was thrilled when he said afterwards, 'Hey, Mom, they said three of *our* scriptures in Conference!' "

Our scriptures—isn't that the way we would like our children to think of them? By memorizing them, they truly become *ours.*

Many parents we interviewed felt that incentives for scriptural reading and memorizing can be motivating and helpful. One mother offers her children a treat when they can recite a scripture by memory. Another mother offered her sons five dollars to memorize fifteen scriptures which she felt would give them strength all their lives. The Calvin Heiner family had a tradition that any child who finished his first reading of the Book of Mormon would receive a ten dollar reward. Their daughter Linda started working for the ten dollars in the 6th grade and finished when she was a sophomore in high school. She says, "When I received that ten dollar reward, it was precious to me because I felt it stood for a great accomplishment. I didn't even want to spend it."

Joye Billings likes to carve and has carved several "gold plate" replicas. Her husband helped her carve little hieroglyphics on them and put rings through, and the children helped paint them gold. Whenever one of the children finishes reading the Book of Mormon he gets one of these carvings for his own.

Whether children receive tangible rewards for memorizing and reading scriptures or not, they will receive lifelong spiritual rewards for doing it. And the more familiar a child is with the scriptures, the more he will love them and identify with them, even if he doesn't completely understand them at the time. Charles and Connie Evans taught their children the ten commandments, and when their little girl recited them back, she said, "Thou shalt not admit adultery!" We must explain what we can now, and realize that the words will mean more later!

LaDawn Jacob said, "I think there is value in memorizing great thoughts, even though we may not fully understand them. Poems and scriptures I memorized as a child mean a hundred times more to me now, and the meaning has come through more and more as I have reflected back on them over the years. I'm so glad my parents had me memorize when I was young."

Giving each child his own copy of the scriptures is another way of encouraging scriptural knowledge. Many families mentioned that they had given their children personal copies as soon as they could read. Michael Bascom repeatedly asked, "Daddy, read it out of *my* Bible," after he had been given his own. Linda Garner treasures a Christmas gift of a white Bible with her name on it in gold, given to her when she was just eight.

But a child's copy needn't be expensive or fancy to be special to him. Each of the nine children in the Leo R. Gifford family have their own paperback copies of the Book of Mormon, and their parents feel it has added a lot to their enjoyment of reading times together.

John and Carol Davis give each child their own personal set of the scriptures (with the child's name on each one) when they are baptized. Carol said, "We don't buy expensive copies because we want them to be able to mark them up, and not feel it's a tragedy if they get torn. We want the children to feel the scriptures are *theirs* and they can use them any time they want. They always use their own copies for our scripture reading time each morning."

Having special family books of scripture can also add to family enjoyment. The Barnes family have a beautifully illustrated Children's Bible that the children love and have become very familiar with. One night in Sacrament meeting, the speaker gave a talk about one of the children's favorite Bible stories, and their little pre-school girl said, "Mama, I wonder if he has the same book we have!"

Charles and Connie Evans purchased a set of the Illustrated Book of Mormon series (which are also available at many libraries.) Connie offered a small reward for each volume a child completed by themselves. She also arranged time for the child to review the book for the entire family.

"Tonight, Holly will tell us about Volume Six of the Book of Mormon Stories," Connie would say. Then Charles and Connie could see how well Holly comprehended and remembered what she read, and Holly would get a chance to be in the spotlight and have her efforts appreciated and applauded. Connie's plan worked so well that the three older children made it through all the volumes in a few weeks. Then she encouraged them to read the more difficult Church History material which is found at the first of the Book of Mormon Story Books. They all accepted the challenge and the program was going along fine. Then school started and eight-year-old Kelly announced, "I'm going to start again after school is out. This is pretty hard—and after all, I'm just a little girl!"

Tapes and Records Can Be Storytellers

Scripture tapes and records, as well as books, can increase family knowledge in an enjoyable way. Many families have purchased sets of dramatized scripture tapes, and found tapes to be a great teaching tool. Many children choose to listen to these tapes in preference to other activities.

Listening to scripture stories can be interesting background for play activities or for bedtime. On a typical day Kelly Evans asked, "Mommy, where's the record about Moses and the Red Sea?" She found it, turned the record on and happily colored as the record played. Kelly hummed as she took the record off and put on the story of Daniel to listen to while she played with her dolls.

Darla recalls, "It was story time at our house the other night, and I didn't feel like reading stories. Then it occured to me that my six- and seven-year-olds might enjoy the Book of Mormon tapes I had checked out of the library for my own use.

'Mark and Brian, I'm too tired to read stories tonight. How would you like King Benjamin from the Book of Mormon to tell you a story?'

'Oh Mom—you're silly!'

'No, really! I have a tape with a man talking who says he is King Benjamin. I'll get it.'

"The boys like King Benjamin as a storyteller and now the Book of Mormon storytellers are used often. A few days after I played the tape about the circumstances on this continent when Jesus died, I found out that Brian, who is six, remembered what he had heard. The light in his room burned out and he said, 'This is just like the three days and nights of darkness in the Book of Mormon—it's awful!' Scripture tapes at bedtime can be another of those precious times when gospel concepts can be neatly tucked into little minds. The atmosphere is right so that the stories and concepts they hear will later evoke pleasant associations. Imagine yourself slowly drifting off to sleep to the accompaniment of deep, rich voices telling gospel stories." Linda Garner often puts her children down for their naps listening to Bible story tapes. She said that many teaching moments arise from the stories. Her children ask questions like, "Mama, why did Jesus say he was a shepherd?" "Mama, what does 'verily' mean?"

Recently, Linda and her husband, Marshall, decided it would be fun to make their own scripture story tapes. They were living close to Marshall's family at the time and decided to make it a family home evening project with his brothers and sisters. They chose a Book of Mormon story, collaborated on the script, and assigned parts. They figured out appropriate sound effects and background music, and had a great time making the tape. Linda feels that even adults relate more to the feelings of scripture characters when they play the role.

Scripture Games to Liven Up Learning

One mother said, "On Sundays when the dishes are cleared away, my boys might say, 'Let's play Seek!' or, 'I want to play Exaltation!' 'Seek' and 'Exaltation' are two of our favorite religious games." Games can be a wonderful tool for motivating children to learn about the scriptures. Even small children can have fun learning if parents enthusiastically record the points they are earning or cheer for them when they give a correct answer. Scripture games make excellent Sunday activities, and original ones can be even more fun than the commercial ones.

On Sunday afternoon, a casual observer would be rather mystified at the scene in the living room of the Despain home. Brandon, age five, is swinging a "sling" and throws an imaginary rock at Mom, who is towering above him. She falls to the floor moaning, and then lies very still. "David and Goliath!" shouts Brenda. "Right." Brandon responds. Then Brenda takes a slip of paper from the hat Daddy is holding. She reads it carefully, and asks Derrick and little Melissa to come into the bedroom with her. They plan their "play" and act out the story of Mary and Joseph and the baby Jesus. And so it goes. Their Sunday scripture charade tradition has become a great motivation for the children to learn new scripture stories so they can act them out.

The Eddington children have often built forts with blankets and chairs and acted out various Book of Mormon scenes. Vera Eddington chuckled as she remembered what great fun they had

had doing it. Acting out scripture stories can help children identify with the characters and sense that they were real people. A
good knowledge of the scriptural characters, such as the prophets, adds a lot of interest and appeal to scripture reading, as well.

One week in a family home evening, Charles Evans said,
"Let's list all the prophets we can think of and see how many
there are."

"I know one, Daddy," said Laurie (not quite four), "President
Kimball!"

"Good, Laurie! He's a very important prophet to us, isn't he?"

"Isaiah!" adds eleven-year-old Tracy.

"Joseph Smith!" said Kelly.

When they had finished, and Mom and Dad had added a few
that the children left out, they were all surprised to find they had
listed about one hundred prophets! Then Dad said, "Now, let's
see how well we can do in putting them where they belong under
four different headings: Old Testament, New Testament, Book of
Mormon and Modern Day."

The reason the Evans family could have such fun playing this
prophet game is that for years they have played a game they call
"I'm thinking of a Prophet." They have played it in cars as they
travelled, in family home evenings, and any time they wanted to
do something fun. The rules are that one person thinks of a
prophet and everyone else asks questions about him that can be
answered with yes or no until they guess the right one. So it goes
like this:

"I'm thinking of a prophet."

"Is he a Bible prophet?"

"Yes."

"Did he live before Noah?"

"No."

They have to talk and read about prophets to make the game
fun and to know what questions to ask! Planning to have a prophet's picture up each week and reading things about him each
day could be helpful to prepare children to play the Evans' game!

Whether through games, tapes, records, reading sessions or
conversations, parents *can* make scriptures an integral and rewarding part of family life!

Ten Things to Try

1. Establish a Sunday firelight scripture-reading as a bedtime tradition.

2. Read scriptures under the stars (with a flashlight).

3. Try a regular scripture-reading time each day and discuss and explain as you read.

4. Act out situations which reflect the importance of using scriptures, such as a traveller using a map, etc.

5. Have a "Bible" day and have the kids dress the part, eat typical Bible foods and act out Bible stories.

6. Apply scriptures to everyday circumstances. Try substituting your children's names for those of scriptural characters.

7. Have a "scripture of the week" for the whole family to memorize.

8. Have good scriptural picture-books, records and tapes accessible to the children. Make it easy for them to choose scripture-learning activities.

9. Put your kids to bed with scripture storytellers. (Use dramatized tapes and records anytime to help the children learn scriptures.)

10. Play scripture games—"Seek", "Exaltation", "Scripture Charades", "I'm thinking of a prophet", etc., to give children an incentive to learn scriptural information, and have fun doing it!

7

Family Traditions Can Teach Values

Have you ever thought of yourself as a tradition-builder? Every parent is, you know. And we should be, because traditions can be great tools for building family unity and teaching a family's true values. Traditions give children a sense of security, a feeling of belonging, and help build memories which can be a potent force in influencing their behavior.

Think of the things you remember best from the home you grew up in. One common memory is coming home from school to the tantalizing smell of freshly-baked homemade bread or cookies. To some of us the memory is important because it happened often and it meant mother was there and that she cared. How many of your memories are simple things which your family repeated over and over until they stuck in your mind as something your family "always did"? You might remember things like going to church together each week, and making a fire in the fireplace every Sunday evening during cold weather and munching popcorn as you talked over the week's activities.

Traditions, as you can see, are not necessarily activities which are repeated only once a year (such as Christmas traditions), but any acts, words, rituals, procedures or even food which your family repeats until they are predictable and expected. A tradition should portray, without words, that which we value enough to do regularly. Traditions such as having family prayers around the smallest child's bed at night, reading aloud together each night after the evening meal, holding home evening each Monday, and having family councils around the kitchen table help us teach values by the very fact that we take the time to do them. This is important because of the probability that values must be "caught" rather than "taught."

Cotton Candy Traditions or Lasting Memories?

Asking ourselves "What kinds of memories do we want to make for our children?" can help us choose the traditions we want to have in our own families. Experiences are like the programs fed into a computer that later determine the computer's performance. David O. McKay said that special memories from the home in which he grew often gave him the strength to resist temptations in his life. Parents can plan for and make such memories in their own homes.

Good traditions can teach values and at the same time develop closer family ties or smooth family routines. However, if not carefully chosen, we may develop "cotton candy traditions" that taste sweet at the time but give little of lasting value. It is even possible to drift into traditions such as eating dinner around the TV every night which deter family progress rather than foster it. Other traditions, such as participating in sports activities, camping, etc. may bring closer family ties, yet may not further spiritual progress. These need to be added to and balanced with spiritual traditions.

Sundays to Look Forward to!

Almost any time is a good time for families to get together to make traditions, but Sunday is a special time for traditions. All the families we interviewed mentioned that family church attendance was one of their traditions, and most of them said that Sunday was traditionally a family day.

"My parents always went to church and expected us to go," said Rachelle Safsten (one of eleven children). "We went to church together and I liked to go because they made it seem special. I feel my testimony started and grew because we always went to church together."

Some mothers admitted that Sundays were sometimes difficult days, but they had improved their Sundays by doing two things: 1) preparing adequately and 2) including activities that everyone enjoyed. They stressed what their families *could* do on Sunday rather than what they couldn't do. This helped make Sundays a positive family experience.

Helen Sharp exclaimed, "Sundays I love! Sunday is our time together as a family. We go to church together and we enjoy the day together. It is a tradition at our house that the children don't have friends over during the day because Sunday is our family time. We sometimes do scripture things, and I like the children to be creative, so I often put a record on and everybody takes a turn performing to it."

Joye and Terah Billings often have company on Sunday and also make Sunday a day for visiting. In the summer they try to include a bouquet of flowers with their visits! The Billings have the regular Book of Mormon cassettes, and the older children often get their Books of Mormon and follow the words in the scripture while they listen. Then they get the illustrated Book of Mormon stories and read the same verses in the simplified version. They also play quiet games, read books, play "school" and, in the summer, sit on their patio and just enjoy being together outdoors.

Linda and Marshall Garner said, "We try to make Sunday a pleasant family day in our home. We listen to Bible tapes, read stories; things like that. But if the children get too restless we let them go out and play for awhile. We never want them to associate Sundays with being miserable." Alma and Clea Burton shared this philosophy when they said, "We often let the children play, but usually Sunday was a day to visit the grandparents and other relatives after our meetings; and the children really enjoyed it."

After Sacrament meeting Roy and Deanne Despain play "Scripture Charades" with their five young children and have great fun acting out and guessing scripture stories. Then just before bedtime they have a firelight scripture-reading tradition which ends their Sunday with warmth and some special family memories.

Planning and preparation can often make Sunday more special. Sandra Covey, in an Education Week lecture, said that on Saturday they prepare "Sunday Projects" for the children in manila folders. They assemble everything they will need for projects (ranging from genealogy to art, to filling scrapbooks) and set them out on the kitchen table. Saturday evening the dining room table is formally set in preparation for the Sunday meal.

The Leo and Katherine Gifford family have some traditions that keep Sunday special for their nine children. They often have films and filmstrips which the children really look forward to. (Leo works in the Seminary program and is a regional librarian for the Church, and has access to a great many.) He said that filmstrips are available in most meetinghouse libraries, and many of the church-produced films can be checked out by any church member through stake and regional librarians. Also, most Seminaries are happy to make their films and filmstrips (such as a whole series of Book of Mormon and Bible filmstrips) available to families upon request. The Giffords encourage other families to take advantage of these great visual aids for teaching the gospel at home and also for making Sundays and family home evenings extra special!

Another Sunday tradition the Giffords have really enjoyed is "grass-roots" genealogy projects. They have sorted and divided all the family's pictures and mementos, and are now organizing and putting them in scrapbooks and Books of Remembrance. They have also made it a family project to get their personal history sheets up to date. Katherine says it has been fun for all the children to remember who their teachers were and where they were living when they each started school, etc.

Focus on the Family Home Evening Tradition

Two other important traditions unanimously mentioned were family home evenings and family prayer. Both were an integral

part of home life for the families we visited. But while the varia-
tions of family prayer were only those of time and place, families
had many differing ideas to share concerning their home evening
activities.

We found family home evening to be a central tradition of
the families we interviewed. Many used family home evening to
talk over family problems, make decisions, begin new programs,
check on progress made, etc. Family home evening seems to be
one of the most important organizational tools for families, in
addition to giving the expected benefits of increased unity and
spiritual strength.

Robert and Jean Porcaro have a philosophy that the gospel
doesn't have to be somber, and that we should teach it with a
"spoonful of sugar" to make it palatable to the children. They believe there should be testimony bearing traditions, but also fun
and crazy traditions such as mid-winter picnics in the basement
with foil dinners, or early morning breakfasts in the canyon in the
summer with everyone dressed as pioneers. Their family home
evenings are also varied and interesting because they believe
variety is the key to keeping the children excited about home
evening, and about the gospel.

Each Monday after dinner, the family gets together for a
short lesson geared to the younger children. The older children
often give the lessons, help with activities, refreshments and
visual aids. Then, after the younger ones are in bed, Mom and
Dad and the older children sit around the kitchen table and discuss the lesson concepts which are pertinent to teenagers; and
they may play a game such as a budget game if the goal that
week is to help the children understand money management.

One home evening idea they have repeated, because it is a
favorite, is one introducing "Be Kind to_____Week." Jean
makes a poster of a family member who may need some extra
attention or encouragement. On the poster she puts a picture of
the person and a special tribute, and the poster is displayed at
home evening. The person to be spotlighted is seated on a chair
of honor in the middle of the room, and the family takes turns
saying something nice about the honored person. Then the parents might talk about that child's talents or abilities and what
makes the child special to them. During the following week, the
family tries to do special things for the person of the week, such
as helping him with his work. This person is also given the big-
gest serving of dessert and the chance to choose the dinner
menu several times during the week. They may even have the

privilege of staying up late some night or choosing where they would like to sit at the table or in the car.

Another fun family home evening project the Porcaros enjoyed together began with a Weekly Reader story on ecology which one of the children brought home from school. (This was during the time our country was experiencing a gas shortage and Americans were being asked to be more careful of their consumption.) The story told how the school children in an eastern town had decided they wanted to go for a whole week without using gas or electricity, as an ecology project. The parents agreed to it and the whole town tried it. The Porcaros' children thought this sounded like fun, so the family decided to turn off their power and gas for twenty-four hours. It was winter, and the next morning when they got up it was dark and freezing cold. Everyone used candles, and Dad shaved with a straight-edge razor by candlelight, and Mom prepared a cold breakfast. Everything they wanted to do that day seemed to require power, and they gained a greater appreciation for the conveniences we all enjoy. By the end of the day, the family was more than ready to turn the power back on but they all felt it was a good learning experience!

Reading family histories together is still another favorite home evening of the Porcaros. During the bicentennial year it was a natural to introduce the family to some American Revolutionary ancestors (about whom Robert had collected the information). Also, some home evenings have been held where the whole family is involved in filling out family group sheets.

Sharing the Home Evening Spotlight

The Richard and Betty Ellsworth family were typical of many who reported that in their homes each family member takes a turn giving the lesson. "My husband assigns the lessons, and it's been a good experience for everyone," said Betty. "I think some of the best lessons we've had have been from the children. Even the littlest ones have presented thoughts that each person has added to and talked about and it makes a beautiful lesson. Best of all, the child giving the lesson feels important. The next time it is their turn, are they ever excited to do it again!"

Rachel McOmber said, "Sometimes we have enjoyed writing our own family home evenings. The children decided what they wanted to do and some of our better lessons have been the ones they have written themselves. (My sons have also made up original religious games for home evenings that we have enjoyed.) We've also had fun with other families with whom we have planned family nights. These families have given us a lot of good ideas, and the children really enjoy seeing how other families do things."

Rachel continued, "Last month we all went to the genealogy library together. We looked in our family histories and each person chose an ancestor he didn't know much about. Then we tried to find out what their lives might have been like. At the next home evening we acted out incidents in their lives and we felt a greater closeness to them. We also felt a closeness to each other, for we were not only doing research together, but we were learning from each other. We became so interested in the histories and we are now writing them up and giving each other copies to put in our Books of Remembrance. This project also led us to share excerpts from our son's missionary journal, which was so much fun that we decided to write our own histories and give copies to each other.

"Actually, I don't think we've had our very favorite home evening yet," Rachel concluded. "It's like the artist who always thinks his best picture is yet to be painted."

The McOmber's married daughter, Marilyn Skousen, recalls that they have always had the tradition of holding a weekly family home evening. She commented, "I remember when we were younger, before they had any manuals, our family nights stressed scripture stories and sharing talents. My father would always tell a Bible or Book of Mormon story and sometimes we would act them out, like charades. (The kids at church used to call me "Quiz Box" because I knew all the answers to questions about Bible stories because we'd learned them in these lessons at home.) Then we would have talent time and one of us would sing or play an instrument (we were usually taking some kind of lessons). We always had a good time together."

Adapt the Program to the Need

Leo and Katherine Gifford try to gear their family home evenings to their present needs. If one child is nearing baptism age, they have a few lessons to help that child prepare and help the others appreciate baptism more. One time, when they were very concerned about some of the bad language heard in their neighborhood, they had a lesson on the value of good language and manners. They have also done a number of timely projects together in home evening, such as making emergency candles and rolled bandages for storage, making gingerbread houses and other gifts at Christmas time, working in the yard and garden in the summer, and practicing fire safety programs in the winter. To begin one fire safety night, Leo started their fire alarm while Katherine burned something in the kitchen. Everyone was curious, but no one wanted to follow the instructions to run and get out of the house. They casually went into the kitchen and said, "What's burning, Mom?" That reaffirmed their need for a fire safety lesson! In the course of the evening they talked about and practiced an actual fire drill, established a place to meet outside and put up fire extinguishers around the house.

The Giffords have a "letter writing to missionaries" tradition as part of their home evenings. When everything else is over and the refreshments are being served, they pass stationery around, and everyone writes the main events of their week. They have been doing this since their oldest son left on a mission four years ago. They feel this letter writing has built a missionary spirit in their home; it also boosts the missionaries' morale and keeps family members closer.

Veldon and Thelma Jones also found that it is important to adapt their home evenings to the changing needs of the family. Thelma told us, "After all our children except the youngest had married and left home, we faced the problem of how to make family home evening interesting enough for our teenage son to want to continue joining in with us. There always seemed to be other things more interesting to do and gradually we quit having home evening completely. One day the thought came to me that we should see if our two sons who had recently married would like to join us and bring their wives so we could all have home evening together. They had been neglecting this duty also and it took a while for everyone to adjust their activities so we could spend every Monday night together, but everyone liked the idea. We took turns having the meetings in our homes. The husband usually prepared the lesson and the wife served the refreshments. We soon began to look forward eagerly to Monday nights and our youngest son joined right in and was enthusiastic and glad to be with his brothers. The young couples were students at the University and whenever something interesting was to be scheduled on the campus we would pile in the car and go up for it; then back home for refreshments and the lesson, or just visiting. It seemed that these occasions were even more meaningful after having been separated, and because of these special home evenings we established a feeling of closeness and love that we may never have had otherwise. One of our sons recently moved to New York and has mentioned several times how grateful he was for those home evenings and the chance it gave him to know us better."

Get Away Together

Planning for and taking family vacations together is another worthwhile tradition which can bind the family with bonds of love and shared memories.

In adult retrospect, many days, weeks, and months of childhood memories seem to blur together without leaving any special impression. But a vacation, camp-out or outing often makes an indelible etching that remains vivid and clear over the years. Family togetherness memories are often framed in the reference of "Remember the time when we went...."

Herb and Virginia Riley (parents of ten children) said, "Vacations are highlights in our lives. We will never forget the togetherness or the fun we have had as a family on trips to Yellowstone, Flaming Gorge or Idaho. We still take vacations together every year, even though most of our children are married. *Everybody* comes (in-laws, grandchildren, etc.) and we all look forward to it. One year we planned a vacation to Yellowstone and one daughter said she couldn't make it because she had a new baby. But the first morning we were there, my husband came back from a little walk and said, "Guess who is camped across the road!" Our daughter had felt so left out that she had packed the day we left and they travelled at night to join us! And we all had a wonderful time together, new baby and all."

"It is traditional for us to do a lot of things together, but one of the things our family did that has made us a closer family was to just get away from the whole ordinary routine of life occasionally and do something completely different together," said Rachelle Safsten, one of the eleven children of Robert G. and Mary Safsten. "We went on a three-month trip back East when I was fourteen and lived for the whole time in a tent! It was a lot of fun, and we really got to know each other! We went on a lot of trips, but the first thing we did was plan. We would sit down and say, "Now, what do we want to accomplish by going on this trip? Where do we want to go? What do we want to see? How much are we going to have to pay? What sacrifices are we going to have to make to do it?" She also commented, "One of the first things I remember the family talking over was buying a new car for a big trip. We discussed it as a family (although I was the oldest and was only six) and I still remember talking about it."

"Remember when?" reminiscing is almost as much fun as the trip! Also, being together in new circumstances often fosters closer relationships. Darla recalls, "I first got to really know my brother, Steve, under the stars in Bryce Canyon when we were both in our teens. We had decided the campfire was so inviting and the stars so bright we wouldn't sleep inside the tent with the others. That special outdoor atmosphere seemed to invite a sharing of thoughts and feelings as we began talking, and we established the basis for a closer brother and sister relationship."

"Some of the most meaningful experiences we had as a family happened when we went camping," said Linda Garner, "Under the pines, with the stars bright above, we seemed to feel closest to each other and to Heavenly Father. We inevitably had our best talks then, and I can see now what good teaching times those were."

Melba Flandro said, "I think one of the sweetest memories I have concerns a vacation we took several years ago in our trailer. We stopped in New Mexico for Sunday and we said to the children, "We can find a Ward if you'd like to, or we could have our own meeting here." They thought it sounded really exciting to have our own, so we got all cleaned up and had a testimony meeting in our trailer. We said things to each other that we *never* would have said any other time."

"We have travelled all over the United States together as a family," said Clea Burton. "Of course we had to plan and save for the vacations, but we felt it was well worth it, and especially good for our children to have time together." In the rush of regular routine, with each family member hurrying to their own commitments, it can be difficult to keep a close family feeling. But on vacations where we spend uninterrupted time with family members, a great feeling of unity and renewed closeness can be recaptured. The Malin Lewis family enjoy a tradition of going to their cabin in the mountains together. Part of the tradition is to hold "Pineball" tournaments where they use pine cones for balls and limbs for bats. They also have badminton and "Pit" (a card game of speed) tournaments. Another tradition their family all love is their yearly Family Olympics which includes everything from an egg-carry event, to swimming, to free-throw events. They make charts of all the winners (and make sure everyone wins in at least one event), then give gold medals in a special ceremony.

"The week before the deer hunt each fall, I used to take my children up in the woods," said Elvin Christiansen. "We would pitch a tent and camp for two or three days. We would go hiking, watch the deer, learn the names of plants and even manage a little fishing." His wife, Elaine, said, "The kids talked about those camp-outs all year long. And they think that their dad is the best cook in the world because they remember how good his pancakes and stew tasted in the open air. I think those experiences really helped them stay close to their dad."

Traditions Can Make Any Day Memorable

Doing something together often makes even ordinary times into special memories. One ambitious family has a traditional "Green-Thumb" party in the spring to get the yard work done. After a morning or afternoon of working together, a special green meal or refreshment is served. Laughter and nonsense are mixed in generously with the allotment of work, and the parents effectively get across the message that working together *can* be fun!

The Porcaros have a Saturday tradition which also helps get the work done! Every Saturday when the weather is nice, they get their work done at home and go somewhere together. They go tubing, to the sand dunes, swimming, or to the school playgrounds where they play soccer or baseball or have a picnic. Kathy, their married daughter, enjoys those Saturday outings so much that if her husband is working, she comes home and goes with them!

The Richard and Betty Ellsworth family had a similar Saturday tradition. Betty said, "When our children were little, we would say, 'Whoever has all their Saturday work done by noon can go with us to get an ice-cream cone.' We didn't do it every Saturday, but oh, the excitement when we did! The kids never worked so hard as on those days. The teamwork was great because the older kids wanted the younger ones to be able to go too, and they would get their own work done and then help the little ones so we could all go as a family."

A "Last Fling" picnic with a neighbor family in the late fall to enjoy the riotous colors of falling leaves is a favorite tradition in the Gary Bascom family. The traditional food for this picnic is Sloppy Joes and homemade caramel apples. The whole autumn season seems more special, and is something they share with more delight because of this yearly tradition.

Summer is more special to the Moore family because they have made it a tradition to take their children on tours such as to a dairy, a bakery or a cookie factory. Julia feels the tours have been educational and really given the children something to look forward to.

Early Morning Traditions

Oman and Helena Evans have carried on a tradition which has been handed down for three generations. Helena tells how President Antoine W. Ivins promised the Saints in the Mormon colonies of Mexico that if they would sing a hymn and have a prayer with their children every morning, their children would never leave the church. Because of this promise, morning song and prayer became a tradition in many colonist homes, and Helena expresses gratitude that in their home, and in most of their married children's homes it has been continued. She remembers the sweetness of their mornings when her husband called their children from their beds with a hymn. He would start singing the first verse, and by the time he got to the end the children were out of bed and ready to join in. They feel it is the best possible way to start a day, and find they all sing snatches of the hymn all day long.

In the Richard and Betty Ellsworth home, a variation of this idea has helped them start the day cheerfully for years. Richard plays a hymn when it is time to get up. By the end of the third verse everyone is assembled and ready for family prayers. Betty said, "When we used to go and awaken the children, they would come down grouchy and resentful, or want a few more minutes sleep. But somehow hearing a hymn encourages a better spirit. If a child doesn't come one morning, that's fine; we go ahead with prayer without him. But none of them miss very often, because it is a terrible feeling to be left out."

Pick a Bouquet of Birthday Traditions

Traditions brighten birthdays and communicate special messages in much the same way as flowers do. Without a word they can tell the birthday child he is loved and important.

Some families traditionally have special parties for their young children, each following a special theme; a pirate party with a treasure hunt, a cowboy or Indian or Cinderella party, etc. Other families prefer making a family dinner or a restaurant dinner the tradition. If it's a dinner at home, the birthday child might choose the menu, and plan and help make the centerpiece and decorations. (Or the other children might do the decorations for a surprise!)

The Wayne Ursenbach family began a unique birthday tradition when the youngest of their seven children was a toddler. They take the birthday child shopping to buy little remembrances for all the *other* children in the family. This solved the problem of little ones feeling left out at present-opening time, but more important, helped the birthday child learn through experience that it can be as much fun to share and give to others as it is to receive.

Many families have special traditions surrounding the 8th birthday, the 12th birthday and the 16th birthday. In one family the eighth birthday is the time to invite grandparents to join in a special home evening where the birthday child is the guest of honor. The grandparents are invited to share their testimonies with the newly-baptized child and let him know how happy they are that he has become an official member of the Lord's church.

This birthday is also a good time to present the child with his own set of scriptures. Other gift possibilities are his own journal, Book of Remembrance or perhaps a card file of "missionary recipes" which he can learn to cook.

Joye Billings is going to make it traditional to continue the idea she started with her oldest daughter, Tonya, of presenting the flannelboard missionary lessons to each child in the weeks preceding their baptism. She says the children all loved it, and Tonya learned a lot and felt much better prepared to be baptized.

Another family begins giving the eight-year-old his own money so that he can learn to pay tithing, save for a mission and budget for the things he needs and would like. One way to do this is to give him a silver dollar for each year of his age, and go with him to the bank to open his first savings account. They start that day to give the child a regular allowance, with instructions telling how he is to divide and use it.

Whether a child is turning two or twenty, the Bascom tradition is to make the whole day special for the birthday child. At breakfast he is greeted by some kind of Happy Birthday poster or sign and one gift to open as everyone sings "Happy Birthday" to him. During the day, each family member tries to do at least one thing to make the birthday child feel special, and the day is culminated at a family dinner where he opens the rest of his gifts and everyone enjoys the birthday child's favorite food.

It's Never Too Late to Make Traditions

Grandparents with all their children married can still start traditions! Jim and Colleen Pinegar hold a traditional family get-together after April Conference, and a camping reunion later in the summer where all the children, grandchildren and in-laws can enjoy each other.

One family has the tradition of holding two musical evenings a year with their married children and their families. Each of the families is responsible to provide three to five new numbers each time. These may be anything from solos to the whole family singing or playing together. This tradition keeps the families learning new songs and gives them a very special sharing time to look forward to.

Malin and Myreel Lewis, parents of twelve children, have a tradition that fosters family unity as grown children move away from home. Myreel said, "Ever since our oldest daughter went to college we have asked each child to write home weekly and we have had great joy in hearing from them. Now it is a family tradition that everyone writes home, and to each other, each week. Each child knows that he will get a graduation present of a typewriter for this purpose." Myreel and Malin also write a weekly letter and run off copies for each family member on their own ditto machine. (For a smaller family, carbon copies would work equally well.) Myreel said, "We had to laugh when one daughter-in-law chose a ditto machine over a washing machine one time, she wanted so much to be part of this tradition." Myreel continued, "This weekly letter-writing tradition has been a great way to increase family unity. We each tell what we have done the past week, any exciting news, humorous anecdotes and funny comments of the children, spiritual experiences, etc. We abbreviate radically, for speed in reading and writing, but each person knows how to 'interpret.' I keep a copy of my own letter and each of the children's letters and have all of them bound once a year. This is our way of keeping the commandment to write a journal or family history."

Oman Evans has organized a traditional yearly testimony meeting for his four sons, one daughter and their mates. "Grandpa" Evans always presides and begins the meeting, which sometimes continues for several hours. The children feel this testimony meeting is one of the spiritual highlights of the year, and the best way they have found for staying close as a family. Such experiences can help a family sense their true "spiritual kinship," which is the basis of lasting unity.

It is possible to find this unity with our extended families as well if we establish traditional times to do it. Each Fast Sunday evening, the Delbert Eddington family piles in the car and goes to Grandpa Eddington's or Grandpa Evans' (on a rotating basis). There they have special Sunday family nights with their grandparents. They enjoy a variety of lessons, programs, testimony meetings and refreshments. The grandparents are especially encouraged to preside, teach and share experiences. One of the Eddington children said, "Mom, I'm so glad we've been going to Grandma and Grandpa's house on Sundays. Even though we used to visit them a lot, we never knew all those interesting things about them. I feel like I really know them now." "Yea," their 7-year-old chimed in, "It's so funny to me to think of Grandpa being a little kid like me once! He tells really neat stories about when he was young, and about when he was a missionary, too!"

In the hurry and hassle of our modern life, it seems we need to structure and plan for opportunities to really get to know each other; otherwise special experiences and feelings remain unshared. Spiritual closeness and unity in our families does not happen automatically, but can be fostered by family traditions.

Melba Flandro said, "One thing that has been very important in our family which has given us a sense of unity second only to our testimonies of the gospel, is family traditions. Our children who have moved away from home have come back, sometimes at great effort, for some of these events. Traditions are the things that make our family special to them!"

Ten Things to Try

1. Choose and plan for a new Sunday tradition (such as playing Scripture Charades, having films or filmstrips, or firelight scripture-reading) to make Sundays more special to your family.

2. Introduce a "Be Kind to_____Week" in a family home evening.

3. Plan a special outing or vacation with your family. Go places and do things together—traditionally!

4. Try a "Green Thumb" party each spring to get the yard in shape or a "Last Fling" picnic each fall to enjoy the autumn leaves together.

5. Start a Saturday outing tradition to provide motivation to get work done faster.

6. Consider a traditional morning hymn to waken the children in a more pleasant way and get the family together for family prayer.

7. Start a new birthday tradition to make the birthday child feel more special.

8. A weekly family newsletter could become a tradition to maintain family closeness even after children move from home. It can also provide a permanent family history!

9. Make it a tradition to have a yearly family testimony meeting.

10. If grandparents live close by, suggest a monthly Sunday family night with them, perhaps including lessions, programs, testimony meetings and refreshments.

8

Traditions Make Holidays Special

Any holiday is a ready-made opportunity for traditions. Even a minor holiday, such as Labor Day, can be a memory-maker. There is a special spot in Millcreek Canyon where the Wayne Ursenbach family goes every year on Labor Day. They get up early and go there to cook a special breakfast and enjoy a hike afterwards. One of their married daughters wrote them recently and said, "It's Labor Day today, and we thought of you and knew what you'd be doing. Wish we could have been there." This sense of "knowing what the family will be doing" promotes closeness even after the children leave home.

"We have a Fourth of July tradition which the children still come home for," says Melba Flandro. "My birthday is on the Fourth, and every July third for fifteen years we have slept out in our backyard in one big family bed. We have chocolate donuts and milk for refreshments—that's part of the tradition. Then we have fireworks before we go to bed. The next morning the girls and I get up and prepare breakfast to eat on the patio." The Flandros also have a fun Easter tradition of making Easter baskets for each other out of shoe boxes, Clorox bottles, etc., then leaving them out for the Easter Bunny to fill and hide.

Another family has developed a whole set of spiritual traditions for teaching their children the meaning of Easter. Two weeks before Easter, special religious pictures are displayed and special lessons are given in home evenings to teach the children what Jesus has done for us. The children learn Sacrament hymns and every effort is made to show the spiritual meaning and beauty of Easter.

Halloween evening brings a traditional dinner at Grandma's house for one family. All the children come dressed in their costumes, have supper and enjoy being admired by the family before they go "Trick or Treating" in their own neighborhood.

Adding More Thanks to Thanksgiving Traditions

Thanksgiving is a traditional time to gather our families around us, set a bounteous table and give thanks for all our blessings. A non-traditional approach to Thanksgiving has become traditional with one family, who decided to make it truly a time of giving thanks, not only to the Lord, but to others as well. They send out thank-you notes to express appreciation to people they might not remember to thank at other times—such as the bishop, their children's teachers (both church and school), Dad's boss, the mailman, etc. To say thank-you to close neighbors and friends for their friendship, they make a thank-you gift and deliver it personally on Thanksgiving Day. The gift is usually a plate of peanut brittle wrapped in plastic wrap and topped with a colorful bow.

The Terah and Joye Billings family also make Thanksgiving a time of thanks in a special way. Before Thanksgiving, Joye and her young children make a number of little apple pies and deliver them to Primary, Sunday School and nursery teachers and also to babysitters. They sing a thank-you song and the appropriate child says, "Thank you for being my teacher!" The effects of such a tradition have been gratifying. A few weeks after Thanksgiving one year, a counsellor in Primary told Joye that one of the teachers they took a pie to was feeling unappreciated, not sure she was doing a good job, and was ready to quit. She added "You know, when your kids took that pie to her it made all the difference in her attitude. That experience was so moving to her that she decided to keep trying and now she's one of our best teachers." The mother of a teen-age teacher said to Joye, "You have no idea how much that meant to my daughter to be thanked." Another time Joye met an inactive mother whose daughter had been a recipient of a pie. Joye didn't recognize her, but the lady said, "Well, I can tell you one thing, I'll never forget you or that delicious pie, or those bright-eyed children you brought to our house!" Joye said, "Even though the pie project is a lot of extra work and never easy, experiences like that make it all worthwhile.

"The children all want to help with the pies, and all feel a personal pleasure in delivering them. Each child holds the pie for his own teacher, and one time in the excitement of the moment the four-year old presented his teacher a pie upside down on the floor in front of her. But the dear lady scooped it up and said, 'Oh, this is just the kind of pie I like—the kind that holds together!' "

Last year the Lynn Hanks family started a Thanksgiving tradition of taking little sacks of homemade goodies to their neighbors and hanging them on the door knobs. They attached notes with the message, "We're thankful to have fine neighbors like you."

The Bascoms have a tradition which turns the thoughts of each family member to their blessings at Thanksgiving. After the traditional meal, Gary takes a kernel of corn from a nut cup, placed by his plate, and starts a "round robin" expression of thanksgiving. He might express thanks for their home and then Arlene continues as she takes a kernel from her cup telling the blessing she is most grateful for. The reciting of blessings continues as each in turn states one blessing they feel grateful for. As a climax to this tradition the family kneels together in prayer to thank the giver of all these blessings. (They found that family prayers at the end of the dinner are most effective because the children feel more grateful at the end of the meal, and can enjoy a somewhat lengthy prayer more than when they are hungry and all those delicious smells are distracting their thoughts.)

Thanksgiving dinner cooked on a big woodburning stove with the family dressed up like pioneers is part of the unusual Thanksgiving tradition of the Johansens. Trent and Margaret explain to the children that the pilgrims were pioneers, too, and talk about how different life was for them and how grateful we should be for what the pilgrims did to make it possible for us to live in such good circumstances.

Food Adds Flavor to Traditions

Food is not a fad. It will never go out of style, and it often adds a memorable flavor to traditions (such as Thanksgiving traditions). Perhaps it is because everything tastes better when we eat food in the company of loved ones, but warm memories are often made of such things as turkey and pumpkin pie, heart-shaped cookies and coconut-covered cakes. One family has traditions of pizza and root beer for Christmas Eve supper, chili and crusty bread for the first snowy winter night and homemade root beer and a freezer of ice cream for special family parties. While not as essential as good company and good humor, good food can add "spice" to most occasions and become part of traditions.

Christmas: Great Time for Traditions!

Christmas invites traditions as naturally as hot homemade bread invites real butter. Christmas offers special opportunities to teach and feel the joy of giving and the true significance of Jesus' birth. A birthday celebration is to honor the person whose birthday it is, and we try to please the person we are honoring. As we evaluate traditions included in our Christmas celebrations in the past, we may feel a need to replace some of them with new traditions that better teach the spirit of Christmas and would please and honor Jesus. Other families' traditions can give ideas.

In the Dean and Claudia Black household, Christmas preparations begin with the New Year. They have the tradition of making all their gifts for each other, and begin as soon as one Christmas is over to prepare for the next. Each child is given an apple box to put on their closet shelf in which to collect gifts and keep the materials with which they are working. Throughout the year when the children need an activity, Claudia suggests gift-making. Her philosophy is that when you make something for someone else you are saying, "I love you enough to spend my time doing this." The children get great satisfaction from their investment of self, and there is rarely any last-minute impersonal gift-buying. They have made the rule that all the family presents should be finished by December first, leaving December a less hurried month devoted to doing and making things for people outside the family.

Three weeks before Christmas, the Giffords, who have had sons on missions for several years, have a Christmas family hour which they tape to send to their missionary sons. The sons can play it on Christmas Eve and feel closer to home. All the children look forward to taking part and the one who receives the tape feels it is a wonderful Christmas present.

"The week before Christmas is really the heart of our traditions," said Milt and Helen Sharp. "We call it our 'Christmas week.' The first night we make goodies and take them out to about ten houses on each side of the street in our neighborhood. The goodies are not fancy, but that is not the purpose—the purpose is to teach children that Christmas is a time for giving. The children themselves make the goodies, arrange the plates and decorate the cards. Then one of them carries a plate, and one of them carries a lighted candle as our whole family gathers at each home and sings a carol as we deliver the gift. During that week we also take all the neighborhood children on a hayride and go caroling through the immediate neighborhood, and then over to the church for a program.

"Another night before Christmas we go out as a family, and drive around and see all the Christmas lights. Then on Christmas Eve we have our 'Family Christmas Play'! We use the same costumes every year, and I have the girls memorize their parts from the scriptures. I believe that through all the years of memorizing these beautiful passages, the message will stay with them. Also, I always try to have a Christmas story before the play, and I make this story up. Whatever I feel our family needs that particular night—that is the story they get! Then, instead of having our big meal on Christmas day, we have our special meal on Christmas Eve. All evening we talk about our blessings, and how much we depend on our Heavenly Father. Christmas Eve is really a highlight for that at our house. It was really special this Christmas because we had just gotten our little Cindy (who is almost two) out of the hospital. She played the part of our baby Jesus. She had been really sick, and we were so grateful to have her home and she seemed very special to us. To complete the evening, we all put our arms around each other and have our family prayer."

Family Fun and Service

The Charles and Connie Evans family have a tradition of family fun and service that makes their Christmas more special for them. Together they bake quantities of nut breads (and with four girls and Mom in the kitchen, that can be great fun!); the girls also take charge of making a gift list. Every year the list gets longer, and Connie and the girls get more ambitious. For extra special giving projects, or for those with big families, they cover two-gallon ice cream cartons with Christmas paper, wrap the handle with foil, decorate with ribbons, and fill with fruit, nut breads, etc. The nights when they deliver these home-baked gifts have become some of the happiest memories the family shares.

Music is an important part of the Christmas traditions of the Wayne Ursenbach family. The day after Thanksgiving they begin listening to Christmas records and practicing carols together so that the whole family can participate in a caroling party just before Christmas. They take baked goods to each of their neighbors and other friends and sing carols to them, and their carolling is received with great delight.

Many famiies inc!ude baking large quantities of goodies as part of their Christmas preparations. To simplify this procedure and make it less time-consuming, some families form a baking co-op. Since many recipes take very little extra time to triple or quadruple, three or four families in a group simply make large amounts of one recipe, and then they all exchange goodies, and achieve instant variety with minimum time and effort. A family assembly line is another favorite method used by many families to move the baking along more rapidly and to encourage more togetherness.

Different approaches to a "Twelve Days of Christmas" tradition are enjoyed by several families. The Porcaro children have enjoyed preparing and anonymously delivering small surprises every day for the twelve days before Christmas to a needy family or a person they feel needs cheering up. They read about this idea in a *New Era,* and felt that it was a special way to give a person who is alone or sad something to look forward to and brighten their Christmas season.

Bernice Ursenbach tells how they carry out their own special family "Twelve Days of Christmas" tradition by drawing names.

Beginning twelve days before Christmas they each try to do something special each day for the family member whose name they picked. When they had all seven children home and one set of grandparents living with them, it was really hard to guess who might have drawn their name—but the children had great fun trying! Bernice says, "With so many surprises happening each day, there was a great feeling of love, cooperation and appreciation, and everything else we did for Christmas that year seemed even more special."

Bringing the Married Children Home

One special tradition which the Herb and Virginia Riley family enjoy together is a buffet supper on Christmas Eve to which the Rileys invite all their children and grandchildren. Each family takes part on the program and the evening is remembered with fondness all year long.

One family and their married children (and their families) have a traditional Christmas family home evening the first or second Monday in December with a religious program which always includes acting out the nativity scene.

A four-generation family tradition is enjoyed by the Oman Evans family. Everyone looks forward to getting together on Christmas day for a luncheon and program. All the married children and their families meet together at Grandpa Evans' home. One year recently, they had a memorable program, written by Vera Eddington, entitled "Gifts the Savior Has Given Us, and Gifts We Can Return to Him."

December Scripture Traditions

The whole month of December is a special time for one family as they teach the children about the Savior. They read together each day, not only about the birth of Jesus, but about his life and mission. They found the children especially interested in the Book of Mormon account of the events on this continent at the time of Christ's birth. To involve the children more, each older child is assigned days to be in charge of choosing and reading the story. Also the children take turns picking out and displaying pictures of the Savior. The family also dramatizes special times from Jesus' life and discusses how he must have felt about these experiences. After one of these discussions their six-year-old said "Daddy, Jesus is a real person, isn't he?"

To help their children understand the importance of giving and serving, Bob and Mina Larson help their family learn special service-oriented scriptures in December, such as "When ye are in the service of your fellow-beings, ye are only in the service of your God."(Mosiah 2:17). The Hanks family's favorite December scripture is "Inasmuch as ye have done it unto one of the least of these, my brethren, ye have done it unto me." They post this scripture on the bulletin board, say it together each day, and talk about what it means. This year Darla suggested to the family that they think of this scripture as it applies to the way they treat each other. She told her children that Jesus loves us all so much that whether we hurt or help each other it is as though we are doing it to him. She said, "This made the children more aware of trying to be kind to each other. This scripture was also a great motivator to get us to put into action our good intentions to help and give to others less fortunate."

Let Them Feel the Joy

Last Christmas the Hanks and their neighbors, the Hendry family, learned of three little boys in a shelter home who desperately needed help in order to have any Christmas at all. The two families accepted the responsibility for these boys' Christmas gifts. The Hanks and Hendry parents have a total of seven little boys of their own, and encouraged each one to give some of their new toys and give up one gift so that they could give more to the needy boys. Two days before Christmas, the families held a gift-wrapping party and soon had three big boxes full of gifts ready to deliver to the Home. They bundled boxes, boys and parents into the car, and Kathy Hendry suddenly ran back to her house and got a big turkey out of their freezer to add to the gifts! At the Detention Home (where they handle the gift distribution) the man in charge gathered the Hanks and Hendry boys around him and said, "I want you to know this is really a neat thing you have done for these boys. They wouldn't have had much of a Christmas at all without your help—but now they will have an extra nice one! You should feel very good about that." They did! The three little boys were the main topic of conversation in both homes for the next week. The Hanks boys on Christmas morning said, "Mom, do you think Terry, Kenneth, and Ted are happy now?" On Christmas Eve seven-year-old Tony

Hendry wrote his Mom a note about the three little boys. It read: "Dear Mom, What I want for Christmas is more brothers-THEM." Love, Tony.

Such first-hand experiences could become special highlights in a family's Christmas traditions. There are countless others which are meaningful to the families who have experienced them. For example, one family we know bakes a birthday cake in honor of the Christ Child each Christmas, and shares it with someone in need of some loving attention. Another gives a gift of money to the Bishop with the instructions that it should be given to a person who needs help.

Some families give up a gift in order to contribute to a CARE package. Others do anonymous giving to needy families, neighbors, widows, or shut-ins. Some families invite missionaries, foreign students, or a lonely single, divorced, or widowed person to share Christmas with their family.

The Bascoms' most exciting Christmas experience this past year was "adopting" a grandma who lives in a Rest Home near them. They called the Rest Home early in December and asked if there was someone who could use an "adopted" family. The lady in charge said there were many in the Rest Home who could benefit from the attention and care of an adopted family, but that they would choose someone who would especially enjoy the children. The first Sunday evening of December the family was all excited about meeting their new "grandma", except eight-year-old Michael. He wanted to stay home and play, but they convinced him that his new grandma needed to meet all the children so she would know the whole family. When they came home, Michael was the first to say, "That was fun! She's nice. When can we go again?"

When they arrived for their first visit, their new grandma invited them to a TV room where they could talk, and she led the way in her wheelchair. When Gary asked her how she would like to adopt a family, she looked blank for a moment as if she didn't understand, then she raised both hands to her face and said emphatically, "Oh! Wouldn't that be FINE!" Gary introduced each member of the family to her. Then she said, "Now! Let's play a guessing game. I want you to guess how old I am." After they had each guessed, she pointed to Michael (who had guessed ninety), and laughingly said, "You're the winner honey! On the 22nd of December I will be ninety-two years old." They made a mental note that her birthday was coming up, and from that moment they began to love that dear, sweet, cheerful lady. They visited her several times during December, remembering her on her birthday and at Christmas with small gifts. Arlene says, "We didn't stop loving her simply because Christmas had come and gone, and we are continuing to visit her. We learn so many things from her. She tells us about her childhood in Missouri and about the things she misses, and the things we should be grateful for. But most of all we learn from the cheerful, fun-loving spirit she radiates in spite of all her hardships. Each time we visit her she asks us to join hands and have a prayer before we leave. She is a devout Baptist, and loves the Lord and praises him for the things he has done for her during her life. We leave after each visit feeling as though we have received a special gift from her."

Darla recalls, "When I was twelve years old, I had an experience I have never forgotten. We moved to a house across the street from a neighbor we soon began to call 'Grandma Woodhouse'. We didn't get to know her well until her husband died the next spring, however. Then she was very lonely because she had no church ties, and only one married daughter who lived in a distant city. We needed a Grandma, and she needed a family so we 'adopted' each other.

"The next Christmas season, everyone in our family was concerned about making Christmas less lonely for Grandma Woodhouse. As soon as the first snow fell, we started making plans. First we decided to make decorations for a little old-fashioned tree to take to her. We had all noticed the gloomy absence of a tree in her house the previous year. We also decided on some useful little gifts we could make; and began to cut, paste, sew, color and wrap with great excitement.

"On Christmas Eve, gift-laden, we made our way across the snow-covered street, excited and breathless. The tired look in Grandma's eyes when she opened the door was quickly replaced by surprise, then lightened with joy. Soon her eyes glistened with tears as we all shouted 'Merry Christmas!' and filled her quiet, unadorned kitchen with love, good wishes and a little tree complete with gifts.

"The smell of pine filled the air, and I was filled with a new kind of joy I had never experienced. We stood around the lighted tree and sang 'Silent Night' and the spirit of love and peace warmed us all. Concepts such as 'the joy of service', and 'the happiness that comes back to you when you make someone else happy' were no longer just words, because I had now *experienced* what they meant." Some of the most precious gifts we can give our children at Christmas (or any time of the year) do not cost money but are given by encouraging and providing positive experiences of this kind.

In our overly-busy lives, finding the time to do these truly meaningful things may be a real challenge. Advance planning is important in order to make it possible to help our families experience more of the true Christmas spirit. A plan called "Countdown to Christmas" can eliminate much of the hassle and confusion of a household where there are too many demands on everyone's time.

Countdown to Christmas

We can begin our planning by making a list of all the baking, sewing, decorating, shopping, cleaning, visiting, gift-making, etc. that we want to do before Christmas, and make this list as early as possible (several months ahead, if possible). The next step is evaluation. How many of these activities can we honestly work into our regular schedule, and still have time for the children? Ask two questions:

1. How time-consuming will each activity be?
2. Is it worth the time and energy it will take?

This perspective helps us shorten our list and give the most time to the most important things.

Now for the Fun and Action!

With the planning accomplished, we can start on the projects which can (or should) be done far in advance such as making the fruitcakes, cleaning, and gift-making. Also, this is the time to purchase and prepare all the materials for the next part of our plan—the COUNTDOWN CALENDAR. The countdown calendar is a take-off from the advent calendar. The purpose of the calendar is to make the children both a part of the planning and the doing of those Christmas preparations which they can help with, and to keep them constructively busy while mother accomplishes projects she cannot involve them in.

After Thanksgiving, the children help make a large December calendar on butcher paper. In place of the daily "surprise" or treats of the regular advent calendar, we place clues which will lead the children to a new "hidden surprise" each day. Mother keeps a master list of the clues and surprises, and each morning during December she looks at her list and hides an object or kit in the place the clue indicates it will be found. The surprises are fairly simple and inexpensive and have usually been purchased or made before December. They include such things as a fresh supply of creative materials (which the children will think much more exciting before Christmas as a sneak preview of what's to come), crayons, marking pencils, chalk, water-colors, clay, etc., or inexpensive puzzles, books, and games—anything which keeps children constructively busy. The second type of "gift" is the pre-assembled kit which the children use in making Christmas cards, decorations or gifts. The third type of hidden surprise is the "let's make cookies together" type. For this kind of "gift" the instructions and materials for any project which can utilize the children's help are hidden for the children to find. (Baking cookies becomes an adventure for all rather than a chore for mother.) Other ideas for this type of surprise are: silverware (all ready for some willing hands to make gleam), all the materials for making centerpieces, placecards, or home-made invitations for a holiday event, or perhaps the frosting to decorate the baked cookies. The fourth type of "gift" is the promissory note for some of mothers' time to be given for a special Christmas story reading hour, or a shopping trip with each child, or time for each child to stay up alone with Mom and Dad to wrap presents, etc. after the other children are in bed. One last kind of thing which helps round out the fun is a goodie for the children to eat with parents' permission, and share with friends. Popcorn balls are the favorite here.

The children love the excitement of following the clue each day to find what they are to make, do, or eat that particular day. We notice that when the children are not being inadvertently pushed onto the sidelines the T.N.T. feelings (troublesome, not tender), which nearly always explode into misbehavior, are replaced by "I Can Do It" feelings which usually result in helpful behavior. Here's a typical list of things to be hidden:

Date

December   1. Present—notebooks.
                2. Kit for presents for Grandmas. Cover and decorate little boxes with felt.
                3. Popcorn to pop and string.
                4. Gift—new books.
                5. Yarn to wrap around juice cans to make pencil boxes for Dad, Grandpa.

6. Foil wrapping paper cut in strips to make paper chains. Include glue.
7. Kit to make Christmas mobile decoration—felt, cardboard, string.
8. Present—Christmas coloring books.
9. Gift certificates for 1 hour of shopping time with Mom.
10. Paper, rick-rack, magic markers, old greeting cards to make hand-decorated stationery.
11. Popcorn ball treats to eat and share with friends.
12. Animal crackers, shellac, pin backs to make friend's presents (extra box for creators to consume).
13. Present—construction paper, magic markers or new crayons for art work.
14. Large piece of butcher paper, old Christmas cards, glue for making large Christmas scene or collage to hang on their wall.
15. Gift certificates for each child: one night each to stay up late and help Mom wrap presents.
16. Kit to make tree ornaments with cardboard, glitter, glue, cookie cutters for patterns.
17. Kit to make bookmarks for presents.
18. Gift certificate for story time.
19. Dough to make Christmas cookies.
20. Frosting to decorate them.
21. Silver polish to use to polish silverware, goblets.

Alternate ideas: make jewelry boxes from egg cartons, homemade puzzles, decoupage or modpodge pictures, shrink art jewelry or plaques.

Ten Things to Try

1. Make a major tradition of a minor holiday, such as a family outing on Labor Day, a family sleep-out on the Fourth of July, or a Halloween dinner at Grandma's before the "trick or treating."

2. Try adding "thanks" to Thanksgiving by writing thank-you notes or delivering thank-you gifts to a few people you may not ordinarily thank at other times.

3. Try starting Christmas gift-making for family members early. It can give activity ideas for the children's spare time all year.

4. Plan for some special activity each day during the week before Christmas. Choose a traditional time to do the things your family enjoys most to insure they will get done.

5. Try forming a baking co-op with relatives or friends. Decide what each will bake in quantity; next, exchange. Result: instant variety!

6. Try a "Twelve Days of Christmas" project to do something special for a family member or needy family, every day, the twelve days before Christmas.

7. Bring the married children home for some type of special Christmas get-together.

8. Begin a December scripture tradition to read about the life and mission of the Savior, and memorize scripture passages with special meaning.

9. Give your children firsthand experiences with service by planning a project to benefit others with your friendship and love during the Christmas season.

10. Examine the "Countdown to Christmas" plan to see if it would help you have more of the true Christmas spirit in your home.

9

"It's Time to Master Time"

*"If we would master time,
we must first master ourselves."*

Time is an asset more valuable than money, and more easily spent. In fact, we cannot avoid spending it. We might think of time as a perpetual bank account from which we draw twenty-four hours each day which must be spent immediately. With this "coin" of time we can pay the price of any goal we choose, or we can let the "coin" slip through our fingers and be lost.

Each of us is free to choose how we will spend these precious days we are given. Yet we may avoid recognizing our free-agency in the matter of our time use. We may be like the mother who said, "I have so much to do, I don't have any choices. I just do what has to be done each day." If we feel our choices have already been made for us by circumstances, or by other people, we will feel little responsibility for the results of our time use. The first step of time management is to recognize and accept the fact that our own choices determine how our time is spent, and the value we will receive from it.

Arlene recalls with amusement the first evening she and her husband invited his parents to their home for dinner. She was anxious to show them she was a good housekeeper as well as a good cook. She laughs, "I spent almost the entire day on my hands and knees removing old wax from the hardwood floors in the living room, and then re-waxing. I barely had time to change clothes and put the dinner together before my company arrived. My new in-laws probably didn't even notice the floor, but I'll bet they noticed how disorganized I was! That day I felt that the clock was an enemy conspiring against me, because I didn't want to accept the blame for my own poor choices!"

When we are keeping up with the demands of life, we look at the clock with satisfaction, and it seems like a friend, but when we get behind or have "too much to do," the clock seems like a tyrant with unwanted power. Many couples mentioned it takes time to be good parents, and confessed they had to learn better time management in order to continue to enjoy life as their responsibilities grew with parenthood.

For instance, Mary Wright (who had fifteen reasons for managing her time well—yes, we mean fifteen children!) even found ways to make the clock work *for* her when teaching her family. If one of the children would say something like, "I don't have time to make my bed this morning; I'll do it when I get home from school." Mary would say, "I'll bet you have one minute, dear. Let's take the clock in your bedroom and I'll time you for one minute, and we'll see how much of it you can get done." Mary explains that many jobs actually take only a minute, and once this is proven to them, the child is more willing to do the job because in good conscience he can't say, "I don't have time to do it." This principle can work for parents, too. Timing jobs and finding out how long they actually take is one good way to start taking control of our time.

For Priorities Sake—Keep Track of Your Minutes

When we really become serious about the matter of time management, we may want to keep a record of our time, so that we can see how we are spending it. We must know how our time is presently being spent before we can determine what changes we need to make in order to improve its use. Most people think they already know how they spend their time, and they skip this step. However, time management experts have said that keeping a record of time use can be our most helpful aid to mastering time. We may find when we do this that we haven't known as much about our time-use as we thought we did.

Janice Burton said, "When my tenth baby was three months old, I started feeling like all the things that matter weren't getting done (things that don't matter always seem to get done!). I made a chart that broke my day into fifteen minute periods, so I could see where my time was going, and try to get control over things again. I faithfully recorded what I was doing in each time block of my day, and through this analysis was able to work out a new schedule for myself that did allow time for the things I really wanted to do."

One author suggested making a list of all the things we need time for, then keeping track of how much time we actually spend on each activity during a weeks' time. Then we can look at this list and see whether we found time for the things that really matter to us, and we can make certain that our values are reflected in our time-use.

When one mother began to keep track of her time, she made some interesting discoveries. She often let the hours from 2:00 to 4:00 p.m. vanish because she did not quite dare to begin any big project which would need to be interrupted when the children rushed in from school. Also the time after the children were all in bed was rarely used productively because she was too tired to decide what to do. As soon as she put her finger on these problems, she began to plan ahead to make use of this time, and learned that to have a definite plan for each time block could make these some of her most valuable hours.

Our time-use may not further our own goals, but we can be unaware that it doesn't unless we make a specific evaluation of how we spend our time. For instance, while we might say, and truly believe, that family comes first, when we do this evaluation we may see that other commitments actually take precedence.

One couple decided to analyze their time use with simple daily charts. They wrote down on the chart not only what they were doing at 15-30 minute intervals, but also why they were doing it then. They reported that this activity was very revealing, and helped them evaluate and analyze priorities. The wife found she was spending too much time on housework, and was putting priorities on "getting things done" rather than on people and their feelings. She noticed she spent her evenings doing chores she didn't find time for during the day, even though her husband might request her to spend some time with him. When her children asked for a story, she often had something which she "had to get done." Her husband was disturbed to find that he was shooing his pre-schoolers away as they clamored for his attention, in order to read the evening paper as soon as he arrived home from work. When he recognized what he was doing, he looked for alternatives. The couple agreed that the awareness they received from this evaluation helped them get their priorities straight. The wife began to try harder to leave her evenings free to spend with her husband and children. This forced her to manage her days better, and she admitted that her free evenings made her feel less like a drudge. The husband shifted his reading of the newspaper until later in the evening so that he could give the kids his complete attention when he first came home.

Time-Use Keys From a Mother of Ten

Janice Burton, outstanding mother of ten children said, "When I first started my family, I felt I would have to postpone my personal, self-fulfilling goals until my children were older. But I was not happy with that conclusion, and saw that I was getting busier all the time, not less busy. I decided the answer was to learn to organize my time better. I learned that organization is a must for parents in order for them to meet the needs of the family, and at the same time meet their own needs." Janice has become so successful in developing her organization skills that this is now one of her strengths. She explains facetiously, "Managing a family is easy. You just divide the day into fifteen minute periods, and then cram thirty minutes worth of work into each period!" Her key words and philosophies for time use are:

"1. *Balance:* There must be a time planned for everything: work, play, self-improvement, teaching the gospel, showing love for children and husband, cleaning, studying and reading, baking, music, meetings, gardening, genealogy, family togetherness and every needful thing. If I allow too little time to any one pursuit, there is no progress, but too much time given to any one thing will throw everything else out of balance. I try not to let time scheduled for one type of activity be usurped by another.

"2. *Perspective:* Trying to do too much leads only to discouragement. A master schedule helps me know how much time I can afford to give to any one activity and what I can realistically hope to accomplish each day.

Part of perspective is being able to look at a situation and decide how to take advantage of the circumstances instead of fighting them. Whenever you make a plan, you have to face the fact that *any* plan will sometimes collapse and will at least require revamping now and then (especially when you have babies and small children). When my tenth baby was a few months old, she was keeping me up until 2:00 a.m. every night, and I was in tears thinking of having to get up the next morning, and how my schedule would be ruined. I finally decided to find something I was so excited about that I'd be glad to stay up. The baby slept all day, so I started taking her with me to the genealogy library, and I would gather materials and plan projects to do that night when she was awake. I also made sure I got a good nap during the day while she slept, and then I got all kinds of long-put-off genealogy done in the late night hours I had been wasting in frustration before. Perspective and flexibility can often turn a disaster into a productive experience.

"Sometimes I think we try too hard once we have a plan. We want so much to be perfect parents that it is hard to face days that are disasters. We need to be more compassionate with ourselves.

"When the seasons change, I find myself with a garden to keep up, a houseful of children out of school, and no lovely time all to myself. You may get to the end of the day with none of the special, creative things done-only the drudgery tasks. Rather than seeing yourself as a failure, you need to see that the time has come to revamp your plan!

"The temptation is to decide it's not worth the work of planning when no plan works for very long, and just try to plough through each day. But for me that means endless drudgery and I really don't feel that's the way life was meant to be.

"3. *Priorities:* I don't let my home own me. I can't keep a spotless house and have time to teach and enjoy my children and husband and also develop my own talents. But, I can't be happy in a messy house. The answer for me was to find a happy medium. We share the load to keep a straight, but not an overly shiny or fashionable house. Also, I've found that I can't teach twenty piano students and have patience left for ten children of my own. So I teach only one church organ course each Saturday morning. I can't watch TV and also have time while I iron or sew to memorize scriptures, learn a language, or teach my pre-schooler the alphabet. So I watch only special programs. I try to spend time doing what is important to my family, myself, and my church calling, and not waste time impressing people or keeping up with the neighbors.

"4. *Organization:* Without a plan which determines the amount of time to be spent on each type of activity, and when it will be done, the most important things may not get done. So I plan everything. My plan includes work lists, menu and grocery lists, gift lists and schedules. I have a master plan, and weekly and daily schedules.

"5. *Self-Discipline:* Nothing important gets done without the specific intent to accomplish it at a particular time, and the discipline to do it. One secret I found to make my schedule work is to have the discipline to stick to my schedule as much as possible. When it is time to stop an activity and go on to something else, I stop, even though the drawer may not be quite cleaned out. (I can finish it in my cleaning time tomorrow.) But if I let any one thing take up time planned for something else, it is invariably important things like time with the children that suffer, and I end up feeling dissatisfied and frustrated. Another time-gobbler I avoid is letting 'extra' jobs creep in that would get me off schedule—you know how one thing can lead to another!

"6. *Procrastination:* I procrastinate, but with a plan! All the housework which is not on my daily schedule is placed on a list and dated with a deadline. I choose one or two projects from this list each day, and then I don't worry about the dozens of others waiting to be done. This helps me avoid much frustration." (Another mother called this principle "selected neglect", and time-management expert Alan Lakein has said, "The typical busy person wants to do more than there is time for, and inevitably is going to slight something. The successful busy person is the one who makes conscious choices as to what to slight, and does it in such a way that things balance out.")

"7. *Delegation:* I recognize that I can't do everything myself, so I try to utilize the help available. Each child is taught his responsibilities. I have found assignment sheets and check-off lists help the children establish good work habits.

"8. *Self-Esteem:* I have to see myself as a competent, intelligent person. I accomplish a great deal more for my family if I take at least an hour a day for self-improvement. I do some things well, and others poorly. I try to spend as much time as possible doing things I do well, because as I do things which are rewarding to me, my self-esteem is increased."

Activities which increase self-esteem should be considered priority time. When we feel good about ourselves, we are more likely to be a good example to our families, and to treat our families in ways that will help their self-esteem grow. It is a beneficial chain-reaction.

Twice the Mileage from Your Minutes

Janice summed up her philosophy about time by saying "Time becomes more precious as we grow older and see it flying by, so I try to make time do double duty whenever possible. While I am cleaning the kitchen or ironing, I mix my bread in the electric mill and mixer, and make necessary phone calls." (Many mothers mentioned how valuable a phone with a long cord is because it enables them to take care of telephone business while doing other tasks).

Other ideas for making minutes count, and to make the day more interesting and productive are:

1. Listen to scripture tapes, language records, operas or plays from the library as you work.

2. Tell rhymes or stories to the children or listen to them read while doing chores which do not take concentration.

3. Recite the alphabet with a pre-schooler, give an older child arithmetic combinations to work out, or teach a child to do the same task you are doing.

4. Spend one-to-one time with a child while doing a necessary task. (Assign the dishes to one child, rather than several, so you can work with that child and have time alone with him. Children seem to open up and talk better while their hands are busy.)

5. Prepare a lesson by taping it and listening to the tape (as well as practicing your presentation) while doing dishes, etc.

6. Play educational tapes or general conference tapes while eating. Or read from an etiquette book or a good children's novel to double the value of time spent at the night meal.

7. To make letter-writing time serve two purposes, write a detailed weekly letter to missionaries, parents, etc. and keep a copy for your own journal.

8. Make double and triple recipes of favorite casseroles, desserts, or baked goods and freeze the extras.

9. Take a book or some handiwork in the car to put waiting time to good use.

10. Spend waiting or shopping time teaching pre-schoolers to pick out shapes, numbers, or letters of the alphabet from signs, or ask them to identify foods and objects or sound out words.

11. Keep note pads handy to jot down thoughts about lessons, letters, schedules, lists, etc.

Another new thought on saving time was expressed by Janice. She said, "A lot of teaching time can be saved if I use example instead of words only. If I want the children to learn to use a schedule, I use one and try to keep it. I keep my budget book carefully because I want them to keep a budget book and present it to me for their next month's allowance. I want them to study, so I let them see me do it. I want them to practice their music, so I practice mine."

Snatch the Value from Snatches of Time

Perhaps one of the greatest enemies to accomplishment is the idea that we must have large blocks of uninterrupted time before we can begin a big project. One thought which was repeated by many productive people was that we can use bits and pieces of time if we learn to start a project even when we have only a few minutes. This can help us sense that any progress is worthwhile, rather than feeling frustrated when we are not able to finish a project at one sitting. Shirley Andersen says, "One thing I have learned from having a large family is that if I have five minutes—I should use it!" She does many things in five-minute snatches of time such as sewing on a button, making a phone call, cleaning a drawer, addressing a letter, making a list, making a journal entry, or darning a sock.

This reminds us of Daryl Hoole who tells how one summer she made several dresses "one seam at a sitting". Marlene Rosen, mother of five, who teaches a clothing and textiles class at a University, also finds that much of her sewing must be done in small snatches of time. In order to use this time productively she stores everything she needs for each sewing project in a small cardboard box. Then, when she wants to sew on a particular item, everything she needs is in one place and she doesn't waste valuable time searching for them. This idea could be adapted to any project which might require more than one work session.

Miscellaneous Time Management Tips

To round out our understanding of time-management principles, we have collected a list of miscellaneous tips which have been valuable to us and to others who have tried these ideas and shared them.

1. *Try using a To-Do list.* A list for each week and each day which itemizes the projects which need to be completed can be a valuable aid to organization. Make it a point to include everything which will need special thought or attention. For instance, when you have a lesson to prepare, write this down on your To-Do list and think about the various things you will need to do to prepare adequately. As you look at the commitments you have for the week, and divide them onto To-Do lists for each day, you can see at a glance which days will accomodate extra projects, or special activities. You might look first for a day when you will have time to read and study the lesson thoroughly. Another day you may only need time to type a stencil, or make a visual aid, or call the librarian. Another day, in bits and pieces of time, think about and practice the presentation. The To-Do list makes it possible to find the most logical time to prepare without feeling pressured or neglecting other important tasks. The same principle applies to any big project. Breaking the project down into steps and deciding when you will do each step is a basic part of accomplishment.

Most of us are pretty good about clicking off the routine low priority tasks, but when it comes to high priority tasks, we may have a harder time getting started. Routine jobs are done

quickly and easily because we have done them many times before, and they give us a feeling of efficiency and accomplishment. On the other hand, our high priority activities are often
new things that take thought and creative energy (and most likely
can't be completed in one time slot), so we avoid starting them.
Unconsciously we may fill our schedule with routine tasks to
excuse ourselves from starting the harder high priority jobs (such
as preparing a special family home evening lesson.)

When we put these jobs on a list and discipline ourselves
to start, we soon feel an excitement that keeps us going on these
harder tasks (and the value and satisfaction of the activity usually
overcomes our inept feelings). The To-Do list is actually a guide
and a memory tool. If we list long term projects like writing our
personal histories, as well as short term ones like preparing a
lesson, it will also serve as a prod and a reminder to start them.
But best of all, it will help us sort our priorities and make in-
formed decisions as we organize our jobs according to order of
importance. When we do the tasks in order of importance, there
is the added benefit that the things we don't get done are the
least important anyway! Also, it helps to overcome the feeling
that we should be doing everything at once when there is a great
deal to do. A list can give us assurance that we are doing what
is most important right now, and the other things will get done at
the proper time! It is surprising the energy we save when our
minds are free to concentrate wholly on the job at hand.

Not everybody enjoys being a list maker, however. If you
prefer to plan things in your mind, that is the way to do it. We
must each find what works best for us. But if you love to cross
off jobs as you complete them—and need the plans where you
can see them— a To-Do list is great!

2. *Give yourself some deadlines.* A realistic yet challenging
time limit can give the motiviation to discipline yourselves to
get a job done, and get it done faster. Most of us can do more
than we are presently doing in any given time period. One mother
confessed that simply by writing down what she needed to do in
a day, and how much time she will allow for each activity, she
has nearly doubled her output.

Carol Jeanne Ehlers, who has twelve children, says that
setting little deadlines for herself really helps her finish her work
quickly so she will have time for the fun and creative activities
she enjoys. She determines a certain amount she will have done
by the time the children leave for school, and then decides what
she will have done by 10:30, when she takes a break with her

pre-schoolers. Her next deadline is lunch time when she plans to have all her housework done so that she can spend the afternoon following her own pursuits such as book illustrating, and spending time with her family.

Time limits give us a challenge and alert our senses to what must be done. Also, if our time limits are realistic, and we declare that we will accomplish a certain amount by a specific time, we increase our faith in our ability to do. It is positive thinking. However, in using time limits, keep in mind one tip from time-management experts. It is wise to add 10% to any time estimate to allow for mishaps and unavoidable delays. One author calls this 10% his "mishap margin", another labels it a "ten-minute time-cushion." Either name implies being in control, and can mean the difference between peace of mind and frantic frustration (especially if there are young children in your home). If you have allowed extra time and delays do not occur, you are ahead and can re-invest the time in something else. Arlene adds, "I mustn't forget to mention how the "time-cushion" has helped me learn to be on time. I had heard it said that you either plan to be on time, or you plan to be late. I couldn't understand what was wrong with my planning, I knew I wanted to be on time, but there were so many last minute things that could crop up (the baby would need to be changed again, Julie would spill milk all down the front of her Sunday dress, or someone would go wading in their only good shoes). When I learned to include an extra ten or fifteen minutes getting ready time, it was possible to handle last-minute problems, and still be on time. It was a great feeling to be in control. If you have ever felt inadequate or pushed around by time, the time cushion could be your answer. It is a relief to find that you need not be at the mercy of the clock!"

3. *Learn to say NO.* Learning to say no to low priority demands on our time is a necessity for managing time intelligently. One of the best hints we've heard on how to say no graciously came from an Education Week class. Kay Edwards, the instructor, said we don't need to give detailed explanations when we must say no. Instead, a polite statement such as "I'm sorry, but I have other commitments at the same time" removes the temptation for them to judge your reasons. (We all have such different priorities that even if our reason seems very important to us, someone else may judge it a poor excuse). It is a sign of maturity and good time management when we learn to avoid letting other well-intentioned people rob us of the time we need to reach our goals. Sometimes we have trouble saying no because we expect

so much of ourselves and we feel inadequate if we can't fill everyone's expectations. Several women told us that they had to learn that their first responsibility was to be true to their own values and goals. This is part of integrity, and when we remember that being true to ourselves is not being selfish, it helps us to overcome feelings of inadequacy and guilt when we must say no.

4. *Please don't excuse my excuses!* There are times when we *are* making excuses. In some cases, we use "lack of time" as an excuse for lack of accomplishment or lack of involvement. We must be honest with ourselves and discover if our "no's" are really only excuses. When we say "I don't have time" do we really mean:

1. We would rather spend our time doing something more interesting?

2. It takes too much effort?

3. We don't know how? (We would rather do something we already know how to do?)

4. We are afraid we might fail? (If we don't try then we can't fail!)

Stephen Covey, outstanding writer, lecturer and teacher, has said that he feels our real problem is not one of time, and that blaming lack of time for lack of accomplishment is a cop-out. He feels the real problem is one of personal discipline and organization.

One More Tip

Progressive people seem to have one thing in common—they get up earlier than they absolutely have to! As we have talked to numerous people, it has become apparent that those who are accomplishing special things are usually the ones who use the early morning hours productively. Getting an unhurried and controlled start to the day seems to be half the battle in using time to advantage.

Betty Lou Lee, mother of 7, who has many accomplishments to her credit, echoed what many others said when she explained, "The early morning hours are the key to a good day for me. If I get up early, I find I have the time to do the extra things that make the difference in my life."

As Daryl Hoole says, "An ounce of morning is worth a pound of afternoon."

LaDawn Jacob feels that one of the most valuable lessons she has ever learned is to arise early and have time for exercise, scripture reading and prayers. She said, "I don't think the importance of this principle can be emphasized too much. We tend to overlook the scripture "Retire to thy bed early, that ye may not be weary; arise early, that your bodies and your minds may be invigorated." (D&C 88:124) I believe this principle is a vital part of successful living."

Time-Management Can Be Child's Play

Many parents have never thought of deliberately teaching their children about time management. However, since time management has eternal significance, perhaps we should consider ways to help our children learn early to make wise choices in the use of their time. One scripture says: "....behold, if we do not improve our time while in this life, then cometh the night of darkness wherein there can be no labor performed." (Alma 34:33)

We are already teaching time management or mis-management in more ways than we realize because example is a potent force in this area (as in most others). One natural way we can teach time management is to make sure we are doing well in managing our own time. Verbalizing our time-use choices and explaining the reasons for our choices can also help. Making plans with children, and helping them to carry out those plans is good training. One educator feels it is important for parents sometimes to ask children what their plans are for the day, to encourage them to plan. As the children get older, we can help them learn to use a To-Do list to encourage thinking ahead and help them evaluate their choices.

"Work Before Play" is What We Say

Rules and consequences can play an important role in teaching children how to manage their time for their greatest benefit and satisfaction. In many homes there are rules such as "work before play", and "homework before TV". These are sensible rules which help children gain the self-discipline necessary to manage other aspects of their time. Many parents set time limits for their children's work, so that they don't get in the habit of putting it off. Children appreciate this type of direction which helps them gain in self-discipline. (They may not appreciate it now—but they certainly will later!)

Clock Work Can Be Fun!

To help teach the value of planning time-use, how about holding a "Beat the Clock" family home evening? Time-use principles from this chapter could be discussed so that the children realize they are free to choose how they spend their time, but that they will be held accountable for their choices. Then a game could be played which shows them how much fun it is to "Beat the Clock" by timing themselves and trying to beat their best time on a task.

One family held a "Be Kind to the Clock Week" where they practiced taking responsibility for their own choices and not blaming the clock (lack of time) for lack of accomplishment.

Who's Afraid of the Big, Bad Clock?

A "Get Control of Our Time Week" could be held appropriately in January where list making, goal setting, priority setting, and schedule making are the main thrust of the week. One family concluded such a week by playing a game they called "Who's Afraid of the Big, Bad Clock?" Each family member reviewed his goals with the family, and made specific commitments about how he was going to overcome the problems of "the big, bad, clock" and make the clock his friend. There was a prize for the person the family voted as having the best plan.

You Can Do It!

Management of time is an individual thing because priorities vary widely. Therefore, no one can tell us exactly how we should organize, plan, or schedule our time. But we hope these guidelines which have helped others can help you to keep the clock from being a tyrant, and to find time for the rich, rewarding, activities you desire most.

These principles work! But to make them work for you, you must try them!

Ten Things to Try

1. Keep track of your present time use to see if you are using it to "buy" the things you really want from life.

2. Make the clock work for you by timing jobs to see how long they really take—then try to beat that time.

3. Analyze your schedule with the key words: balance, perspective, priorities, organization, self-discipline, planned procrastination, delegation, and increased self-esteem.

4. Make time do double-duty such as: While cleaning tell stories or practice ABC's with the children, while doing dishes

practice giving a lesson, when ironing or setting hair memorize scriptures or listen to educational tapes. Try a long cord on the phone so you can do telephone business while working. Watch for other ways to do two things at a time.

5. Learn to use snatches of time: try sewing a dress a "seam at a sitting", learn a lesson a paragraph at a time. When you only have five minutes, find a way to use them!

6. Try using a To-Do list. Organize tasks in order of importance.

7. Try a new way to say "no" to low priority demands on your time to avoid letting well-intentioned people rob you of the time you need to reach your goals.

8. Try getting up a few minutes earlier to get a good start on your day. It will be one of the best things you ever did for yourself.

9. Check the rules in your home to see if they are geared to teaching your children good time-management.

10. Try a "Beat the Clock" family home evening or a "Get Control of Our Time" week to help make the children aware that they have responsibility for the way they use their time.

Epilogue

When I was a child, time stretched like an endless sheet of untouched parchment waiting to be written upon.

When I grew to be a girl with dreams of writing an immortal story upon the waiting whiteness,
The parchment seemed infinitely available.

When I became a woman, a wife, a mother, the parchment was suddenly jammed with new and untried words.

When my children were small, the pen daily duplicated many words, it seemed the story would remain forever the same,
But the pages filled unbidden.

Then one day my eldest left home to begin to write his own story.
I stopped abruptly and stared at the untouched parchment ahead.
It was no longer an endless sheet.

Panic gripped me. "Time, time," I implored. "I must have more time."
And while I plead, the parchment filled inexorably.

God heard my plea and whispered in my straining ear
"There's all the time you need—use what you have."

I paused and thought of what I'd heard. "I have as much as anyone.
Why complain when I yet have breath?"

My pen moved then with firm resolve, my imperfect story to improve.
And the parchment once more stretched into eternity!

Arlene Bascom

10

Parents Can Be Practically Positive!

One night Darla wrote in her Journal: "This could have been one of those days. In order to get a head start on the canning, I got up at 5:00 a.m., but by 5:15 both babies were awake and crying. Later, Mark fell down the stairs, and then missed the bus. Benji dunked his teddy bear in the toilet, and David got a bee sting and cried for an hour. I cried with him. It was my car pool day and when I delivered the Kindergarten kids I backed from Paul's driveway into a parked truck. To top the day off, I didn't have supper ready when Lynn got home. In fact, so many things went wrong that I didn't get everybody fed and bedded down until 10:00 p.m. Then I had to finish the chili sauce, clean up the kitchen and fold the clothes.

But interlaced through all the hassle and frustration were some beautiful moments! I saw the sky turning pink above the mountains and shared the view with the children. Mark gave me a kiss and said, "I love you, Mom!" David and Benji's giggles warmed me as they chased me around the room during morning exercises. At nap time I read a beautiful article by the Prophet that lifted my spirits. And tonight little Benji came with outstretched arms wanting to be held. As I looked at that dear smudgy face so full of love and trust, I felt a surge of joy that said, "life is good." I picked Benji up and gave him a big squeeze and this time cried some happy tears."

The Positive Approach Defined

Perhaps Darla's feelings at the end of that day describe the "positive approach", suggested throughout this book. It's not a magic formula that saves you from the problems and frustrations of living and coping with growing children, but some healthy attitudes which help you meet the problems without collapsing, and stay aware of the joys and satisfactions that are there each day in all the little things. When love shines over the mountains of laundry (and around the endless demands), making you want to try a little harder tomorrow—that's positive parenting. When your little ones write on your glass doors with crayons and smear baby food all over the kitchen; when your bigger ones swarm around you like pesky flies buzzing, "Mama, Johnny won't play with me!" "Give me that—it's mine! "Mom, David hit me!"; yet you still believe that life and kids are basically good—that's being positive. When you earnestly try to use positive tools of love, kindness, and cheerfulness to build and encourage your children, yet you keep your faith in yourself when you throw all those tools away and act like a grouch—that's being positive. The positive approach is simply expecting and making the good outweigh the bad.

Why Be Positive? Because It's Practical!

Being a parent is wearying if we get grim and negative about it, but the positive approach can make parenthood more than tolerable—many times even fun! The positive approach works because it is based on principles of the gospel of love. A positive approach makes a person capable of influencing other family members to behave in a more positive, contributing way.

Carol Jeanne Ehlers tells of a time when her little girl, Collette, learned an impressive lesson about the power of the positive approach. She said, "I had my first little girl after five boys in a row, and in later years this little girl sometimes had a hard time with all those big brothers. When she was about nine, we decided to have an experiment one winter day when they were all cross and things were a bit hectic. We wanted to see if just one person out of that many could have a real influence to change the atmosphere toward the positive just by being kind, cheerful, and helpful (even though *they* were acting the opposite). I remember she started by saying, "May I take your dish over to the sink for you?" The most amazing thing happened—the positive spirit caught on and everyone started being nice. It was contagious! It really was! Here was this small girl among all those big brothers and she learned that she could wield a great influence on the atmosphere of the entire family. We continued to try our "experiment" for a week, then pointed out what we'd been doing in family home evening, and talked about the exciting power each individual has."

But no matter how well we know that the positive works, there are still many times when the negative creeps in to frustrate our efforts. We want to be positive, but don't always know how. So let's discover some How-to's to help us use the positive approach more and more of the time.

Give Your Children a "Happiness Insurance Policy"

One of a mother's prime responsibilities is to teach children to become independent and personally resourceful. Productive independence and getting along with others isn't a happenstance, however, we must teach it! Teaching a child skills that will help him to be independent and live successfully is a definite part of the positive approach. It includes showing, telling, and explaining what you *do* want children to do. Adults often forget that every detail of correct living must be learned. They somehow assume that a child should know (without being taught) how to greet a guest or clean a sink or resolve a dispute. An impressive but simple way to teach simple skills (and solve many misbehavior problems at the same time) is called modeling. Arlene and Gary went to a class one evening where the teacher defined modeling as acting out or explaining in detail a behavior we want a child to adopt. The teacher explained that many times a child is misbehaving because he honestly does not know the proper way (or a better way) to act in the situation. Arlene and Gary began analyzing various problem areas in their home and were surprised to realize that in several instances they had never been specific with the children about how they wanted them to behave. They went home and tried out some of the modeling suggestions. Arlene said, "Michael, I know it makes you angry when your little sister gets into your things and messes them up. I'll pretend that I'm Holly and Daddy will pretend that he is you and we'll show you some things you can say and do when Holly does this." After they had acted out several situations (to the great enjoyment of the children) they asked Michael and Holly if they would like to try acting out what they could do next time they were angry with each other (instead of hitting and hurting as they had done previously). For a moment the children giggled and acted silly, then enthusiastically replayed what they had seen their parents say and do. The next few days Arlene watched and reminded the children to practice this new way when they forgot. Soon she noticed them trying one of the pretend solutions without a reminder!

The Kent Krzymowski family initiated "Family Training Sessions" when they began to realize they were sometimes reprimanding for things the children had never been taught to do correctly. They decided to make the training sessions a regular part of their family home evening agenda. Some of the specifics they taught were:

1. Etiquette and table manners such as how to eat soup, what to do when you meet someone, how to answer the telephone correctly, etc.

2. Good personal habits such as how to wash your face well, how to do a good job brushing your teeth (including how to squeeze the toothpaste correctly and put the cap back on), how to take a bath, etc.

They outlined the procedures in steps. For example, for taking a bath—first go get your clean clothes, then run water, put dirty clothes in hamper, be sure you have soap, then get in. Lather and scrub all over, rinse, dry, dress and make sure you put towels in the proper place and leave the bathroom in order.

3. Personal organization such as planning their days, budget planning and goal-setting.

Claudia Black, two-time winner of Young Mother of the Year awards, said, "I believe a mother should be a child's best, and favorite teacher." (She practices what she preaches, and has taught her children everything from breadmaking to quilt-tying.) "I made a list of skills I felt my children would need to know before they left home, and have tried to systematically teach these skills to each child." Claudia's list includes cooking, cleaning house, sewing and mending, handiwork, quilt-making, meal-planning, shopping, gardening, carpentry, house-painting, and leatherwork. She uses the list to give the children ideas for activities to do in the thirty minutes a day she tries to spend with each child. Claudia says, "Learning skills is my children's favorite activity. It is the one they choose most often." Claudia believes that parents who teach children the skills of living give them a "happiness insurance policy". Her special brand of teaching includes methods which make it easy and fun for the children to learn. She draws picture recipes on posterboards that children can follow before they can read! (She draws a picture of the size cup or spoon they will need, and a picture of the ingredient next to it). Claudia teaches her beginning seamstresses to use the sewing machine by letting them "sew" without any thread on paper which has a simple pattern traced on it. When they develop the control necessary to succeed at staying on the pattern, she lets them try straight seams (such as on pillow cases).

Teaching skills in the positive framework they deserve increases the fun and satisfaction of family life for both parent and children alike.

The Leaven of Learning

Have you noticed that when children are learning, they usually rise to the positive level? Learning in a warm atmosphere is a leaven that lifts us. We seem to sense that as we learn, we become more like our Heavenly Father who knows everything. Perhaps this is why drudgery flies away and excitement replaces it when we become teachers to our children. Most mothers feel they're doing what they are really meant to do when they lay aside policeman's uniforms and teach their children. It is rewarding to feel a child's positive reaction when we help him feel more adequate and more at home in the world.

LaDawn Jacob, mother of six, enjoys teaching as a part of her parental role. She often records poems and songs that she wants her children to learn and plays them at breakfast time and through the day. LaDawn says: "My mom and dad taught us to memorize scriptures and poems. Dad would ask, "How many synonyms can you name for this word?" These things were such fun for us that I try to do the same things with my children." Before a recent trip to historical spots in the United States, she and her husband prepared reports for family home evening, checked out history books and visual aids from the library, and tried to find stories to make U.S. history interesting to little children. LaDawn said, "Although the children are small, I feel the preparation helped them get more out of the trip and gain more of an appreciation of their country." To keep the children occupied and learning while they travelled, they read books, memorized scriptures and played word games.

Kent and Marleen Krzymowski have done some fun educational things with their children, in addition to their family training sessions. They placed stars on the bedroom ceiling in the pattern of the constellations and made a model of the solar system to hang down from the stars. (They got the idea from an astronomy book.) They also do various experiments with the children with ideas gleaned from science books and from their own college experiences.

Dean and Claudia Black do many enjoyable educational projects with their children. For a time, they selected a country, such as Japan, to study each month. During that month they would learn one thing about the country each night at dinner. If there were any university students from Japan, they invited them to one of the meals they had during the month which would be typical of that country. They often featured appropriate decorations and pictures of the country the night of the special dinner to make it more festive.

They also post pictures of various things the small children are learning to do (like brushing teeth) and talk about them. On another part of their bulletin board, they post pictures of their "Animal of the Week" and assign one child each week to make this another interesting dinnertable learning experience. In addition, they post a "Temple of the Month" and a "Word List of the Month."

Richard and Betty Ellsworth use their bulletin board in a way that proved to be a real boon to keep their family learning. Betty said, "We have a bulletin board which we use for sharing ideas. It is really neat because if we find something we would like our children to read or think about, I post it and they read it: but if I said to them, 'I would like you to read this; this is exciting,' they would turn right off, no matter how important or wonderful the material was. Now the whole family puts things up (although they usually don't admit who did it). When we see something new, it is exciting, and we discuss the thought at the dinner table. Sometimes at family night we write the message and post it to remind us to focus on the message throughout the week. The whole thing has been so much fun for our family—and a good learning experience."

Clyda Blackburn has initiated a fun learning project with her three older boys. Each boy chooses a poem to memorize each week and the poems are taped on the mirror in the bathroom. Clyda memorizes all three poems, as well as one she chooses for herself. She feels that memorizing poems sharpens mental abilities and fills the mind with vivid imagery and worthwhile concepts. It also gives them something fun to share with each other. Every week when they pick new poems, they recite some of their old ones, (which are kept in envelopes with their names on them). They also review and recite at odd moments during the week, and Clyda mentioned that travelling in a car is an especially good time for this.

Public libraries are treasure houses of ideas and materials to use to teach children, as are church libraries (which are often overlooked). Many ward library materials (such as film strips, projectors, and all kinds of pictures) can be checked out by ward families for home use. We need not feel limited by our budgets when such an array of quality learning materials are available to us at no cost from the libraries.

Perhaps there has never been a time in our history when so much good was available for us to learn....and teach! LaDawn Jacob said, "I feel a strong motivation to use every minute possible to get positive information into my children's minds. There is so much of worth in the world, and if my children know a lot of good, I feel that they will have a much greater shield against the bad."

Experiences Are Teachers Too

We learn through positive participation and many experiences that make a difference in our lives do not come to us by chance, but by planning.

Parents have the ability to help children by positively structuring the environment and providing the opportunity for good and needed experiences for them. Many times a parent can plan special experiences that will not only teach, but solve some problem a child cannot handle well by himself.

For example, Michael was in the second grade when he began coming home from school grouchy and upset.

"It's not like Michael to be so cross," his mom commented to his dad. "Something must be wrong at school." They questioned Michael, but he said little.

A couple of weeks later, parent-teacher conferences were scheduled, and Michael's mother talked the problem over with his teacher.

"I wonder if it could be a problem on the playground?" Mrs. Parry began. "There's a boy, James, in Michael's class who's a real leader! It upsets Michael when James refuses to play with him. I've noticed that happening lately."

Michael's mother thanked the teacher and left, wondering what a mother could do about some little boy not playing with her son at school. But the next day, she came up with a plan.

"Mike, how would you like to invite James over to your house to play with you and have some ice cream?"

"He doesn't want to play with me."

"Ask him tomorrow and see what he says."

James came, and Michael and James had a good time together. Mike asked him again the next week, and James came. Mike's cross behavior disappeared, and he came home from school happy.

As we analyze our childrens' problems and needs, we don't need to wring our hands and feel that we are helpless. Although your "James" may not want to come to play, or may have a terrible time and go home crying, there will be many times when you *can* provide experiences for a child that will help him over a rough spot, and save you a lot of wear and tear on your nerves as well!

Control the Context

In a class at B.Y.U. Education Week, Lynn Scoresby stated that he believes the most compelling influence on behavior is the context or set of circumstances in which it occurs. He said that parents have no idea how great their control of behavior can be simply by controlling the context through very simple means. The dinner hour is an example that Lynn used. Purpose for being together is a major factor in context and one we can control. If we determine to enjoy each other and maybe even learn something new at suppertime (not just stop the hunger pangs)—and "set the stage" accordingly, the results can be gratifying.

"There is a great difference in the probable behavior of the children when we seat them at a bare table with paper plates thrown in front of them, in comparison with inviting them to a table covered with a lovely cloth, pretty dishes, and lighted candles," Lynn said.

Naturally we can't have candlelight dinners every night, but there are many things we can do to create a positive atmosphere at the table. Who would want to fight or quarrel if Mom is reading "Where the Red Fern Grows?" Dad might even forget to chastise the children for slurping their soup! The result is a more pleasant mealtime and better digestion for everyone. Some of our best reading and teaching moments can be at mealtimes. We have a "captive audience", and the children listen without resistance. (This practice can also improve the parent's waistline!) The key to controlling context in many situations is to take positive action yourself in order to avoid negative behavior from children. Travelling in the car with children is another good time to explore the possibilities for controlling and improving the context.

Mary Safsten, mother of eleven, planned varied seating arrangements for the children when the family was going on a long trip with Grandma. As they travelled, Mary's mother was amazed at the good behavior of the children. Mary said, "It's strategy, Mom! I know which children bring out the best in each other and what combinations will be most likely to cause problems. So I just plan seating arrangements accordingly!"

Clyda Blackburn, mother of four boys, takes a purse-full of pennies when they go on a trip. She promises the boys a penny for finding unusual sights along the way. They keep busy watching, and arrive at their destination with spending money.

After some traumatic trips with four live-wire sons, Darla decided to change the context for their next trip to Idaho. Her "strategy" was gift-wrapping snacks and materials for activities. She let the children open one gift for each hour they behaved well. The boys loved the "gifts" and kept busy, full, and happy.

When things do get out of hand in the car (or anywhere!), we can often change the context by telling a story or having the kids listen to a recorded one. When travelling overseas with two small children, Lynn Hanks got the idea of taping his boys' favorite stories on a cassette recorder. The children listened to these stories and kept happily occupied for long periods, leaving Lynn and Darla free to enjoy the scenery and visit. They had controlled the context.

Harness the Horses and Hold the Reins

If we don't decide what we *do* want children to do, our time will often be spent stopping behavior we don't want! The positive approach can make the difference between standing in the road and trying to direct a stampede of horses, or having the horses harnessed to your cart with you holding the reins and travelling together in a positive direction. Both approaches take time and effort, but it's so much more pleasant and productive doing good things rather than just stopping bad ones. Instead of saying, "Susy, stop kicking the dog; Johnny, keep your feet off the table; Julie quit throwing paper on the floor," we can say, "Here's some colored chalk to use for your new blackboard," or "Here's you favorite book, Susy; sit right here and look at the pictures and tell me which one you think is the prettiest." Gayle Whiting has a whole file of activity and lesson ideas for young children which she collected, using the Relief Society Nursery lesson materials as the starter in each category. She uses her file to initiate positive activities when things begin to get out of hand with her four pre-schoolers.

However, we don't want to give the impression that it is necessary to *provide* a constant stream of activities for children. There are many things a parent can do (such as having creative materials and ideas handy and using music to advantage) that can keep the atmosphere positive and help children initiate their own projects with no direct guidance. One mother has an arts and crafts cupboard where the children have access to all kinds of paper, paints, paste, etc. Many families have story records and tapes which the children may use freely. Narda Woodford, mother of five, keeps a list of possible activities (one for summer and one for winter) which the children refer to for ideas:

Summer List	*Winter List*
football	look at picture books
baseball	do crafts
frisbee	ping pong
jump rope	games and card games
roller skate	spin top
four square game	do puzzles
badminton	play piano, play recorders
tennis	call Grandma or friends on phone
croquet	play jacks

swimming
hop scotch
bicycling
marbles
walkie talkies
fly kites
pop caps
hammer and nails
butterfly net
visit Grandma
skate board
B B gun
stroll baby
weeding and watering
Barbie dolls
Annie aye-over
dress-up

chess and checkers
play doh
cut up old catalogs
do collages
color or paint
work with colored paper
play with trains
erector set
tinker toys
building blocks
play with cat
go to the library
play records
play with walkie talkies
get Mom to read stories or poems
look at the *Friend,* do activities in it
play store, post office,
doctor, beauty shop, etc.

Make it Easier for Them to Behave!

A change to a late Sunday morning meeting schedule proved potential dynamite at the Bascom house. With too much free time, the children became restless and rowdy and the Sunday feeling was quickly lost. Arlene thought about what kind of a morning she would *like* to have and made plans accordingly. First, she discussed some rules with the children. "You are to make your beds, get dressed and come to breakfast in time for scripture and prayer just as on a school day," she said. "When everyone is ready for Sunday School and the house is in order, you will be rewarded with a special project you can work on together until it is time to leave." The children agreed.

The next Sunday (which was in November) the children fulfilled their part of the agreement and then asked, "What do we get to do today, Mom?" Arlene produced a large sheet of newsprint, a stack of magazines and catalogs, and scissors and paste. She wrote in big letters across the top of the paper "Things We are Thankful For." She said, "Find pictures of things that you are thankful for and paste them on this paper to make a collage. We will hang it on the wall in the dining room, and discuss it at dinner time." The children were enthusiastic and the feeling was a great contrast from the previous Sunday.

Arlene could have focused on simply stopping restless, rowdy behavior. But the positive approach of showing her children what *to* do stopped the negative behavior automatically while furthering other family goals at the same time.

The Positive Approach to Children and Church

Marshall and Linda Garner (who have four children, four years of age and under) believe there are two "positive" principles involved in teaching children to behave so that the parents can enjoy church:

1. Proper preparation (making positive expectations clear)
2. Lots of positive feedback.

One thing Linda feels has helped her a great deal is a book by Carol Lynn Pearson called, *"Sounds and Shh"* which talks about how Heavenly Father made our wonderful bodies capable of making many sounds. But it explains that there are times when we need to be quiet; when someone is sleeping or on the telephone, or when we go to church. Linda often reads this book to her children just before they go to a meeting. She reminds them what they will be doing at the meeting and how she wants them to act. She tells them how important it is for them to be quiet and reverent so that Mom and Dad and all the other people can hear the speakers and feel Heavenly Father's spirit. She explains the Sacrament in simple language, and lets them see the little picture of Jesus which they always take to church. Linda said, "I feel that just telling tiny children to think about Jesus during the Sacrament is a little unrealistic. But a picture of Jesus which is brought out only during the Sacrament helps them direct their thoughts, and make Jesus more real to them."

Before they leave, each child is allowed to choose one thing to take, a quiet book, paper and pencil, or a story book. On the way to church Linda asks the children, "How are you going to act today?" They recite back to her the "behavior expectations" she has taught them. If a child has to be taken out during the meeting, they find an empty classroom and give the child a serious talk or a spanking, then go right back in. They are never allowed to stay out and play in the foyer.

After the meeting, Linda always finds something good to say about each child's behavior, even if it wasn't perfect. She might say, "I noticed you had a hard time sitting still today. It is hard when it's so hot, isn't it? But I noticed that you folded your arms during the Sacrament, and that made me proud."

When they do well, she makes it a point to praise them. She says things like, "I was so proud of you today. You were reverent and remembered what we talked about. I appreciated so much that you were able to sit still and be quiet so I could hear. Maybe I can tell you more about the talks now because I know it was hard for you to understand."

Spiritual Implications

When it comes to staying on a positive level, parents are put to the test in a difficult and peculiar way. Who else must face lost socks, sibling conflicts and spilled milk twenty-four hours a day with no route of escape? No wonder negative feelings so easily creep in! Even though we may be convinced that the positive approach works best to motivate children, we may keep looking for easier ways, or fall back into negative patterns. Days when one thing after another goes wrong, the effort required to stay positive may seem to be more than we can manage! It takes *no* effort to yell, hit, or threaten because the negative is the path of least resistance. But to rise to the level of the positive, where we actually put into practice the principles of the gospel, takes self-control and the help of the Spirit.

In Proverbs 15:1 we read, "A soft answer turneth away wrath." Does anyone ever find it easy to stay positive and give a soft answer when someone else is in a rage? Yet the beautiful results when the challenge is met, lifts one from the level of the natural man and offers a taste of spiritual control. Only when we are in this positive frame of mind can we be open and receptive to the promptings of the spirit.

Ten Things to Try

1. Be specific in showing, telling, and explaining what you do want your children to do.

a. Try modelling or acting out a behavior you want from a child.

b. Try family training sessions where you teach etiquette, good personal habits, and personal organization.

2. Keep your children learning! Record poems, songs, or scriptures that you want the children to learn and play them at breakfast or through the day.

3. Check out pictures, tapes, records, filmstrips, and new books from your library this week. Let the children benefit from the library's wealth.

4. Choose a "country of the month" to study, and learn new things about it every evening at the supper table.

5. Try a special bulletin board to be used for sharing your thoughts and ideas. Encourage family members to post things on it and discuss them together.

6. Plan a success experience for one of your children that might help solve a problem or fill a need.

7. Control the "context" in your home. Tell a story or sing a song when things get tense. Read uplifting stories at the dinner table to keep things on a positive level.

8. When travelling with your children, plan "strategies" such as seating charts, or gift-wrapped treats and creative materials for good behavior.

9. Organize an arts and crafts cupboard or start an activity file to provide your children with ideas for constructive activities.

10. Give your older children an "idea bank" by providing them with a list of ideas of activity possibilities (one for summer and one for winter).

11

Building Faith and Overcoming Discouragement

One particularly beautiful summer night, four-year-old Holly Bascom joined her mother who was sitting on the front porch. She sat down and looked up at the sky. An expression of awe came over her face and in an amazed voice she said, "Oh, look at all those stars up there. Those must be lights in the sky to help us find Heavenly Father!"

All of us need "light" to help us find Heavenly Father, and the light of faith shines the brightest. Faith is the first principle of the gospel and the prerequisite to all progress, power, and spiritual living, and in its purest form is often exemplified by little children.

One night four-year-old Richard Buck was very sick. His mother, Deanna, was holding Richard on her lap when her husband, George, got home from a meeting. As soon as George came into the room, Richard said, "Daddy, where's that medicine you put on my head so Heavenly Father can get me better?" George explained to little Richard the purpose of the consecrated oil, and gave him a blessing. Immediately after the blessing was finished, Richard jumped off Deanna's lap and said, "I feel better now."

"When our oldest son, Bruce, went on his mission, he was given a blessing that his family would be protected and watched over while he was gone." said Thelma Jones. "Later, our dog, Tippy, who was a dear family pet, got very sick and the Vet said he probably wouldn't live. I talked to our youngest son, Steve (who was eight at the time) and explained that the dog might die. 'Oh no, Mom,' Steve replied. 'Tippy will be all right. He's part of the family and Bruce's blessing said we'd all be protected.' Tippy was alive and well when Bruce returned from his mission!"

When two-year-old Owen Wolfgramm was sick, his brother, Louie (who was three) put his hands on Owen's head and said, "I'm going to give Owen a blessing, Momma, so he will get better." His mother, Joella, explained that you must have the Priesthood to give blessings, but that he could pray to Heavenly Father and ask Him to help Owen. "What a sweet sight that was," said Joella, "To see my three-year-old kneeling by his little brother praying sincerely that Heavenly Father would help him."

What does it take to develop that kind of faith in a three-year-old child? Parents can learn from the sweet faith of little children; but children must first learn from us. A child who is not taught of God has little chance to develop faith in Him.

Teaching Moments Matter

Elvin Christiansen and his wife, Elaine, believe that faith is built step by step...and a great deal of it comes from living with parents who have it. They have always tried to take advantage of special teaching moments. When they would go up in the mountains, Elvin would say to his little ones, "If you had the faith, you could even move that big mountain! There's nothing you can't accomplish if you have the faith—and if it's right." He also said things like "With all his knowledge, no man can change the color of the leaves. But the highest power, God, knows how to do everything. Look around at these beautiful mountains and the colors you see—this is the kind of beauty that God alone can make." He taught lessons from observations of the animal life and everything they saw in nature.

Karen Reilley said, "One day we were talking with the kids about recycled water. They wrinkled their noses at the thought of drinking it. So we explained how all water is recycled by nature over and over and over again. My oldest son, Franky, thought about that and then said, "You know, that makes you know there has to be a God. The earth couldn't think to itself, 'I'll just recycle this water, now what is the best plan to use?' " Karen feels even the simplest processes of nature can be faith-building to a child as parents help him see the necessity for intelligent direction behind it all.

Alma said it this way,

> Yea, and all things denote there is a God; yea, even the earth, and all things that are upon the face of it, yea, and its motion, yea, and also the planets which move in their regular form do witness that there is a Supreme Creator.   (Alma 30:44)

Dantzell Lewis Allen said, "My Dad always used the teaching moments well. I remember one time we were up to our cabin, and the family walked over where we could see the whole valley. We sat down and looked at the city below. It was just beautiful. Dad talked to us about having faith in our country and keeping it free. Another time after I was married, I went with the family to visit my sister's grave. My father sat us down around the grave and started teaching us about the plan of salvation. I realized then that this type of thing had happened all my life."

Marilyn Ursenbach was ill a great deal as a child and had to have many operations. When she was four, she asked her mother, Bernice, "Mama, will we be sick when we live with Heavenly Father after we die?" Bernice reassured her that we wouldn't; that we will all have perfect bodies, so we have a great deal to look forward to. After years of physical problems, Marilyn said, "Mom, I know the Lord has something special for me to do or I wouldn't still be alive and as well as I am."

Connie Evans believes that a natural time to build faith-nourishing thoughts in little minds is bedtime. Every night she rocks her smallest child and sings and talks with her. She often sings church songs to reinforce spiritual ideas and lead into conversations about gospel concepts. She has talked about the pre-existence with each of her children at an early age. One night two-year-old Holly asked her, "Do spirits have legs?"

Things of a spiritual nature *can* be very puzzling to children. When Brian Hanks was three he said, "I wonder how Heavenly Father gets someone to heaven. I know, He reaches down His arm and makes a hole in the sky and pulls them through...or maybe He gets a cloud and climbs in it to come and get them!" Children need to be taught, and parents need to grasp each teaching moment.

Connie said, "The responsibility for teaching a child the gospel and helping him gain a testimony falls primarily on the mother. Mother's teachings can be reinforced by dad and the church organizations, but she should teach him first when he is just tiny."

Building Faith by Sharing Faith

Thelma Jones believes you should share faith-promoting experiences with children and remind them often of how much the Lord loves us. She said, "Share experiences, point them out; let children see demonstrations of your faith."

Carolyn Plain agreed: "I feel it really builds children's faith when you share spiritual experiences with them. My children ask to hear their favorite ones over and over again. I always try to talk about anything that happens to me that shows the help of the Lord or the benefits of living the gospel."

One mother said that she believes a child's faith begins to grow when they are very young if they see it and feel it in the lives of their parents. Margaret Bosch tells how the faith of their whole family grew because of the faith of her husband. He suffered from a steadily worsening kidney disease and finally became an artificial kidney machine patient. The A.K. maching (although it required intensive training and long and tedious hours for its use), gave him a new lease on life, and for eighteen additional months his family enjoyed his influence in their home. Margaret said, "We shared in his great faith and superb attitude. We watched him go about his life in as normal a fashion as the A.K. would permit. I never went down to the A.K. room without silently saying a prayer of gratitude for his life, for his strength of character, and his great faith that kept us all going. He simply refused to give up." When a second catastrophic disease took his life, that same faith sustained Margaret and their seven children.

She said, "In the eight years of his illness, the Elders had responded to our plea for help many times, and had exercised priesthood power in his behalf. But this last time there were no promises made, and instead of additional strength he was granted release from pain. But how could we quarrel with it? We knew it had to be for the best! Even if we had been granted the power to call him back to us, we wouldn't have wanted him to come back to such pain. Miss him?...Yes! Daily. But even these intervening years are made sweeter by having a sure conviction that this is but a fleeting moment of separation before we share the eternity with him!"

"I taught my children from the first, that the Lord would always watch over them and take care of them no matter what happened," said Mary Wright. "When something bad *did* happen, they saw I really meant it because the first thing I wanted was to have them administered to right away. I told them after they had been given a blessing that I knew they were in the hands of the Lord and everything would be all right. One time my boy, Earl, got kicked in the face by a horse and when they brought him to me, I couldn't even tell who he was. He was an awful sight. We sent for the nearest priesthood holders we knew of (men working on a house next door) and as soon as he had been blessed, I knew all would be well; and his face healed without a scar. The children all shared in this miracle and many other such experiences."

It seems that there is a great deal of non-verbal as well as verbal communication that helps a child build faith. When the parents have deep feelings, it gets across to the children. One mother said, "In the home where I grew up, we didn't talk about the church a lot; yet there was still this underlying feeling—we knew the church was the most important thing in the world to Mom and Dad because their lives centered around it."

Focusing our Faith

We also need to build faith in specific ways concerning specific principles and aspects of the gospel. For example, we can encourage our children to experiment with gospel principles, to really try them out.

> ...awake and arouse your faculties, even to an experiment upon my words....
> (Alma 32:27)

Living the Commandments. When Linda Garner was quite young, her family talked it over and decided none of them would do school studies on Sunday. When Linda got to college, she found that this was a real issue. Many of her friends had similiar policies, but when the pressures mounted, and they had really important tests or assignments, they would end up doing them on Sunday anyway, and they would say, "What else could I do?" Linda thought about it and made a commitment to herself that no matter what the circumstances she would keep the Sabbath day holy. She said, "That commitment brought me a feeling of great peace. I created a sanctuary for myself; a day free from pressure. I knew that no matter what the other demands, I would have Sunday for rejuvenation; for scripture study, prolonged prayer, letter-writing, genealogy work, writing my personal history—things that would lift my spirit. I kept that commitment to myself, and even though I sometimes had to start at midnight on Sunday and work through the early Monday morning hours, I always got everything done I needed to without encroaching on my special day of rest."

Keeping the commandments builds faith; and increased faith builds strength to keep more commandments! If we can encourage our children to *try* living a commandment, it is almost certain to become a faith-building experience for them. One way to encourage them is to talk about our own experiences in living the commandments. Julia and Walter Moore talked to their children many times about how they had been blessed for paying tithing and how much their finances have improved (even with so many more children) since they were first married when they didn't pay their tithing for a short time. They feel sharing their experiences concerning the law of tithing has strengthened their children's faith in this principle.

John and Carol Jeanne Ehlers take every opportunity to tell their twelve children the blessings they have received from their faith in the commandments. People often say to them, "I'd like to have a big family, too, but I just can't afford it." John said, "We have decided that you don't afford any of your children, because you don't provide—your Father in Heaven does. (The earth is His and we only have a stewardship.) If we just keep His laws, all will be added according to our needs." Carol added, "Really, you are being presumptuous anyway if you say 'I did it, I provided' or 'I can't do it,' because He will bless us and provide ways for us to fill our needs if we keep His laws. We have found a lot of help in the promises for paying tithing, fasting, and keeping the Sabbath holy. We have been blessed from trying to live these laws. So we feel it would have been a lack of faith in the Lord's promises, not a lack of finances, that would have been the deciding factor if we had limited our family."

Scriptures. One family always encouraged their children to find answers to their problems and questions by searching the scriptures. Their daughter said, "As a little child, it was so impressive to me when my parents would read answers to my problems from the scriptures that it really developed my faith in their value and motivated me to turn to them frequently as I grew older. For instance, they frequently referred me to D&C 122:7,8 where the Lord said:

...know thou, my son, that all these things shall give thee experience, and shall be for thy good.

The Son of Man hath descended below them all. Art thou greater than He?

That scripture helped me as a teenager and it has been a source of comfort to me numerous times since."

Testimony and Church Attendance. Linden Hurst, a member of a stake presidency and father of seven, said, "It really is hard to pinpoint what builds a child's faith. In our home, well...sometimes it's really hectic. Yet when I see the faith the children have, I'm just amazed. I see my children, right from an early age, show love for the Lord and enthusiasm in church activities; one boy loves to read the scriptures, one daughter is totally involved in seminary, and all the little kids are thrilled with primary and sing primary songs all the time. You wonder what makes the difference, and I think it isn't so much things you do on rare occasions, but what they see every day. Two specific things I believe do make a difference:

1. If you can take them to church regularly to hear all those good lessons.

2. If they hear Mom and Dad bear testimony. When I was bishop, the kids would really listen to me when I bore my testimony from the pulpit. And I often tell them in daily conversation things like, 'You bet I know the church is true!' I don't stop and say 'Now I'd like to bear my testimony.' But whenever the conversation is right, I just tell them the way I feel."

"Bear testimony to your children often," Diane Pace suggested in a B.Y.U. Education Week class. "Share your feelings and experiences. Don't slight your children by thinking that they won't understand. They are touched by the spirit to know the truth of what you say no matter how little they are. Share every tender feeling of your heart."

Some parents write their testimonies and give each child a copy for his own Book of Remembrance. Parents and grandparents can also make cassette tapes of their testimonies and the

things they would like their children and grandchildren to remember. The impression and significance of these faith-building
words may be even greater if the children are able to hear the
testimonies in the voices of their loved ones.

The Dangers of Discouragement

To share faith we must have it...children's believing attitudes seem to blossom naturally when they live with parents who
set the right example. But we can't lead children where we are
not going. It is often the parent's lack of faith which makes life
less productive for the whole family. Faith is an action word;
without it we may teach the gospel verbally, but the moment-by-
moment application may be missing...along with the joy!

Discouragement and negative thinking are some of the greatest enemies of faith and positive action, and we need to fortify
ourselves as parents so we do not let these forces keep us from
having the kind of family the Lord wants us to have. Conscientious Latter-day Saint parents can seldom be swayed by temptations to indulge in the things of the world, but all of us are
vulnerable to discouragement! Satan and his angels must rejoice
when good people yield to the temptation to become discouraged; for when we choose to let negative thoughts and actions
take over we are, in fact, choosing to follow the promptings of
the adversary. One perceptive church member we will call Karen
put it this way:

"Sin is sin because it keeps us from progressing and becoming all we have the potential to be. Because of this, I believe giving in to discouragement and negative thinking is a sin. I know I
certainly don't make any progress when I'm caught up in black
thoughts and I have never lifted or inspired anyone else when
I've been 'really down' myself. I finally had to come to grips with
the fact that I was not following the Savior when I allowed myself to be filled with gloom and depression. The Savior said,
'Doubt not, fear not, but be believing.' Yet I often used to hear
myself saying, 'I can't do it; it won't work; we couldn't possibly;
something will go wrong, it always does.' This kind of thinking
is the very opposite of faith. How could I pretend to be living the
gospel with such a pessimistic view of life?

"So I started studying the scriptures more and began to see
that the Lord has counselled us repeatedly to avoid negative
thoughts. ('Look unto me in every thought; doubt not, fear not.'
D&C 6:36.) 2 Timothy 1:7. Philippians 4:4-8. I learned from the
scriptures that faith is a gift of the spirit (I Cor. 12:9) and is in-
separably connected with the power of the Holy Ghost. In Ro-

mans 15:13 Paul offered this comforting assurance: 'Now the God of hope fill you with all joy and peace in believing, that ye may abound in hope, through the power of the Holy Gost.' When I really thought about it, I had to admit that I could never remember feeling depressed at the same time I felt the sweet influence of the Holy Ghost. In fact, those two feelings are opposite! I could see the price we pay for negative thoughts and discouragement is far too high. I decided I must learn to master my thoughts and take advantage of all the ideas I could find to help me avoid and overcome discouragement. That decision has made a great difference in my life."

How To's for Overcoming Discouragement

Almost all techniques for overcoming discouragement and negative thinking are also faith-builders. As our faith barometer rises, our discouragement barometer falls! (And, we cannot remain discouraged if we succeed in pulling our thoughts to a positive level!!) Many people have found specific things that work for them in overcoming discouragement and negative thinking.

1. *Cling to the Shining Moments.* Get out scrapbooks, Books of Remembrance, diaries or journals and re-live spiritual experiences and times when you felt the best about yourself. One mother keeps a special notebook called "My Book of Triumphs," where she records her personal successes. She reads it often to build her up when she feels her faith and confidence slipping. (When we lose faith, we also lose confidence!)

Virginia Riley, mother of ten, said, "One of our youngest daughters got married recently and it was a great occasion in our family. Two daughters decorated her cake, all helped with the catering, one played the organ at the reception. Everyone in the family was there and at their best. I couldn't help thinking that although we can't escape problems when we are raising a family, by clinging to such shining moments, we can make it through!"

2. *One Day at a Time: "Line Upon Line."* Sharlene Tyler said, "One day I remember I was so discouraged and I called my mother long distance and told her all the things that had gone wrong and how I was behind on everything and just felt overwhelmed. Mother said, 'How are the children?' I told her they were well and happy. She replied, 'If you've gotten your children one day older and they have had a happy day—your time hasn't been wasted! Just try to take one step at a time, one day at a

time.' That advice has snapped me out of a depression many times!"

With our lofty expectations for ourselves, it is easy to lose perspective, and feel discouraged about our rate of progress. But we need to remember that our conscience beckons us to come and do better; it is the adversary that prompts us to condemn ourselves and feel discouraged. We need to be compassionate with ourselves and be content with progressing one day at a time: "line upon line: precept upon precept."

3. *Start Again and Again!* One enthusiastic mother of four said, "I used to get discouraged with myself when I would start creative programs and ideas but didn't follow through on them consistently. I finally realized I was spending more energy reprimanding myself for negligence than it would take to make great progress by starting again and trying harder. So my new motto is "start again...and again!" Many times we feel it is too late to do anything about it if we have neglected a goal for a day, a week or a month. But this is another trick Satan uses on us to keep good things from happening. If we do start again, we can redouble our efforts and sometimes even make up for lost time! Because we didn't accomplish what we had intended this morning doesn't mean we can't work harder this afternoon! If we let our exercise program or scripture reading slide for a week, there is no reason we can't start again...and again...until we reach our goal!

4. *Use Mottos.* Mottos can be a great help to fortify our determination and confidence when we feel discouraged. One mother said, "Everytime I find myself getting discouraged (and when my goals seem impossible to reach) I try to remember to say to myself in enthusiastic tones, '*I can* do it, and *I will* do it!' If the problem of procrastination is adding to my discouragement I remember:'If not now, when? If not me, who?' This simple method often gives me determination to keep trying and overcome my discouragement when I backslide into old habits."

5. *Try an "Affirmation List."* One personnel counselor, (whose specialization is helping businessmen develop positive mental attitudes) recommends using an "Affirmation List". He suggests you write a list of virtues you most desire (wording them as though you have already achieved them). For example: "I am patient, I am loving, I am kind, I am cheerful, I have great faith." Then read this list or say it aloud to yourself several times a day to keep your thoughts on the positive qualities you *want* rather than the negative ones you may be displaying. One author

calls this "auto-suggestion" and implies that we can change our reaction patterns and measurably increase our faith and abilities by consciously feeding our minds these positive affirmations. When your sub-conscious is given such statements, it sets about to help you make them become reality! One mother said, "I have seen more measurable change in my life through using the affirmation technique than through any other method I've tried. When I'm thinking over and over 'I am kind' it influences me strongly to behave that way. Because most of our actions depend on how we see ourselves, I think this process has a lot of potential."

6. *Read Inspiration Material.* Helen Sharp said, "One of the best ways I have found to get myself back into a spiritual frame of mind when I am discouraged is to read things that inspire me: church magazines, scriptures, great thoughts, etc. That approach always uplifts me and I feel one of the blessings we have in living today is the wealth of inspirational material we have access to."

7. *Listen to Good Music.* Our spirits are often lifted by listening to inspiring music. If you enjoy singing or playing, active involvement in music can be even better therapy! Many people also mentioned that they try to memorize their favorite hymns so they can sing or recite them when they feel discouraged.

8. *Work, Work, Work!* "Do something!" is a good motto for overcoming discouragement. Betty Ellsworth said, "Too many times we get discouraged when things get hard and say, 'Oh this is too hard, I can't do it, or maybe I'm not supposed to do it.' But this is probably Satan working on you, and if you have prayed and received that warm feeling that what you are doing *is* right, you must gather all your forces and all your prayers and say 'full speed ahead and give me lots of help!' "

It has been said that during our greatest trials the perfection process is at its height, and often the greatest temptations to discouragement come just before periods of growth and triumph! So the time we are most tempted to give in to discouragement is the time we need to work, work, work!

Hard work can improve our situation in many ways. Filling our physical, social, spiritual, and mental needs requires work, and if we *do* something to improve things, we are sure to feel better. We may not be able to change a specific problem we are concerned about, but there are many other things we *can* change for the better. Those are the things on which we should focus.

Active exercise can also be a helpful way to fight discouragement. Feeling the action of our bodies can help us regain a sense of aliveness that will overcome mental lethargy.

9. *Do Something for Someone Else.* It's hard to remain depressed when we are doing something for someone else. Doing something that makes a difference to someone else affirms our own worth, increases our faith in our power to change things for the better, and gives us the uplift of association with other people. (See Chapter 8)

10. *Look Ahead.* One mother said, "I have noticed in the scriptures that the phrase 'it came to pass' is used frequently. It never says, 'it came to stay!' I try to apply that to my worries and problems when I get discouraged. Whatever it is that's bothering me I think 'this too will pass' and I immediately feel better." We can look ahead, past the problems of the moment; think of achieving some of our most important goals and how we will feel when we have reached them. Even saying, "tomorrow will be better" can often help. Julia Moore said, "When I feel discouraged, I say, 'it won't be as bad tomorrow!' or 'Things will get better soon!' Sure enough, they do. I think the best thing to help when we are discouraged is to use phrases like this in order to regain our perspective."

Setting new goals and making plans to reach them, reading our patriarchal blessings and "pre-experiencing" or imagining ourselves acting and feeling as though we had already achieved the promises made to us, are other ways we can regain enthusiasm for living!

11. *Activate Faith.* One root cause of discouragement it seems is to be not truly believing at the moment that things are going to improve. However, most of us actually have a much greater store of faith than we give ourselves credit for—we just forget to use it! We can sometimes challenge ourselves out of mental depression by simply saying to ourselves, "O.K. now, do I honestly believe things are going to remain just as they are or get worse! Do I really think that the Lord won't help me improve things if I honestly seek His help?" This brings our thinking to a rational level; and helps us out of many of our discouraged feelings.

For example, a couple we will call Joan and Bill found themselves in very trying financial circumstances, and for months nothing seemed to improve, and they became more and more discouraged. One night when Bill was especially despondent, Joan wrote him a letter. It began with scriptures like:

Come unto me, all ye that labour and are heavy laden, and I will give you rest.

Take my yoke upon you and learn of me;...for my burden is light.

(Matthew 11:28-30)

Cast thy burden upon the Lord, and he shall sustain thee....

(Psalm 55:22)

If God be for us, who can be against us? (Romans 8:31)

All things work together for good to them that love God....

(Romans 8:28)

Then she said, "Do we *really* believe, or are these promises just words to us? Life only needs to be burdensome when we *let* it be, when we try to shoulder the whole load without the Lord's help. I'm so worried about the example we've been showing to the kids. We profess to believe these scriptures and the gospel as a whole, and we obey all the outward commandments. Yet we are unhappy and depressed. I'm afraid the kids will begin seeing our version of 'gospel living' as a drudgery; as an unhappy way to live. They may want to look elsewhere for a 'happier' pattern to follow."

Because they both really *did* believe the promises in the scriptures, they *were* motivated to change their attitude. As a result, their circumstances soon changed for the better.

12. *Make a Needed Change.* A great principle for overcoming discouragement is recognizing a need for change and doing something about it, as Joan and Bill did. A big part of discouragement is usually related to mistakes we have made, things we have not done that we should have, and discrepancies between values and actions. Our only freedom from the heaviness this brings is to take advantage of the Lord's atonement through repentance. George Pace said in a B.Y.U. Education Week class, "If we continue in sorrow it means we haven't accepted what Jesus has done for us. It is His design that we be happy." We have been counselled that "despair cometh through iniquity." As we humbly repent (of even our very smallest iniquities) and gain the Lord's help to improve our lives, faith will gradually replace despair.

Live the Law—Reap the Blessings

We *can* consciously choose to change our lives. Too often people lose faith and feel that unfair circumstances are causing their problems and there is nothing they can do about them. This happens especially if they have done things they think *should* make a difference—and have really *tried* and worked hard to solve a problem with no favorable results.

Some of us might identify with the English student who went to his teacher after receiving a low grade on a paper and said, "How could you do this to me? I worked so hard; put so much effort on this paper—and you gave me the worst grade I've had all year." The teacher said, "If you build a boat and put forth great time and effort but it is still not seaworthy, and leaks when you launch it—can you explain to the ocean so it won't sink?" Every spiritual, mental, and emotional process is governed by law, just as the physical processes are. All laws are meant for our blessing and growth, and are irrevocably decreed: (D&C 130:20) The laws of nature never pay an unearned account and never fail to pay one that is earned. We must pay the price for the blessings we desire by living the laws on which they are predicated. If we try to discover what law we are not living, and are willing to change our lives to comply with that law, solutions *will* come. This willingness to search and to change is part of being honest in heart, and part of the process of repentance.

Betty Ellsworth explained how she applies this idea to improving things in her home, "I have learned that when you try and try and something is just not working with your family the way you want it to, it does no good to blame the family or get upset; what you need to do is change the plan! You just say, 'O.K. that plan isn't working; I'm not getting the results I want. What will work?' Then I try another plan."

When we are honest with ourselves, we quit blaming outside circumstances for our problems and bad attitudes. We realize that discouragement is based on the false feeling that we are not responsible—that fate or something "out there" is making us unhappy, not our own bad choices, or attitudes. Once we accept our responsibility, then through the guidance of the spirit we will learn what we need to do that *will* make the difference in our lives—and then do it!

We soon learn that it is our *reaction* to circumstances and not the actual situation which determines the quality of our lives and the level of our faith. Someone said, "What happens to us may not matter very much or for very long; but what we do about it may matter for all eternity." It is an exciting thing to realize that we *always* have a choice concerning what we *do* about what happens to us. The gospel makes it clear to us that we are *free* to choose for ourselves. (2 Nephi 2:27, 2 Nephi 10:23).

This means we can have a tremendous amount of control over our environment by the power of our attitude, and we have the potential to develop total control over our own thoughts (which determine our attitudes). Once we experience the power we have over our lives when we control our thoughts, our faith in ourselves will grow and we will not linger in the spiritually barren state of discouragement and depression.

Nourish the Word

> But if ye will nourish the word, yea, nourish the tree as it beginneth to grow, by your faith with great diligence, and with patience, looking forward to the fruit thereof, it shall take root; and behold it shall be a tree springing up unto everlasting life.
>
> (Alma 32:41)

Our greatest source of help to build faith and overcome discouragement is spiritual. If we pray, fast, meditate, read the scriptures, ponder promises in sacramental prayers, and ask for special blessings, the Lord will give us the faith and strength we need to improve our thoughts, attitudes, and circumstances. When the Savior said, "Peace I leave with you...Let not your heart be troubled, neither let it be afraid." (John 14:27) He really meant that no matter what the circumstances in the world, we can accomplish our own life's mission and have peace in our hearts if we try to keep the commandments and stay close to Him.

The Book of Mormon repeatedly tells us "Whatsoever thing ye shall ask the Father in my name, which is good, in faith believing that ye shall receive, behold, it shall be done unto you." (Moroni 7:26) The Lord has given us so many beautiful promises, and we have so much assurance of His help, that we can always bolster our faith by "nourishing the word", putting the Lord's promises to the test, and feeling His power and influence in our lives.

Darla said, "A certain scripture has come to mean a great deal to me and has really been a faith-builder. One day my little one-year-old Benjamin came up to me with his chubby arms outstretched, wanting me to pick him up. His expression and whole countenance were especially appealing, and he had an almost pleading sound in his voice when he said, 'Mama! Mama!' I leaned down and picked him up and held him close. At that moment a scripture came to my mind:

> Or what man is there of you, who, if his son ask bread, will give him a stone?
>
> Or if he ask a fish, will he give him a serpent?
>
> If ye then, being evil, know how to give good gifts unto your children, how much more shall your Father who is in heaven give good things to them that ask him.
>
> (3 Nephi 14:9-11)

"When my little ones come to me and they are thirsty or hungry or in need of comfort, there is no way I can shove them aside and not help them. Thinking about this scripture gave me a warm, comforting assurance that when I go to my Father in Heaven and reach up to Him and plead for help, He will not ignore me!" He is there, He hears us, and He will respond.

Carolyn Plain said, "When I am discouraged, I just pour my heart out to the Lord; really tell Him every feeling I have and why I feel that way. One time I was discouraged about a problem my daughter was having with her friends. I had prayed about it repeatedly, but one day when I felt I couldn't stand it any longer, I sobbed out the whole story and told the Lord how much we needed His help. Two hours later something happened that made a great difference and really eased the problem." Faith is not just a principle—it is a power!

If we "try an experiment" on His words, and nourish them, the seeds of our faith can grow and grow until discouragement has little power over us and faith becomes the great motivating power in our lives and in the lives of our children.

"...and this is the victory that overcometh the world, even our faith." (1 John 5:4)

Ten Things to Try

1. Share your faith-promoting experiences with your children. Talk about your experiences that show the help of the Lord and the benefits of living the gospel.

2. Take advantage of teaching moments to build your faith through observations of the orderliness and wonder of God's creations.

3. Bear testimony to your children whenever the situation is right. Write your testimony and give a copy to each child, or record it on a cassette recorder for them. Encourage the grandparents to do this also.

4. When you feel discouraged, get out scrapbooks, Books of Remembrance, diaries, or journals and re-live meaningful and spiritual times in your life. Focus on your successes.

5. Make an "Affirmation List" of the qualities you most desire. Read it every day.

6. Read inspirational material or listen to good music to lift your spirits and build your faith.

7. When you feel you are not making progress in one area, change your focus and work hard in an area where you **can** make

a difference. One of the most effective forms of work is to make something better for someone else. Service is a good antidote for depression!

8. Look ahead. Set new goals and plan how to reach them; read your patriarchal blessing and contemplate the blessings you have been promised. "Pre-experience" or imagine yourself acting and feeling your best and achieving your goals!

9. Challenge yourself to activate your faith! List your favorite scriptures and apply them to your present situation.

10. Try an "experiment" with the Lord's promises; "nourish the word" through practice, prayer and patience, and watch your faith grow.

Making Greatness the Goal

"Mommy, is the six-million dollar man really as strong as he is on T.V.? Wow! I'd sure like to be strong like that!"

T.V.'s make-believe super-heroes have been very popular for years and have become idols to many young viewers. What fun to identify with someone who, with little effort, can triumph over the mundane, irritating limitations we all experience. The super-heroes have powers as varied as their names and costumes. But they have one thing in common. Their powers are not real and their greatness is based on a false premise.

The gospel encourages us to seek excellence and promises the help of the sustaining power of God—which is the only power to help us rise above human weakness and limitations. Children need to know of people who triumph through the real power of faith, persistence, and reliance on the Priesthood of God in order to identify with true greatness. Someone has said, "We become what we think about." If we can touch our children's minds with stories of greatness, these thoughts can be their daily fare and will influence what they become.

Heroes Children can Follow to Heaven

The scriptures are a rich source of good examples we can share with our children. Betty Ellsworth said, "When our children were little, my husband began to tell Bible stories at the table. 'Oh, Daddy, tell us a story!' the children would say, and storytelling became a tradition. Of course, Dad didn't get much eating done, but the stories he shared made mealtime so special! The children learned to identify with the characters, and I think their favorite is Joseph of Egypt because he had so many problems, but overcame them and developed character and strength."

Some writers have said that it takes courage to be happy! Perhaps this is because it takes courage to learn new things, face new situations, and continue to grow and progress. The courage of the Davids and the Daniels, the strength of Moses and Abraham, can inspire children to develop the courage and strength they need for successful living.

While the Old Testament offers a rich and varied supply of heroes, the New Testament is unparalleled in its contribution. Our children should be taught to admire and emulate the Savior more than any other individual. There are many things we can do to help our children sense His true stature. We can display pictures of Him, study His life, and talk of His central importance and influence in our lives. No other pattern of greatness is without flaw, and no other example in history can proclaim so confidently, "Come follow me." The concluding chapter in this book discusses following the Savior's example.

In many homes the Book of Mormon has become a great favorite for stories of adventure and strength of character. Nephi, Alma, King Benjamin, Moroni, and many others offer us their exciting and inspiring experiences in overcoming the forces of evil and triumphing through the power of the Lord. Learning of this caliber of man can motivate us to seek that power in our own lives.

The Greatness of Early Church Leaders

The Lord chose great leaders to guide His church in the early days of the restoration. The Prophet Joseph Smith's life is full of stories of faith and courage which we can make a part of our children's experience. A favorite story of the Hanks boys is the one about Joseph Smith's courage when riding in a stagecoach when the horses became frightened and began running out of control. Joseph Smith climbed through the window, up to the top of the stagecoach, and made his way to the driver's seat as the stagecoach veered wildly. He leaped onto the back of one of the horses and calmed him and was able to get the whole team under control and stop the stage!

His prowess at wrestling and other sports and his great love for socializing also make good stories for children.

Joseph Smith's birthday, on December 23rd is an appropriate time to remember him. Since his birthday comes at such a busy time of the year, it might be fun and practical to start in the fall and post a picture of the Prophet on your bulletin board, along with a picture of a birthday cake. Then add a paper candle to the cake for each story you read about the Prophet's life, so the cake is full of candles by December 23rd. You can undoubtedly think of other ways to celebrate Joseph Smith's birthday that will help your children gain a testimony of his calling and be motivated to emulate his qualities of greatness.

Older children can gain a foundation for understanding the character traits common in outstanding church leaders by reading the Doctrine and Covenants and studying church history. The exciting, trying, and frightening experiences many of them faced could be a fruitful source of reading material to share with children at dinner time, bed time, family night, or anytime.

The courageous leadership of Brigham Young in the days of the Saints' exile from Nauvoo and their suffering in the camp at Sugar Creek is a good example. Brigham Young entered the camp prepared with a year's supply of provisions for his family. But he felt a personal responsibility to care for the poor and destitute among his people, and within two weeks, he had nothing left. He had given freely to try to alleviate the suffering of his people and he trusted the Lord to provide from there.

Many of the women who lived through these trying days were also exemplary of many of the traits we would like to encourage in our children. Their unselfishness, determination, and cheerfulness in the face of unbelievable hardships can motivate us all to cheer up when our own way seems rough. Eliza R. Snow was a woman well known for her compassion and industry in serving the church and her fellow men. Her writings give us some of the finest insights into the conditions of that time. She said, "Many of our sisters walked all day, rain or shine, and at night prepared suppers for their families, with no sheltering tents; and then made their beds in and under wagons that contained their earthly all. How frequently, with intense sympathy and admiration, I watched the mother, when forgetful of her own fatigue and destitution, she took unwearied pains to fix up, in the most palatable form, the allotted portion of food, and as she dealt it out, was cheering the hearts of her homeless children, while, as I truly believed, her own was lifted to God in fervent prayer that their lives might be preserved."

Walter Bowen, an outstanding Institute teacher, said, "No make-believe story or plot could offer as much true excitement as real stories from the lives of our early church leaders." He encouraged his students to learn these adventure stories so they could tell them to their own children and give them *true* heroes. His excitement with the potential power for good such stories can have in our children's lives was the inspiration for this chapter.

The Powerful Lives of Modern Prophets

One of the valuable experiences of studying the truly great is learning that they didn't achieve by having an easy life! Recognizing the realities of obstacles, and seeing how others have surmounted them can help us overcome our own.

The courage our present prophet, Spencer W. Kimball, has shown in overcoming difficulties qualifies him to be a hero to our children! We can share the stories of his difficult health problems and his triumphs in each area of his life.

President Kimball also exemplifies another trait common to true greatness: concern for the individual, illustrated by a story told by Ross and Judy Richins. Judy said, "Ross's parents met President Kimball when Ross's father was in the stake presidency. When he stayed in their home, they learned they were related and Ross's mother has sent President Kimball bits of genealogy ever since. They corresponded over the years, and when Ross's father passed away, President Kimball was a special source of comfort to his mother. Because of this association, we have had some choice experiences with President Kimball and have sensed his Christ-like concern for all of us. When our last baby was a boy, we felt we wanted to name him Spencer, in honor of President Kimball and the day he was named was the prophet's birthday. Grandma Richins wrote and told President Kimball our baby had been named after him, and he sent Spencer $1.00 to start his missionary fund! The children feel that President Kimball is the greatest man in the world, and they are sure our baby is going to be just like him!"

The Good Example of Church Leaders and Teachers

Not only the prophet, but any church leader or teacher can become a hero to a child. The Dean and Claudia Black family have, at times, studied a different general authority every week, telling their children faith-promoting and early life experiences from the lives of these great men. They post a picture of the "General Authority of the Week" on their bulletin board, and the children learn to identify the name with the picture. Dean and Claudia report that the children's interest in conference has been much greater because of this project, and they have all developed greater admiration for these men.

Stake presidents, bishops, Sunday School and Primary teachers can also be uplifting examples to children. We have a tremendous opportunity to encourage children to emulate them as we point out their devotion to the gospel and their sincere efforts to serve the Lord.

Every teacher in the church has the potential for influence in the lives of those they teach when they magnify their callings. Judy Richins said, "A Primary teacher has been a great influence on our oldest daughter, Jill. She was unusually thoughtful! She brought doughnuts the day our last baby was born, remembered family birthdays, sent Jill a note of congratulations when she had earned enough money to get her a bike, etc. One day Jill said, "She's really thoughtful, Mom. I hope I can be like that when I grow up."

Pointing Out the Path of Greatness

Greatness knows no boundaries, and we have the opportunity to introduce our children to great people of every age, faith and race because of the books and magazines that are available to us. Karen Reilley gathers inspirational stories (stories of courage, sacrifice, and determination in facing and solving life's problems) from sources like the Readers Digest, Church News, and "Mormon Journal". Whenever possible, before the children go to bed she reads one of these stories to them. Karen said, "I feel such stories give my children good solid people to identify with and righteous examples to follow. The beauty of this bedtime tradition is that it requires little preparation and can be done on the spur of the moment (even when I have only five minutes). But in those few minutes I can give the children something good to think about as they go to bed instead of 'Mod Squad' or 'Three Little Bears'."

There are many teaching moments when stories of greatness are appropriate. Linda Garner tells of her memories of special camping experiences with her family, "My mother is a very good story-teller, and when we were sitting around the campfire she would tell us inspiring, faith-promoting stories of pioneers and prophets and great families. I can remember the special spirit we felt then, and I'm sure those stories influenced my life."

We can help our children gain a sense of patriotism, as well as help them identify with greatness by reading to them about great American heroes such as Washington and Lincoln. Special books, pictures, and even film strips can be checked out of the library to help make these men real and influential in our children's lives. Making a special story-telling day on the birthdays of such patriots might be a good way to teach the children about them.

One father who had been motivated and inspired by the life story of Thomas A. Edison decided to make it a family project to learn more about him. He assigned each of his older children to find stories that portrayed some of Edison's most outstanding characteristics and report back to the family.

Some of the things the children mentioned were:

Edison was ambitious and hard-working. When he was only twelve, he sold candy and newspapers on the trains between Port Huron and Detroit and did chemical experiments in the baggage car in his spare time. While waiting in Detroit for the return train, he went to the public library and read and studied.

He was courageous. As a teen-ager he risked his life to save a stationmaster's child from an onrushing train.

He was persistent and never seemed to get discouraged. This is one thing for which he is perhaps best known. The children were amazed to hear the story of how he had made 8,000 tests on a storage battery without success; yet when an assistant asked him if he was discouraged he replied, "Why should I feel downhearted? We've made a lot of progress. At least we know 8,000 things that won't work!"

With Edison (as with any great person) the little things made him great; his attention to detail, his willingness to work and work and never give up, his curiosity, his wish to improve things and help people, and his constant desire to learn.

Read About Them, Walk With Them

All libraries have a large autobiography section full of life stories of great people. One mother said, "An autobiography that has really impressed our family and made us determined to continue reading this type of literature is the autobiography of Benjamin Franklin. I believe we store everything we read or hear, and knowing how others live affects our lives. When we experience greatness vicariously, we begin to sense our own potential a little more, especially if we can put some of that person's philosophy into our lives. We found we could do this in a very practical way with Benjamin Franklin.

"In his early twenties, Franklin decided he had some weaknesses that were holding him back and would keep him from achieving his goals. So he decided to change. He made a list of the positive character traits he wished to develop and worked on them one at a time, recording and examining his progress daily. These character traits which he developed through conscious decision and pure effort are the ones he became so well known for in later years. Sincerity, justice, and moderation are just a few .

"After reading Franklin's autobiography, we introduced the idea in a home evening for each member of our family to try to follow Franklin's example of character development. We gave each person a little notebook and some 3 x 5 cards and we wrote a list in our notebooks of the traits we most wanted to develop. Then we listed one on each 3 x 5 card and carried one card with us each week as a constant reminder. At the first of each succeeding home evening we shared any successes we had had in putting that trait into action in our lives, and recorded those experiences in our notebooks. It was an exciting time! This plan gave us a focus for our efforts and we all made great progress. Benjamin Franklin was no longer just a name in history books, but a man who had influenced our lives!"

Another family told of the inspiration they had received from reading the autobiography of Helen Keller: a woman whose zest for living and learning made it possible to overcome great handicaps. Her philosophy is well summed up in the story she tells of riding twelve miles on her tandem in one day. She said she rode on a rough road and fell off three or four times which made her awfully lame; but the weather and the scenery were so beautiful, and it was such fun to go scooting over the smoother part of the road that she didn't mind the mishaps in the least. This attitude was symbolic of her total approach to life!

Because we become what we think about, we give our children the opportunity to become great when their minds are exposed to the thoughts, attitudes and actions of those who *are* great.

Napoleon Hill, author, lecturer, and eminently successful businessman, tells how he let great men shape his life. He chose nine men whose lives were most impressive to him, and every night for a long period of years, held an "imaginary council meeting" with them in an attempt to acquire from each man, by emulation and study, their most outstanding characteristics and abilities. He claims that these men had a great influence on his life, and contributed much to his outstanding success.

Great Branches on Your Family Tree

In family home evenings, Donald and Barbara Marshall have been reading family histories to their four children. They have ancestors who knew the Prophet Joseph Smith personally, and their little boys (ages seven and nine) can hardly believe how different life was then and the kind of hardships the people suffered. Barbara told them the exciting story of her great-great-grandmother who braved the danger of panthers when her husband was gone to town for supplies. "That lady was really brave!" exclaimed Jim. "Panthers are really mean, aren't they?" asked Rhett. They had found a heroine!

George and Deanna Buck make it a practice to share special stories of their ancestors with their children. One of their favorite stories is about their great-great-grandmother, Mary, who was born in Denmark. Her father was a sea captain and was lost at sea. Two years later, the missionaries converted her mother and her grandfather. Mary (who was eight), and her brother, Andrew (age six), her mother, and grandfather made passage to come to

America and join the Saints. They landed in New York and journeyed westward. At Omaha, Nebraska, they joined a wagon train for the trek to Utah. Because of lack of funds, they were assigned with several other families to one wagon, and there was room for only food and bedding in the wagon. Every morning after breakfast, the little old grandfather would tie some dry biscuits in a sack and hang it on his belt along with a tin cup. Then he would take the two children by the hand and start off ahead of the wagontrain. (With the young children to consider, they were slower than the oxen.) They would have the biscuits for lunch, along with water if they were lucky enough to find a stream.

The children, Mary and Andrew, became heroes to Bucks' children and they often say, "Tell me about Mary and Andrew walking all the way to Utah!" The effects of a story like this can be very practical as well as inspirational! One day Deanna's car broke down when her oldest child, Jennifer, was four, Richard was two, and her baby was four months old. They had to walk a mile and Deanna couldn't help Richard and Jennifer because she had to carry the baby. But she said, "If Mary and Andrew could walk all the way to Utah, I'll bet you can be good walkers, too." They walked the whole mile without complaining!

Another hero to the Buck family is the man who married this same Mary when she grew up. Mary became the 11th wife of a polygamist named Archibald Gardner, whom she chose in preference to young suitors because he was such a remarkable and truly good man. Archibald owned grist mills, and personally delivered sacks of flour to widows all over the area. In fact, he met Mary when taking flour to her mother. Archibald had 48 children and provided well for them. But best of all he provided an example of love and service. At one time when many were in need, a man came to him and asked if he would sell him a bag of flour for three dollars. He said, "If you have three dollars, go and buy your flour from the other miller. My flour is only for those who have no money." He was so concerned about providing for those who had no food or means that he would not accept cash even when he needed it.

One day Archibald met an old acquaintance who said to him, "I'm a wealthy man, now, Archibald, but what have you got to show for the years?" Archibald replied, "All my treasures are in heaven."

The Bucks have a book about the experiences of Archibald Gardner and they feel that it gives their children a sense of pride to identify with such a great man and they are fascinated with the stories about him.

Very, Very Human Heroes

Handling human frailties with good humor can sometimes qualify ancestors for hero status. It can be a very refreshing thing to adult and child alike to read experiences such as the one we borrowed from the journal of Z.T. Draper:

"In the year 1874 I went to a place called Cedar City (about 50 miles from home). Not having been away from home much, I was very bashful and didn't know how to act when in a stranger's home. Having arrived at Cedar, we stopped at noon and were invited in to dinner. My bashfulness hadn't bothered me much till now, for I stayed around the wagon, and hadn't been in the house. Well, as I said, they asked us in to dinner, and they had quite a time to get me to accept the invitation. Finally not knowing what else to do, I went in and after blundering around and making all the awkward movements I could while standing, I took a seat at the table. I felt sure that there was some awkwardness which could be represented there and that I was the boy that could do that to a tee. So I did. I was no more than seated, till I knocked my glass of water over. That was an act that I hadn't intended to perform just yet so I made a grab to catch the glass! But I caught my plate instead and sent it flying to the floor. I hadn't exactly planned that, either. And in trying to pick up the plate and place it on the table again quick enough not to have its fall noticed, I hit the corner of the table with my head and shook the table so that the soup which was on it sloshed all over. Well, after knocking one thing and another around for some time, I commenced to eat my dinner. I just began to think I was beginning to get along nicely when I dropped my knife. 'Well, you're smart,' said the boy that lived there. At this I grabbed at my knife, dropped my bread, grabbed at it, and knocked my plate of soup into my lap. Somehow or another I didn't feel hungry. And I wanted to see what the wagon looked like, so I left the table and went to the wagon. Well, nothing else of interest occurred as I know of now until after we had reached home again!"

It is a comfort to know that some problems commonly occur as part of human experience whether in a modern setting or one long ago.

Good Examples from Living Relatives

Uncles, aunts, older brothers and sisters, cousins, and grandparents can also have a special influence on the lives of our children. To make their good examples more effective, we can comment on the good traits we see in our relatives and tell of the things they have accomplished in their lives.

Arlene Barnes and her husband, Dale, take every opportunity to tell their children stories about their grandparents. They believe that exemplary grandparents can be heroes for children, and the Barnes children love to do things with their grandparents and often comment that they want to be like them.

Homey little incidents with relatives are often impressive to children. One day Holly, who was four, was watching her older sister prepare a package for a missionary. She watched her intently for quite a while, asking her all about her project. Then she looked up at her and said, "Loree, that makes me feel like doing that when I grow up!"

Heroes are Homemade

Joye Billings said of her mother, Mary Wright, "Of all the people I have ever met in my life (and I've met a lot), there is no one I would rather be like than my mother. She is respected by everyone."

There is nothing more inspiring to children than to have their own parents exemplify the traits they would like to develop. Judy Richins said, "I have appreciated it in our home when our children have said things like, 'I want to be just like you when I grow up, Mommy,' or 'I want to be a nice Mommy, just like you.' It really motivates me to want to set the right example." Mom and Dad can be some of the most effective, influential heroes to a child because they have so many opportunities to teach through word and example. One authority indicates that values aren't taught by words from teachers. They are taught by the lives we see led by the people who love us and who we admire. The most effective way we can make greatness the goal of our children is by making greatness our own goal and moving steadily along the path that takes us there!

Fathers are in an especially good position to become heroes to their children. As leaders in the home, they can have a great influence for good on their children.

"My husband has always been a good example of a priesthood leader in our home," said EvaDean Parcell. "That good example really pays off when you see how it affects the decisions that the children make as they get older. When Polly, our oldest daughter, was planning to get married, I overheard her explaining to her little sister why she had chosen Dennis to be her fiance', 'I wanted someone just exactly like our Dad,' she said, 'and I knew Dennis was the one, because I could see he was that kind of a man.'"

"It's great when we can make Dad a hero to the children," commented Gayla Wise. "One night when I was preparing a lesson on training children to be missionaries, I asked my husband, Joe, to tell the children about his missionary experiences. This is an area where he really shines, and he got out his mission photos and told some of his conversion stories. What an experience! I felt any little boy would want to be like Dad after a night like that!"

Ten Things to Try

1. Choose your favorite scriptural characters, relate their stories and point out their strengths to your children.

2. Use the New Testament stories of Jesus's life to help the children understand and admire the pattern of greatness Jesus set for us.

3. Locate and collect stories of early church leaders, modern-day prophets, and your own exemplary ancestors to share with children at meal-time or bed-time. Challenge older children to do research and find new stories of their ancestors.

4. Point out the good qualities and admirable actions of church leaders and teachers.

5. Introduce your children to great people of every age, faith, and race through books and magazines which tell their stories of courage, sacrifice, and determination.

6. As a family, read autobiographies of great patriots, scientists, and leaders to inspire lofty thoughts and motivate good actions.

7. Study and follow the character development plan exemplified by Benjamin Franklin. You could give each family member a small notebook in which to list the character traits he most wants to develop and have him choose one each week to work on.

8. Encourage older children to choose one great person they admire and earn as much as possible about him; analyzing the qualities that made him great and reporting their findings in family home evening.

9. Celebrate the birthdays of great church and civic leaders as an opportunity to teach more about them. Try putting a paper

cake on your bulletin board well in advance of the birthday and add a paper candle for each story read.

10 Fill your own thoughts with greatness and lead where you want your children to go. If you make greatness **your** goal, you can be your child's best example!

SAVING FOR MY MISSION

Preparing for a Mission: Ways Parents Can Help

The Lord needs more missionaries. Where can he get them? They must come from our homes. Preparing children for missionary service is part of the responsibility the Lord gave us when he counselled us to teach our children to walk uprightly before Him. (D&C 68:28). The quality of our teaching can make a difference in whether or not our children go on missions, and what kind of missionaries they will be if they choose to go.

Guiding Them to the Goal

There are many things a parent can do to help a child prepare to be a good missionary. Actually everything we do that helps them grow and develop in any other way will also help them to be better missionaries. But the first challenge is to orient their thinking towards missionary work—to help them early in their lives to establish missionary service as a goal.

One mother said, "Fill the child's early days with stories of the great missionaries of the past. Parley P. Pratt is an excellent example of a man whose missionary experiences make exciting stories to tell children. Also tell family missionary experiences and missionary stories of your own ancestors." Telling our children our own missionary experiences and the missionary experiences of others is an excellent way to encourage them to be missionaries.

Also, knowing the effect other missionaries have had on their own family can be an exciting motivation. Many families hold home evenings where the parents tell the conversion stories of their parents or grandparents and explain that it is because of missionaries they have the blessings of the gospel and are able to live in the United States.

In encouraging our children to set the goal of missionary service, a principle frequently mentioned by the people we interviewed was "positive expectations". Linden Hurst, father of seven, asked a woman who has raised four missionary sons by herself, "How did you get your boys to go on missions?" "Oh, I don't know," was her reply. "I never once thought that they would not!" Linden decided to use this approach with his own boys, and now says things like, "In just a few years you will be going on a mission, and..." Knowing they will have their free-agency to choose when the time comes, he believes it is a righteous principle to *expect* them to go on a mission, just as you expect them to go to church because you know it is right.

One young man reached missionary age but continued his schooling and didn't consider a mission. When someone asked him why he hadn't gone on a mission he said, "My parents didn't seem to expect me to go, so I figured I wasn't missionary material." On the other hand, Alma and Clea Burton's son, a returned missionary said, "In our home, it was never 'if' you go on a mission—but *'when.'* I'm sure that influenced me." Another returned missionary said, "When I turned nineteen, I wasn't suddenly faced with a major decision, because the decision had been made in my mind years before. I always thought I would go, and I felt good and right about going on a mission when the time came."

A missionary orientation to every phase of a child's life can affect their decisions during all their growing-up years. When one thirteen-year-old boy went hunting with a friend on Sunday (without telling his mother he was going) she had a private talk with him and said, "With every good thing we want to do or be, we need to start early. You want to be a missionary—and now is the time to start. If you can't be a missionary with your friends now by setting the right example, it will be much harder for you later." Her son was impressed with that logic and hasn't repeated his wrong choice.

Effective Missionary Work Begins at Home

The Church needs powerful, well-trained young people to spread the gospel, and our children can be among that force if we follow President Kimball's counsel to prepare them. The importance of preparation at home was vividly pointed out through a survey done by Rosemary Mackay, wife of a branch president at B.Y.U. She asked a group of returned missionaries in her husband's branch to respond to the question, "What preparation did you make before your mission that helped you as a missionary?" and "Looking back, what could you have done before your mission that would have better prepared you?" Some said, "I was poorly prepared and paid for it with the first year of my mission." "I made no preparation. I arrived in the field without a testimony, having not read any scriptures and basically lost—it's *not* the way to go." "It's hard preaching what you've never practiced."

However, one missionary said, "My best preparation was being raised in a strong, active L.D.S. family. Our family talked about the gospel, lived it, and enjoyed its blessings. I was encouraged to read the scriptures and had a good knowledge of them and how they relate to gospel principles before I ever went out. Another great preparation is that my parents helped me decide before I left what kind of a missionary I would be."

The returned missionary survey gave many other excellent suggestions that can help parents prepare missionaries. We would like to combine the survey ideas with the suggestions of

the parents we interviewed, and give you a "summary of suggestions."

A Diller, a Dollar

One of the most-mentioned suggestions was a missionary
fund! Linden and Darlene Hurst start a missionary fund for each
of their boys when they reach the age of six. Linden puts five
dollars per month in each boy's fund and the boys are encouraged to contribute a portion of any money they earn. Hank and
Daryl Hoole's young boys have "world globe banks" to motivate
them to save their dimes and nickels for their missionary funds.
They presented these banks to their sons saying, "Somewhere
in the world you will go on your mission."

Several parents suggested budget training, and missionaries
agreed this was helpful preparation. Willis and Lynnette Brimhall
have their children keep individual budget books, and Willis reviews the children's entries monthly and helps them analyze how
they are doing. Their son, Greg, who just returned from a mission
said, "Home training really was a help in the missionfield. The
first thing I did when I got to my field of labor was to buy a budget
envelope book, and each time I got my check I would immediately
cash it and put the money into the envelopes for the different
categories. That way I never got caught without any food money
at the end of the month."

When motivated by a missionary fund, the disciplines of
working, budgeting, and saving have real purpose! And, in addition to these benefits, a missionary fund also makes the goal
of a mission a more tangible reality to young people and can
motivate them to want to prepare in other ways.

Healthy is Happy!

Good health and physical stamina can be great attributes
to the missionary. One elder said, "A healthy missionary is a
happy missionary!" Those parents who hope to make it onto the
"most appreciated parents" list, will teach their children the good
habits and know-how they will need in order to care for themselves in every way.

Good nutrition is one essential part of good health. "Good
nutrition to build good missionaries" is a concept that can be
established early! One three-year-old said, "If you didn't get me
breakfast no time, I wouldn't grow to be a missionary, huh? I'm

going to be a missionary, so you got to give me breakfast!"

However, no missionary takes his mother along to provide his meals, and one of the most often mentioned suggestions for missionary preparation was "learn to cook!" Some of the specific suggestions were:

1. Have the prospective missionary prepare dinner once each week.

2. Have a "Learn to Cook" week in the summer and have him budget, plan menus, and prepare the meals for the entire week.

3. Have a family home evening lesson on good nutrition and good table manners.

4. Make a file of "quick missionary recipes" and help him learn a new one each week. Teach him how to prepare his favorite foods in the simplest ways possible.

One missionary mentioned that one of the best ways young people could prepare for a mission would be to establish good health habits, such as going to bed early and getting up early *before* a mission; then the struggle is out of the way and they are ready to settle down and work when they get there! Even better, help them establish these habits from an early age; then the struggle of change won't be necessary at all. Many families get their children up at 6:00 a.m. as a general rule. Missionaries from those homes will likely find it a breeze to live the mission rule to get up early!

Teaching a proper balance of rest and exercise, plus personal grooming and housekeeping skills can also be terrific missionary preparation. (One elder had the motto "neat is nice!") Several returned missionaries expressed appreciation that their mothers had taught them simple housekeeping skills, as well as how to do laundry and mending. Sewing on a button, restitching a seam, sorting laundry or ironing a shirt can be a snap to the boy who has been taught how to do them. But to one who has never learned how, they may loom as large and difficult challenges.

Social Skills Bring Security

Since missionary work is a social experience, anything we can teach our children concerning good human relationships will help them be more effective missionaries. One mother had a "Courtesy Counts" week, and each night at the supper table, discussed the value of being polite and courteous in our dealing with other people. Another mother had training sessions she called, "The Magic of Manners", and had her children act out situations in mannerly and unmannerly ways to demonstrate that manners *do* matter and are an evidence of our concern for the feelings and sensibilities of those around us.

Family home evening offers a fertile training ground for many of the social skills a missionary will need. If we provide our children with opportunities to give the lesson, conduct the meeting, lead the singing and take part in discussions from the time they are small, they will feel at home with the demands made on them as missionaries. Family night is also a good place to have impromptu talks that give children practice at thinking on their feet and putting thoughts into words. Some of the subjects suggested for missionary-related impromptu talk assignments were: faith, repentance, baptism, the Holy Ghost, prayer, and love.

Many returned missionaries mentioned the importance of learning communication skills; not only the ability to give formal talks and lessons, but learning to converse in a warm and friendly way with strangers and listen carefully when others are talking. Parents can provide many opportunities for young people to practice these skills. One of the best is through involving them in service projects. (See Chapter 21). Service is also one of the most sure roads to self-esteem, and everything a parent can do to increase their child's self-esteem is helpful preparation for a mission as well as for other challenges he may meet. (See Chapter 4.)

Learning to get along with other people and relate to them in a positive way requires a combination of many things, such as self-discipline, a cheerful attitude, and learning to forgive and forget. All the little lessons parents can teach in the home to help children live happily with others will help them in the missionfield. Learning to give and take, learning to resolve differences, learning to be patient and tolerant with others' weaknesses are a few other areas suggested for concentrated teaching, and if we as parents can exemplify good mastery of these social skills, our children will have a head start!

"The Lord Thy God Shall Lead Thee by the Hand"

Since the power of the Spirit is the most necessary ingredient for the success of a missionary, teaching our children to seek the Spirit and recognize and respond to its prompting should be high on our priority list. (See Chapter 10). Some missionaries who have the great handicap of being almost illiterate and know neither the scriptures nor the discussions well still succeed because they rely on the spirit, bear a powerful testimony, and love the people. Two returned missionaries felt their most important preparations had been spiritual. One said, "I had learned to understand my relationship with God and that relationship is more important than any amount of knowledge I could have received." The other said, "I learned that by fasting and sincere prayer I could get real answers to questions and strength to do what I could not do by myself!" Others said, "The greatest preparation I could have made would have been to establish a real and working relationship with the Lord. I would have benefitted from having more real experiences with the Spirit and receiving personal revelation. I wish I had worked harder to have these experiences for myself."

How can parents help children prepare spiritually? A few suggestions given were:

1. Teach children the power of prayer by example. Share your faith-promoting experiences and answers to prayers with them. Encourage them to pray about their concerns and problems and to view prayer as a very real source of strength and guidance as it is to you.

2. Pray for them and with them. One mother said she constantly prayed that her son's heart would be touched with the spirit of missionary service and that he would desire to do right so he would be worthy to serve.

3. In family prayer, pray for the missionaries, and ask the Lord to make missions possible for your children.

One mother summed up the importance of spiritual preparation when she said, "We must learn to pay the price for success on our knees."

Learning and living any gospel principle (such as repentance and obedience) is part of a missionary's spiritual preparation, as are patriarchal blessings, consistent church activity and knowledge of how to perform Priesthood ordinances. In the mission field, young men will need to know how to baptize, confirm, bless children, consecrate oil, administer to the sick, and possibly even dedicate a grave.

"For in Them Ye Have Eternal Life"

Another commonly mentioned area of suggested preparation was to know the scriptures and really understand them! "I would like to have had the ability to use the scriptures like I use a fork and a spoon," said one returned missionary. "It is especially helpful to know how to use the scriptures to solve daily problems." One good step in helping our children learn the scriptures is providing them with their own copies. A set of missionary scriptures should be provided well in advance of missionary age. (Additional suggestions for teaching the scriptures to children are found in Chapter 6 of this book.)

Additional suggestions to prospective missionaries were:

1. Develop good study habits. Well before your nineteenth birthday start a study system to make sure you have read and studied all the standard works before you go.

2. Instead of just reading and marking the scriptures, memorize the key ones now. Get a list of the most-used missionary scriptures and learn them.

3. Study the Old and New Testament. It helps to be on equal ground with non-members. Many investigators are Bible scholars, and they expect missionaries to be, too.

4. Study and learn the Book of Mormon well. It is the foundation of our religion! Several mentioned the power of the Book of Mormon as a missionary tool as well as an aid to personal righteousness.

Miscellaneous Preparation and Motivation Ideas

Jaynann Morgan Payne suggests that we interview our boys at intervals and talk with them about what they are doing *now* to prepare for a mission.

In a Relief Society presentation, Jaynann told of a young man who made himself a chart to put in his bedroom. It said:

"If I am going to be an effective missionary someday, I must put myself on the spot!"

S   tudy Scriptures

P   onder and Pray

O   bedience

T   estimony

Other ways suggested that parents can help are to:

1. Encourage Seminary training.

2. Have missionary family home evenings and discuss common investigator questions, and present the missionary lessons.

3. Make special events of farewells and welcome-homes for missionaries.

4. Have family projects to write regularly to missionaries.

5. Invite missionaries or recently returned missionaries to your home.

6. Arrange for your older boys to go with the missionaries tracting or to cottage meetings whenever possible.

7. One of the best things a parent could do is to invite their non-member friends to their home and have the missionaries teach them! To watch the actual teaching and conversion process is one of the best kinds of missionary preparation.

8. Teach children to appreciate the differences in other countries and cultures.

Several returned missionaries mentioned that it would have been helpful to them to know more about other countries. Some mothers make it a monthly project to teach their families about the country they are studying that month in Relief Society. They fix a meal typical of the country, relate interesting facts and stories about it, and may even get related pictures and books from the library to make the evening more interesting. Some families invite foreign students to their homes for dinner to tell the family about the countries they are from. Also, many families encourage study of foreign languages.

Darla found a way to combine several of the ideas we've presented. For his eighth birthday she gave her son a file box labelled "Missionary Preparation Kit." Inside were 3 x 5" cards divided into four sections:

1. Missionary scriptures to memorize.

2. Great inspirational thoughts.

3. Quick missionary recipes.

4. Skills that would be good to learn to prepare for a mission. (A different one was listed on each card, and included everything from sewing on a button to learning to lead the singing.)

She plans to spend time with her son each week teaching him a new skill, a new scripture, a new recipe or a new thought.

One returned missionary suggested a good summary thought. He said, "Tell prospective missionaries of the trials and heartstretching challenges a mission offers as well as the happy times. Help them see the hand of the Lord in *all* things and to know that a mission is not a two-year vacation; that there will be hard and challenging times along the way."

The Lord works through parents. While each young person must do a great deal of his own preparation for missionary service, there is much parents can do to help their children prepare to be great missionaries!

Ten Things to Try

1. Help children set the goal of missionary service through your positive expectations. Say "When you go on your mission," not "If...."

2. Start a missionary fund for each child and encourage them to work, save and budget in order to contribute to it consistently.

3. Teach housekeeping and culinary skills! Try letting older children budget, plan menus, and do the cooking for one full week during the summer.

4. Have a "Courtesy Counts" week or a "Magic of Manners" training session.

5. Make a file of "Quick Missionary Meals" and teach the potential missionary to prepare a new one each week.

6. Help the young person establish good health habits such as "early to bed and early to rise," and proper nutrition before it is time for them to go on a mission.

7. Teach children the power of prayer. Share your faith-promoting experiences and answers to prayers with them. Pray for them and with them.

8. Give children their own copies of the scriptures and help them to know and understand the scriptures by consistent scripture reading in the home.

9. Hold special family home evenings where you discuss common investigator questions, give missionary lessons and assign impromptu talks on missionary subjects. Have the stake or local area missionaries come to your family home evenings and give the lessons to your non-member friends so your potential missionaries can see it done and catch the spirit of it.

10. Give each child a "Missionary Preparation Kit" including missionary scriptures to memorize, quick recipes to learn, good thoughts to inspire them, and a list of skills for them to master before they leave home.

Teaching Chastity in a Framework of Reverence

One of the questions parents often ask is "How can I effectively teach my children the importance of chastity, and how it fits into the total plan of life?" Peggy and Dwayne Andersen found one exciting answer which has proven effective with their children, and with the permission of Wanda Hilton (who originated the plan) they have agreed to describe the plan for the benefit of other parents. They have done so in the form of a letter, which follows:

My dear friend,

You have asked me to tell you about the plan I have used to teach my children the facts of life in a framework of reverence. I am happy to share these ideas with you, although I realize the limitations of trying to put the plan into the written word. I wish I could sit down with you and explain it, but since that is not possible, I will do my best to describe it in a clear and understandable way. I hope you will like the idea, and that it will be a help to you in teaching your children values concerning sex which will be a safeguard to them in meeting the temptations surrounding them. This idea has worked beautifully for us, but since it is such a personal subject each must work it out in her own way, and use the parts that will work best in each family situation.

In our family, the book I give the children to introduce the subject of chastity has become a tradition (as well as the whole series of events surrounding the presentation of the book and its contents). This tradition has actually become a bond which builds relationships as well as teaching the children the facts of life. After we had given our youngest son his book, our oldest daughter said with tears in her eyes, "Mama, I really think this is the neatest thing we've ever done in our family. I want to do it exactly this way with my children."

The Plan

The basic features of the plan came from another friend, Wanda Hilton, who gave a presentation on "How to teach your children the facts of life" to a group of sisters in our ward in Walnut Creek, California, years ago. I liked her approach so much I have used her idea of presenting a special book (which is made for each child); and most of the script in my books came from her book which she showed us that night. She has given me permission to share these ideas with you.

The book itself is only a means of opening up a strong communication between you, the mother, and your child. The presentation isn't all in the book. Part of it must be in your own words. What you will tell each of your children other than what is in the book is up to you. It will take some preparation on your part, but I can assure you it will be worth the time you take to prepare to answer your child's questions and give him correct information with accurate terms. You can't teach any child all the facts of life in one sitting, but the purpose of this presentation is to help your child realize that you are willing to talk about anything he may want to talk about, and to build a strong foundation for future discussions. It has been our experience that after we have given our child the book and discussed it, he is not afraid to come back later and talk about it or ask questions.

Some parents say, "When my children want to know something about the subject of sex, they will come and ask me. And when they do I'll tell them anything they want to know." But many times they don't ask. One of my sweetest friends said this to me, and three days later I saw her fourteen-year-old boy at the restricted book section at the market trying to get his information, but from the wrong source. I am a firm believer that you should give children correct information at the right time, and not let them wonder or get their information from the wrong places. Determining the right time takes discernment. My husband and I have to watch each child carefully to decide when he is ready because it can be anytime between the ages of eight and fourteen.

Many teaching moments will come up throughout the life of our children and we should take advantage of them, but we must also create some teaching moments; and this is, in effect, what I have tried to do by preparing and presenting the books.

Putting the Plan Into Action

To put this plan into action, the first thing I did was to make a personalized book for my child. I used sturdy loose-leaf type notebooks, with poster paper cut to size for the pages. I wanted the book to be "custom-tailored" for each child's personality. Although much is the same in each book, there are pages which are completely different, suited to each particular child. I have found and cut out pictures from many sources to illustrate each concept expressed, but your own artwork would be even better if you have that ability.

Making the "Date"

When the book is completed, I make a date with the child. I tell my child this is a very special date, and we (my husband and I) want him to find a time that will be convenient for him when he could forget about everything else while we enjoy some special time together. I let him know that this is important enough to me that I am willing to set aside all my other responsibilities to spend a few hours alone with him. (It usually takes two to three hours of uninterrupted time.) When I present the book to the child, my husband takes the other children away from the home, and enjoys some kind of activity with them. Now this might be different for other couples. Perhaps the husband will want to present the information, and the mother take the other children out, and join the father and child later. But one parent and one child alone can talk about things that two parents and a child or two children and a parent may have trouble discussing.

When the time comes which we have set aside for the "date", we wear our Sunday best, and I present the child with a corsage or boutonniere' to convey the feeling that this is something extra special.

The Presentation

Then we go into a room where we won't be disturbed. We take the phone off the hook, and ignore the doorbell. In the room, I have the book and a table full of gift-wrapped presents already prepared so that it looks like a party. As I begin, I tell the child that "Daddy wishes he could be here, but someone must be with the other children. He is anxiously waiting for us to finish our discussion, so he can return and share some time with you also." (My husband, too, wants to chat with the child.) The gifts are partly to reinforce the presentation, and partly to keep the child excited and enthusiastic about what I plan to present. Sometimes he may not listen to every word I am saying because he may be thinking, "I wonder which page will be the one where I get the next gift?", but this doesn't matter because my purpose is to "open the door", and even if he doesn't remember everything, he can come to me later and ask the things he wants to know. In other words, I want to "set a pattern" for future discussion.

Now I will describe my procedures from here as if you were doing it. You begin by telling the child that you have made this book for him, and you would like to sit down with him to go through the book together. Then you can mention that the gifts are for him, but that you are only going to give them to him at certain places in the book, or at certain stages of the discussion.

As he opens the book, he reads a short statement which you have written about him, how you feel about him, and why you felt he was ready to know more about life and the plan our Heavenly Father has for us.

Build the Foundation

The first pages of the book are designed to build a child's feeling about himself as a worthy individual. (I will give the entire script for boys and girls separately at the end of this explanation).

Then, in word and pictures you help him see that he belongs to a family who cares for him and build up the importance of the family unit in God's plan.

Next, you gradually build upon the development of the boy-girl relationship from the time he thinks girls are nice to be with, until he wants to be with one person most of the time. You then build up to courtship and the excitement between the man and the woman and the thrill of finding the one he wants to take to the temple to marry for time and all eternity. Next proceed to the excitement and thrill of having the first child.

You *stop right there.* Go back in his development and explain that these events are the ultimate in life, but before this happens the Lord expects him to prepare.

With the help of the book you will want to discuss what he must do to prepare for this wonderful time...the time which will be *the most important time in his life*—when he chooses a companion and marries and has children. In this section about preparation I begin with a letter I write to them which personalizes the book even more because I tell the child about his own birth, and how I felt about it from the time I knew I was going to be his mother. I also try to include how Daddy felt.

Hopefully, after finishing the personalized letter section, you have built a spiritual base. Now you are ready to discuss the changes that will occur in his body to prepare him to become a father, and the things he can expect. (Of course, with a girl you will discuss motherhood preparation.) The physiological facts can be presented with pictures and charts. Then he is ready to hear about the things he can do to prepare for this special time of life.

Explain the Lord's Plan

Through all the instruction, the main theme is that the Lord created us, and that it is part of His plan that men and women be different and have different roles. You explain that the *scriptures* tell us that *God* meant for man and woman to be together, to cleave to one another and leave their parents, to be as one flesh. All of us were given the power of creation in our bodies, and this is a sacred power. It is Heavenly Father's plan that the act of creation, the sexual union, should only occur under the bonds of marriage. The privilege of creating children is the most important thing that will happen to us in this life, and the Lord wants everyone to begin marriage in His holy temple. When we do this, we have His love and His blessing and can enjoy marriage to its fullest. Marriage and having children can be the most crowning thing in one's life and be thrilling and joyful, but only if we follow our Heavenly Father's plan.

The final section of the book emphasizes keeping the body pure and clean so that it will be a worthy tabernacle to bring these spirits into the world (that the boys can honor the priesthood and be worthy to bless their own children and the girls can be worthy of a celestial marriage and pure motherhood).

At this point you ask your child if he has any more questions and tell him how excited you will be when he goes to the temple, and when he has his first child. Remind the child this time was a very sacred time that you have shared together and these are things we only discuss in families. It isn't secret, but Heavenly Father intended for this teaching to be done in each home. You can caution him not to talk about it with his friends because it is sacred.

Demonstrate Family Love and Unity

After I conclude the presentation, my husband and the other children return home. Usually the child will have received so much information that he will only desire a few moments in private with his Dad, but that is all it takes to cement the bond of family togetherness for this special event. Then we have a nice family dinner, or do something special which seems appropriate and won't disturb the mood, but will help the child feel the reality of family love and unity. We tell him this is what the whole thing is about—families and the plan God has for us to become families and live together to learn the lessons we need to know to come back to live with Him someday.

The older children are so excited when the younger ones are going to receive their books, and the younger child gets the feeling he has "arrived." ("Now we are all the same" kind of feeling.) As each child receives his book, the other brothers and sisters who have already received theirs know they can talk with him about the things he has learned...with a reminder again that we only talk about these things in our family.

The Script

Now for the script which I promised to give you. These are the words which may be written in the book which you will prepare for your child. This is only a guide, and can be changed to fit the personality and needs of your child. Choose pictures to illustrate each concept, and make each page as attractive to the eye as you possibly can. The writing should be done with a fine-line felt-tipped pen in any color you choose, but the darker colors show up best. You may want to type the messages as my friend did, but I wrote it out in longhand to make it seem more like a letter to my child.

Script for a Girl's Book

1. Begin with a personal statement telling the child how special they are and how you knew this was the right time to tell her these important things.

2. Isn't it fun to be young? It's just wonderful, and then to be a girl, too, is sheer joy!

3. Every girl is a "princess" to her own Mother. But have you ever dreamed of being carried off to a castle to live "happily-ever-after"?

4. Maybe you've even found yourself dreaming of the boys in your classes at school or church—or even about *one* special boy in your own imagination (that boy of your dreams).

5. Boys are many things to girls...fathers, grandfathers, brothers, cousins, and uncles. But boys can also be friends (and lots of fun to be around).

6. Wise is the girl who builds friendships with many boys in high school and early college. She can enjoy the companionship of groups and leave "steady" dating until later. This will give her the chance to understand herself better before she starts narrowing down the selection. Boys are such fun, and it's good to spend a long time looking them all over—until that wonderful day (at college, or after a mission) when you select just *one* to be your sweetheart!

7. Boys make it possible for girls to become BRIDES, and later mothers.

8. Most girls dream of that far-away day when they will finally become a mother. Have you ever dreamed such dreams?

9. But between those dreams and the time they become real are many months...and years. During this time you will want to build and prepare for your future with greatest care. You will be living with yourself forever...in the future you build for yourself. You will want to build wisely in order to be ready to care for yourself and your very own family someday.

10. PLAN AHEAD! You must build both body and spirit.

11. Build with Beauty. See the beauty of nature in all God's creations; beauty in harmonies of grace and color which you can put into your own home someday. Learn all you can about them.

12. Every flower, every creation of God speaks of beauty in its own special way. But nothing can surpass the beauty of the tabernacle of your spirit. It is a beautiful temple built by the Master Builder, God. He created your body in which your spirit dwells.

13. Protect and guard this precious body by keeping your body clean and pure as Heavenly Father created it.

14. Learn to care for your physical needs. Eat proper foods to build a strong body which will be prepared for Motherhood. You can also help your body stay strong by getting enough rest, and remembering the importance of personal cleanliness.

15. Don't forget the beauty that is found in words. The world of literature has its own charm and spirituality...and herein you can gain strong and firm convictions. Build with knowledge and intelligence gained from education and the study of good books.

16. You will want to build with love, love for all God's creations, love for family (an eternal unit created for your security), father, mother, brothers, and sisters...they all need your LOVE. Love for friends. Build with cheerfulness, cooperation, and kindness. Service is the way to show your love. SERVE OTHERS.

17. I know you'll want to prepare with FAITH AND PRAYERS. Gain for yourself a testimony...strong and true. You cannot teach your children the gospel unless you know it, and know it is true.

18. Begin now to develop your talents. Learn to play the hymns, a love song or a lullaby, learn to dance with grace and beauty. Learn the true enjoyment of searching out, studying, and disciplining yourself to schedules. Eventually you will know great, wonderful satisfaction in achieving.

19. Begin now to learn about economy and good judgment in order to help you stretch your husband's paycheck and feed and clothe your family well. Build your kitchen talents; learn to use your hands to create clothing, and furnishings for your

future family and home. Keep your clothes in good repair now. Take care of your possessions.

20. Maybe you'll be...a missionary...a secretary...or a school-teacher.

21. And after all this, you'll be ready to be a beautiful bride... and you'll experience the contentment and fun of being together with your one and only...the thrill of knowing you belong to-gether.

22. Later you will know the thrill of approaching motherhood.

23. And then, at last, you'll know the wonder of holding your own child in your arms! There is no joy to compare!

24. And, best of all, you will know that you are a family unit forever and ever...for all time and eternity. Your temple marriage makes it so, for you will be sealed through the Priesthood of God.

25. The Lord has promised "all He has" to the faithful. I'd give you the "world" if I could, for you are the most precious thing in my world, but God did not intend that all things should come too easily to His children. Never forget that I want only the best things in life for you. I hope you will always be happy and grateful for your life. Let me tell you how you started this life.

26. (Here you include a personal letter expressing how you felt when you knew you were preparing a body for another spirit to enter, the circumstances of her birth, and your feelings at the time of her birth.)

27. I want to help you build the habits and attitudes which will eventually take you back into the presence of your Heavenly Father.

28. So today I have something special to talk over with you. In the coming months or years, your body will begin to change. It will be preparing so that one day you can become a mother. When it reaches a certain phase of growth you will begin to men-struate. You already know something about this flow of blood which means that you are no longer a little girl, but you have come into your womanhood. This is the most glorious thing that your body is capable of doing because this means that you will then have the capacity to become a mother (although you will not be ready to become one). Here you explain in detail about the physiological facts of menstruation.) This issue of blood is like a sign of promise that someday God will allow you to become a mother when you and your husband are ready to become part-ners with God in creating a new body to house one of His spirit children. (Not only do you explain physiological facts of men-

struation at this point, but you must be clever enough to "word these facts" so that your child will actually ask you "How does that sperm get to the ovum?" Then you have the opportunity to explain sexual intercourse—which is the ultimate purpose for the book, the special date, etc.)

29. I hope when you begin to menstruate you will remember these things and will not be afraid. I hope this will help it to be a good experience for you. Try not to speak to others or even think about this special function of your body in an unclean or crude manner, and keep yourself completely clean in every way— mind and body. Promise yourself that you will never violate this trust of potential motherhood...for it is from God. Only those who keep themselves clean and pure in this life, and keep the other highest covenants of God will be given the blessing of parenthood in eternity.

30. Always remember that you are a child of God. Because you are a child of God, you are someone special, and God expects you to love and respect yourself, and stand up for what is right so that you will remain clean and pure.

31. But there is danger ahead (temptations). (Explain.) Guard your way well. Listen to that still, small voice. Never hesitate to come to me, or Daddy, or Heavenly Father for help and advice. You will never have a problem that is too big, or too secret to discuss with us.

32. Remember to be modest always. Clothe your body with proper dress. Do not exhibit it to public view. Do not flaunt it in an unholy manner. Do not use it as an instrument of evil enticement, or pass it about like a plaything. Shelter it and safeguard it as a precious jewel. For one day in the bonds of holy matrimony you will want to give yourself to the one you love. You will want your body to be a holy, undefiled sanctuary where choice spirits from God can make their mortal beginning.

33. Be particular about:
Where you go.
Whom you go with.
What you do.
What you say.
Whom you choose for friends.
Whom you marry.

34. Even though you may sometimes feel that you are alone in being particular about these things, remember there are many other fine girls who are keeping their standards high with you!

35. I'm glad that we are friends. I hope this never changes. How proud I am of you, and how I do love you. I want to share in your life just as much as you will let me. Let me know when you are worried, when you are happy, when you are a bit sad. For God has entrusted you to me until that time when you and your husband become one in His temple.

36. These things we have discussed today are holy, wonderful, and must be kept sacred. We shouldn't talk about them jokingly or disrespectfully, but they should be treated with reverence. Sometimes people don't know the whole plan and they take one part of it and speak of it in an unclean manner. But you and I know that we must be reverent about the things of God. They are not really "secret" for everyone learns about them sooner or later. But they are for mothers and daughters to talk over in their very own homes. I want you to ask me again about anything which you do not remember or even something which we might not have talked about today.

37. Daddy loves you. You are one of our most treasured possessions. I love you. Your family loves you. Heavenly Father loves you!

38. If you are always true, the way of life will be made known to you, and you will never be deceived by Satan...you will surely return in safety and purity to your Heavenly Father.

Script for a Boy's Book

1. Begin with a statement which explains to the child how special he is and how you knew this was the right time to tell him these important things about life.

2. In this fast moving world of ours, a boy must truly wonder and dream. A boy probably dreams of many things. Do you ever think about girls as you daydream?

3. Girls are many things. They are mothers, sisters, cousins, grandmothers, and girls are friends, too!

4. Wise is the boy who builds friendships with many girls in high school and early college. He will enjoy the companionship of groups and leave "steady" dating until later.

5. Girls are for having fun with, and looking over, before you come to that wonderful day (after mission and college) of choosing one out of all those friends to be your sweetheart.

6. Girls make it possible for boys to become husbands and fathers.

7. Have you ever thought of the day when you'll be a father? It's a far-away dream, isn't it?

8. But between these dreams and the time when they will become real are days and months and years when a boy must build his future with the greatest care, for he alone will be the builder who is held responsible for the results, and he must live forever with himself, and in the future he builds.

9. And so, a boy must be wise and begin to look ahead. He will need to prepare his body, mind, and spirit to be able to rule and guide his own home someday.

10. A boy who is really preparing for life will seek knowledge and truth.

11. He will build through gaining an education.

12. He will find wisdom from words and he can build inner strength from scriptures, great thoughts, and biographies of great men.

13. He will gain an appreciation for the arts—perhaps learn to control the body through dance, or the mind through drama.

14. He must build with wisdom and gain an appreciation for the beautiful world which God created for him to enjoy.

15. Nothing can surpass the beauty of the tabernacle of his spirit. It is a beautiful temple built by the master builder, God. Heavenly Father created each boy's spirit, and allowed his parents to assist in preparing the body to house that spirit.

16. He will care for his body by giving it proper nutrition according to the word of wisdom, and proper sleep so that he can build a strong body to be ready for fatherhood.

17. He will build with love:

For family: He will grow in wisdom and self-discipline as he stays close to his family.

For friends: One tends to become like his friends, so he will choose friends carefully.

For all creatures God created for his enjoyment and care.

18. He will build with acts of courtesy and service to others. Service is the way to show your love, and to grow in self-esteem. SERVE OTHERS.

19. He will learn to work. He will learn the satisfaction of a job well done, a game well played.

20. He will learn to manage his money, to budget and save in order to be ready for a mission and later for family life.

21. He will learn to obey his parents and church authorities.

22. And all of this to prepare to become a king to his wife and children. He must try to prepare himself for those glorious events—marriage and children. A noble calling deserves noble

preparation, filled with thanksgiving and joy as he goes along the way leading to exaltation.

23. He will build through faith and prayer.

24. He will build by honoring and magnifying the Priesthood of God.

25. A worthy goal takes effort and brings joy.

26. There will be a mission in his future, and he will build to become worthy of a mission call.

27. He will have the excitement of finding the ONE GIRL (and becoming a handsome GROOM), and knowing she is his.

28. He will have joy in knowing she loves him as much as he loves her!

29. Oh, the contentment and peace of just being together.

30. And then to approach fatherhood.

31. And finally to know the glorious feeling of holding his own child in his arms and giving it a name and a blessing...because of the Priesthood which he honors. THERE'S NOTHING TO COMPARE!

32. He will have his own family unit forever and ever because he was sealed for all time and eternity in God's Holy House by the authority of the Priesthood.

33. The world lies at your feet. The Lord has promised "all that He has" to the faithful. I would like to give you everything, but I don't believe the Lord wanted things to come too easily to His children. But never forget that I want you to obtain the best from life. I want you to be happy always. Let us build together and try to help you develop the habits and attitudes which will eventually take you back into the actual presence of your Heavenly Father.

34. (Here you include a personal letter expressing how you felt when you knew he was coming, the circumstances of this birth, and your feelings at the time of this birth, and how his Dad felt.)

35. Today I have something special to talk over with you, for in the coming months and years, your body will begin to change. It will change in preparation for you to become a father. Some of the outward signs will be the change in the quality of your voice, hair beginning to show under your arms and in the pubic region, and on your legs. It will be such a wonderful time in your life, for these will be indications that you are beginning to come into your manhood, and you are no longer a little boy. Inward signs will also begin to occur and you will find that it is quite pleasant to be around the opposite sex and enjoy their associ-

ation. I don't want you to worry about these feelings. They are just another sign that God has planned that you will soon be a man. These yearnings and desires will become so strong that you will want to choose one girl out of all your associations to become your mate for time and eternity. Because of the wonderful changes that will occur in your body, both outwardly and inwardly, you will be able to become a father. (Here you can discuss the physiological facts, seminal emissions, etc. Also teach them about menstruation of a girl. This helps them respect girls and their sisters and understand this is a sacred function of a girl's body. Then, as with the girl's script, you will need to word it so the question and discussion of sexual intercourse may come naturally.)

36. All of us are given the power of creation in our bodies, and this is a sacred power that we must not misuse. It is Heavenly Father's plan that the act of creation, the sexual union, should only occur under the bonds of marriage.

37. Then you and your wife and your Heavenly Father will become partners in the most glorious miracle of earth life...birth.

38. Of course, it will be a long time before you are ready to become a father, but in the meantime, I hope these signs will remind you that you have a trust...to keep yourself clean and pure. Try not to speak about these things to others or even think about them in an unclean manner or crude way. Sometimes people don't know the whole plan, and they take one part of it and speak of it in an unclean manner. But you and I know that we must be very reverent about the plan which God has given us to bring children into this world. Promise yourself that you will never violate that trust.

39. There is nothing finer than clean, honorable manhood. Your life, to your father and I, is far more precious than worldly power or wealth. We know you will be true to your trust.

40. It will help you if you remember that you are a child of God. Protect and guard your choice spirit by keeping your body clean and pure as Heavenly Father meant it to be. Then you will love and respect yourself.

41. Remember to be modest always. Clothe your body with proper clothing. Don't forget that God expects modesty and virtue of both men and women. There is no double standard in His gospel plan. Your body is sacred.

42. One day you will want to give your body to the one you love in the bonds of holy matrimony, for time and all eternity. You will want your body to be an undefiled sanctuary which can

give spirits from God their mortal beginnings...a royal birth.

43. Guard your way well, for there is always danger ahead. (Discuss the temptations.)

44. Listen to the still, small voice within you. Never hesitate to come to your Dad, to me, to your Heavenly Father, to your Bishop for help and advice.

45. I'm glad that we are friends. I hope this never changes. How proud I am of you, and how I do love you. I want to share in your life just as much as you will let me. Let me know when you are worried, when you are happy, when you are a bit sad. For God has entrusted you to me until that time when you and your wife become one in His Holy Temple.

46. Take time to work and talk with your Dad. Get a man's point of view. No one loves you more than he, nor wants to help you more than he does.

47. These things that we have discussed today are part of God's plan for you, and they are sacred. We should not talk about them jokingly and disrespectfully. They should be treated with reverence. They are for parents and children to talk over together in their own homes. They are not really "secret" for usually everyone learns about them sooner or later. But, sometimes people speak of these things in an unclean manner. However, you and I know that we must be reverent about the things of God.

48. If you will follow the example of your wonderful Dad— then someday your own son will want to follow you.

Well, that's the plan. I hope it will be useful to you. It does take some effort to put it into practice, but as my husband said to me when I was tempted to put off giving our youngest boy his book until I had finished working on a degree, "What is most important—your son or your degree?" I had no trouble deciding, and I put everything else aside for a few weeks while I prepared his book. I'm sure you have learned, as I have, that anything which is worthwhile does take effort and time. God bless you as you try to fulfill this sacred responsibility.

Best wishes,

Peggy Andersen

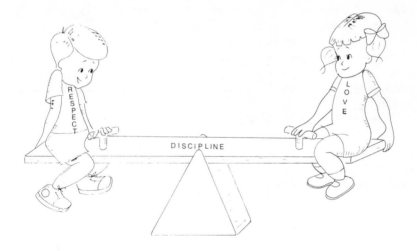

15

Taking the Drudgery Out of Discipline

"On a warm summer afternoon, I left my children with a babysitter and went shopping," one mother related. "I soon noticed I had forgotten my shopping list and returned, coming in the back door to avoid repeating the farewell scene. I got my list and was about to leave when I heard angry voices.

"I can too!"

"You'd better not!"

"I heard a slap and loud crying. It hurt me that someone had treated one of my children unkindly, and suddenly I identified with Heavenly Father standing on the other side, listening. I sensed how he must feel when any of his children are treated badly. In one of those rare moments of insight, I wept as I sensed how he had felt when I had been less than kind in my role as a parent. This brought a new thought: my Heavenly Father is a parent, too. How does he treat me? I realized then that *guidance and help to be a good parent comes not only through inspiration, but also through Heavenly Father's example as a parent!* I felt I had found the best source I could think of for how-to's of discipline and child-rearing in general—the example of our Heavenly Parent."

Discipline is, at best, a controversial subject. There is no one right way or one set of rules that works for every child under every situation. But if we try to discover the basic principles the Lord uses with us as His children, we will have some guidelines to follow.

The dictionary defines discipline as "training which corrects, molds, strengthens, or perfects." That definition seems in keeping with what the Lord is trying to do for us, so we will accept it as our general frame of reference. Basically, discipline should always teach with respect and point a child to a better way; not just punish. Effective discipline turns responsibility over to the child rather than depriving him of it, and builds his self-esteem. Discipline is training which helps a child develop his own "inner controls", which in turn make real obedience possible.

But how does a parent be a good disciplinarian? Helena Evans, social worker and mother of five successful grown children, suggests that parents need training just as everyone needs training for any responsible job. She says, "So many times people expect to automatically be good at being parents, but it rarely happens that way. It is something that must be worked at and learned just like any other skill."

The Golden Thread of Respect

In effective discipline, respect seems to be the basic and essential quality, and the golden thread running through the parental example that our Heavenly Father sets for us. The Lord shows deep and profound respect for his children. (The dictionary defines respect as "to consider worthy of esteem, hence to refrain from obtruding upon; to notice with attention, regard, consideration.") Many authorities feel that lack of respect is at the root of most discipline and relationship problems. Parents sometimes live by a separate set of rules with children and show them less respect than others, especially in trying to discipline.

Helen Sharp commented, "The fact that we came to earth before our children doesn't make us superior to them. In the spirit world they might have been more valiant than we were. I think we need to show respect for our children, and treat them like valiant spirits."

Clear Instructions Clear the Air

The Lord has set the example of establishing clear rules and expectations. In the scriptures and through the voice of the prophets, the Lord clearly states what we should and should not do, giving the consequences for disobedience and the blessings to be received from obedience. To follow this example, we must set standards for our children and let them know what is expected of them. They only feel secure when they know the limits of what they can and cannot do. Children equate limits with caring. Many delinquents say, "My parents did not care enough to give me any rules." The love of a parent protects a child from his own inexperience by keeping him from playing with fire. Author Marabel Morgan said, "It is love that limits—for love's sake. It has been said that if God had wanted parents to be permissive, he would have given us the Ten Suggestions instead of the Ten Commandments!"

In a B.Y.U. sponsored class (for parents of children with reading problems) the importance of having rules, consequences, and rewards clearly understood by children was pointed out. A challenge was given for Mom and Dad to take a single rule and analyze it, by asking these questions: "What is the rule?" "Do we agree on it?" "Do our children clearly understand it?" "What does Mother do when the rule is broken?" "What does Father do when the rule is broken?" "Do we do it consistently?" "What happens when the rule is followed?" (Is there some positive reinforcement?)

Having clear rules can give children a feeling of security (through knowing what is expected) and release parents from the role of policeman. When a rule is clearly understood, the only enforcement necessary may be to ask, "What is the rule?"

Not only does this procedure make the parents' job easier, but it can bring a great improvement in the feeling-tone between parent and child. Consider the following examples:

A. Mom: Dan, get in here immediately and get those school clothes off!

Dan: But Mom, I'm not getting dirty.

Mom: Young man, you've been told a million times that you shouldn't play in your school clothes. What's the matter with your ears? Now march!

B. Mom: Dan, what is the rule about school clothes?

Dan: We are supposed to change before we go to play.

Mom: What do you think you should do about it?

Dan: I guess I should change.

Mom: Come and show me when you have your play clothes on.

Whenever a child clearly knows what is expected, simple questions can be very effective in changing behavior. Jean Orgill, mother of three and an outstanding kindergarten teacher, says that one of the best forms of discipline she knows is to ask questions such as "What should you be doing now?" or "What is a better way to do that?" Arlene had a pleasant success experience with this technique. When company was expected, instead of saying, "Julie, go change the sheets on your bed", she asked her, "What do you think you need to do to get your room ready for company?" Without further supervision, Julie changed the sheets, and also vacuumed and cleaned her whole room. Perhaps the reason this question approach is so effective is that it gives the child a chance to use his own initiative, and not just obey a command.

Thou Shalt Nots Aren't Negative

Heavenly Father includes "Thou Shalt Nots" along with the "Thou Shalt" rules. So should we, for such rules are often necessary guidelines for the safety and well-being of the child and those around him. Rehan Dunnigan, mother of five, says, "Thou Shalt Nots need to be taught verbally not just by example. For instance, we have a large gravel driveway. Our children were taught not to throw rocks. But the children who visited usually had not been taught. Invariably (although *none* of their parents threw rocks) the visiting children would find rock-throwing an appealing pastime. I had to teach them through word, as well as example, *not* to throw the rocks. We cannot be sure our children will avoid negative behavior in any area just because they have never seen us do it. They need clear 'Thou Shalt Nots' in addition to good examples."

One mother found that she was failing to accurately communicate "Thou Shalt Nots" by going to the extreme trying to be understanding. When her little boy made mistakes, she would always put her arms around him and say, "I'm sure you'll do better next time." But when his behavior didn't improve she realized she wasn't communicating her disapproval of his wrong actions. She decided there was a difference between patience, and permissiveness, and as soon as she made her child understand clearly what he shouldn't do and showed her disapproval when he disobeyed, his behavior improved immediately.

The Long and Short of Expectations

Heavenly Father communicates great expectations of us through patriarchal blessings, ordinances, and counsel from the prophets, yet he is always mindful of our present stage of development and does not expect more than we can do. We should be sure our own expectations are realistic and in keeping with each child's stage of development. Discipline problems can be caused by expecting too little or too much of a child.

Most parents readily respect the developmental stage of a new-born. We don't say to a baby, "What's the matter with you? Why can't you talk and run and help with the dishes?" Instead we say, "Look how fast you are learning! Before we know it you will be able to run and jump and shout and play!" However, when he can do all those things, we are inclined to say, "Don't run! Quit jumping! Why can't you hold still and be quiet?"

It seems to be increasingly difficult as a child grows, to respect the limitations his immaturity places on his behavior, (especially when the behavior is inconvenient or irritating to us.) "To every thing there is a season, and a time to every purpose under the heaven..." Ecclesiastes 3:1. If we expect apples to turn red and juicy before it is their time, and become angry because they are still green, it is our expectations that are at fault, not the apples. If we don't understand the growth stages of a child, we may expect behavior he is incapable of. However, it seems that in any area of child-raising, when you talk about one concern, you immediately need to voice caution lest that idea is carried to extreme and balance and perspective is lost. So it is with expectations. While we must be careful to avoid expecting the impossible, we parents often put up with behavior that is frustrating and upsetting to us when we really don't need to. We don't expect enough when the child is perfectly capable of complying with a more reasonable standard.

Expect Reasonable Behavior

Helena Evans feels that firmness when the child is making unreasonable demands can help both parent and child if the parent remains kind. Helena had a granddaughter who had decided that bread and honey were life's greatest delights and refused to eat anything else. This little girl came to stay with Helena while her parents went on a two-day trip. Each meal time she demanded bread and honey, and each time her Grandma placed a good meal in front of her and told her she could have bread and honey when she had finished her meal. The child went the whole first day without eating a thing. The next morning at breakfast the little girl said, "I want bread and honey." Grandma said, "Eat your cereal, and then you may have some bread and honey." She ate her cereal without a protest and ate a balanced diet from then on. Helena believes that a child needs to know you will be firm when it is for their best good, and that you will not allow them to browbeat you. Once you have established your firmness, the spirit of cooperation often flows freely again.

It is a child's nature to test his limits. When these limits hold firm, he feels safe. Good discipline, basically, consists of setting limits in love and correcting a child with love when these limits are ignored. Author Marabel Morgan said, "You may never hear your children admit you were right, but nevertheless you must do for them what you know is right. Parenthood is not a popularity contest. A parent who is fearful to limit, afraid to forbid, and unwilling to train, sends his child into the tanglewood of life without a knowledge of the trails."

Whenever a child's behavior is unreasonable, intolerable, or falls far short of what we know they are capable of, we should feel free to set limits, expect better behavior, and find ways to bring about the change. One mother finds it necessary and effective to lock a two-year-old in the "time-out" room when he passes the limits of tolerable behavior. Another mother puts her child outside in the fenced-in yard when he is impossible, and tells him he may rejoin the family when he is ready to change his behavior. (Depriving a child of an audience when he is acting up seems to be effective!)

Linda Garner sets limits for her pre-schoolers and explains how she enforces them: "The main discipline method I use is to have my little ones sit on a chair when they have done something wrong. It gives me a chance to calm down, and is uncomfortable for them because they hate being out of the action. I always end the chair sitting with a talk to make it a learning experience, not just a punishment. I explain exactly what they did wrong, and what they should do next time. I tell them I want them to learn to behave well because I love them so much and want them to be happy. It really works for us." One mother uses extra work assignments with older children to enforce limits on their behavior. She said, "If the children are squabbling and can't get along, I tell them it must mean they don't have enough work to keep them out of trouble, so I'll give them some more. (If their behavior immediately improves, I don't give them the job, but they know that if it continues even for one minute they will both be given assignments—and I will see to it that they do them.) I also use this procedure at bedtime. Anyone who can't settle down at night can get up and do some work. They usually decide to settle down! If a child complains about an assignment, I give him two. If he leaves his coat lying around, he must clean the whole room it is left in, and if one child interferes with another's work, he must take over and do it for him. Like the day my oldest was mopping the floor and the others were running in and out to tease him. I simply said, 'The next one who steps on the floor will mop it.' That approach usually results in instant good behavior."

There are a lot of pros and cons regarding using work as a discipline, but an outstanding counselor we talked with heartily recommends it. She explains that she feels work is the healthiest discipline you can use, because a child vents his frustrations as he works, accomplishes something worthwhile, and ends up feeling better about himself when he is finished. At the same time, he is contributing to the good of the family if you give him something to do that really needs to be done.

Fewer Words, Greater Influence

"Many of us talk too much when disciplining," said one authority. "When parents pile up words in an unending array, the child quickly becomes 'mother deaf.' " Driekurs, (another authority) has said a fundamental rule of discipline is, "don't talk—act!" Instead of threats when a child goes in the street—take him in the house. When children are fighting, instead of repeatedly pleading for them to quit, separate them. Instead of telling them over and over to quit splashing water when they are in the tub, take them out. Instead of counter-arguing, leave the room. Colleen Pinegar said, "We told our children what we expected and then refused to argue about it. Our philosophy was that we avoid having word battles with our children." It seems to communicate to a child that we are *not* certain or firm in our expectations if we repeat requests too many times, engage in arguments, or talk when we can't enforce.

Kenneth A. Griffiths, in an article in the April, 1968 issue of "Instructor", explained the reason children often pay more attention to Dad's requests than Mom's "seems to lie in the lack of clear expectations" because Mom talks too much. Mothers often bombard children with a constant patter of do's and don'ts without being able to follow through to see whether a child complies with her wishes. Mr. Griffith said, "When we identify a few clear expectations for our children and pursue them consistently, we will find our children meeting these expectations quite consistently."

The Far-Reaching Effects of Expectations

Bernice Ursenbach said she felt the most important factor in encouraging righteous behavior is to expect children to do right. Bernice and her husband have had seven teenage drivers and no problems with cars; yet they never had rigid rules about car-use. Bernice said, "I feel the explanation was simply that the children knew we trusted them and expected them to be responsibile."

Over the years, good expectations of parents (and grandparents!) also seem to have far-reaching effects. Kathy Porcaro Adamson (the oldest of Robert and Jean Porcaro's ten children) said that her parents' expectations had a great effect on her, and still do even though she is married and has a baby of her own. She said, "I've always listened to my parents because I respect them. I know what they expect from me and feel I would hate to hurt them, even now, by not living up to what they expect. For example, whenever I am even tempted not to go to church, I think, 'Oh, I couldn't stay home. Mom and Dad expect me to go and they would be disappointed in me if I didn't.'"

Arland and Fern Larsen exerted a great influence on their children through their good expectations. Their children said

"We always knew they expected us to do what was right, and even though their expectations were largely non-verbal, their genuine surprise if we did make a wrong choice helped us understand the confidence they had in us to live up to their expectations."

Linda Garner said, "Temple marriage was never considered an 'if' when we were growing up. It was always 'When I get married in the temple'. I never even thought of being married anywhere else."

Dantzelle Lewis Allen says "I remember going to family reunions when we were very young, and making promises to our grandfather that we would be married in the temple and go on missions. So far every one of the grandchildren have gone on missions and been married in the temple. Our parents told us how important it was to marry someone we would be proud to bring home. In fact, my father made lists of qualities we should look for in a companion, and emphasized that we should be living up to these standards ourselves. He told us he had looked for those qualities in his wife, and that is why we had such a wonderful mother!"

Routine: One of Discipline's Best Friends

A regular, but flexible routine seems to simplify family life, and shows respect for a child's real needs. Kenneth A. Griffiths said, "For the very young child, nothing provides greater security or engenders more trust in the world about him than an established routine. A regular routine teaches the beginning steps of obedience and self-discipline. Instead of expecting the world to obey his every wish, he learns that the world is a friendly and good place, but it requires a bit of self-discipline."

With this perspective he speaks of the importance of having family and individual prayers, church meetings, and family home evening as part of the regular routine. He said, "Activities that are regularly scheduled part of our lives take on added importance. At the same time, they teach us obedience and self-discipline as we consistently follow our routine of living and putting first things first." Perhaps this is one reason the Lord has given these things as commandments.

When a child gets the concept that we don't go to bed because we feel like it, but because it is bedtime, we don't do our work because it strikes our fancy at the moment, but because it needs to be done, then he begins to realize that life has requirements that bring benefits when we consistently comply with them, regardless of our mood at the moment.

A New Definition of Consistency

However, so much has been said in recent years about the necessity of consistency in relation to discipline, that we often feel guilty for any change in feelings or routine. The truth is, no person is totally consistent; only machines are consistent, and even they break down on occasion! Should we expect to react exactly the same to rowdy wrestling and loud music when we are making out our income tax return as we do during an ordinary evening? Should we expect to give Johnny the same response when he drags every pan out of the cupboard and bangs the lids together when we have a splitting headache and company coming for dinner in ten minutes as we did yesterday when we felt fine and were under no time pressure?

One authority suggests that a more realistic kind of consistency is consistently being honest with a child about our feelings and how we are affected by his behavior of the moment. Then consistently giving the child a chance to respond and work with us in finding solutions acceptable to both of us. Changing moods and circumstances are openly admitted and accepted; children know where they stand. This kind of consistency can teach true respect for the feelings of both parents and children.

Fish Swim, Birds Fly, and People Feel

A child's sense of worth is largely determined by the respect or lack of respect with which he is treated. If a child is treated harshly, with no regard for feelings, he puts up defenses which rob his life of joy and spontaneity. Many parents mentioned the importance of starting when a child is tiny to show respect for his feelings and special needs.

Linda Garner said, "I think that very little children can understand a lot more than we give them credit for and that they feel things deeply. Because of this, I always try to explain things, even to little babies, to prepare them for what I am going to do or what is going to happen to them. Even if I am just going to change their pants or put them in the bathtub, I tell them what I'm about to do and why. One day my husband, Marshall, said, 'Linda, why do the children cry when I put them in the tub, yet when you do it, they rarely make a peep?' I said, 'I think it's because I explain to them what I am going to do before I do it so they know what to expect. How would you feel if some big person grabbed you, laid you down, pulled your clothes off and dumped you in a tub of water...all without a word of explanation?' Marshall thought the point was well taken, and did notice an improvement in the children's behavior when he tried to explain to them what he was doing."

Someone once said, "As you are with them, so will they be with all others." Feelings are sensitive and real, and influenced dramatically by the responses of those whom we care about most. In order to raise compassionate, kind, loving children, it seems logical that we must treat them in a compassionate, kind, loving way. Haim Ginot said, "You can't teach kindness with a sledge hammer." It seems likely that high on the list of parental regrets will be those times when we overlooked the feelings of our children, just for the sake of expediency, getting things done, or venting frustrations.

Correct with Respect

Who can imagine living with a child and not giving him any "negative feedback"? But parents agreed it's the approach and the timing of the feedback that makes it criticism or helpful discipline.

If Johnny is learning to drain the dishes and we say, "Hey, you're doing that all wrong; do it this way", Johnny may get angry or discouraged and want to quit. But if we say, "Let's put the cup upside down so the water will drain off", Johnny will probably not resent the suggestion and be glad to follow it.

Children in the teen years are especially sensitive to parental insensitivity, and may interpret correction to be an indication of lack of understanding. Marie is an exemplary and alert teenager, active in church and school. One Wednesday she came home from school, threw open the door, ran through the living room and tossed her books and coat on the couch. She breathlessly exclaimed to her mom, who had watched her enthusiastic entrance, "Mom! Guess what? I got the part I wanted in the play at school!"

"Marie, how many times have I told you not to leave the door open and not to throw your things on the couch. When will you pay some attention to me? Now you march right out there and come in again, and this time do it right!"

Marie burst into tears. "Oh Mom, you don't even care about me. All you ever do is tell me all the things I do wrong. You won't even listen when I'm trying to tell you the most important thing that has ever happened to me!" Marie ran to her room, slammed the door and threw herself on her bed.

Marie's mother honestly wanted to motivate her daughter to improve her habits. But her timing and approach were not helpful, nor positive. Pointing out faults, weaknesses, and in-adequacies, except in a respectful, constructive way, often hurts feelings and damages relationships. A pleasant tone of voice, sensitivity to a child's feelings, and respect of their need to learn without "losing face" can help us correct when necessary without causing friction and discouragement.

"Our ten children are special people and our best friends," said Janice Burton. "We feel a responsibility to guide and at times correct them, but this must always be done with respect. We are not perfect either, and they are free to correct or try to teach us; but only with this same respect." Janice said they are very open in communication in their home and freely express and discuss feelings. This keeps the air clear and the feeling tone relaxed and happy. They always try to remember to talk with their children as they talk with one of their friends.

We do have the responsibility to teach our children to make right choices and do things correctly, and should never let a child think we don't care about his transgressions. However, part of respect is to overlook the inconsequential things parents sometimes treat as though they *were* transgressions! Imagine being trapped in a situation where your every imperfection was constantly brought to your attention. But isn't ignoring any nega-tive behavior simply not facing a reality? After all, thorns are thorns! Well, roses are as real as thorns, and if you know a thorny child, perhaps someone paid a lot of attention to his thorns. Why not pay attention to the roses instead?

"Catch Them Doing Right"

Marilyn Skousen told us how her mother, Rachel McOmber stressed the positive and corrected with respect. Marilyn said, "We would usually start our family home evening with what we called "Family Business" when we discussed things that needed to be changed. Mother always brought up positive things first. She had what she called "Bouquets" for each family member. At each home evening, she would tell each of us something good she had noticed during the week. She was constantly recognizing the good things we did, and that made it easy to listen when she included an area where we needed to improve. It was a highly motivating thing to me. Mom used the positive approach in her pre-school, too. She taught twenty-seven children, but hardly ever had to reprimand one of them. It was amazing to me the way she could divert their attention from what they were doing wrong, reward them for doing right, and keep things running smoothly. I can see that this approach takes a lot of patience, which mother had really worked to develop."

Lynn Scoresby feels that parents should make it a point to act positively concerning their children, instead of just "reacting". Reaction often turns out to be critical and negative. "Acting" requires control and self-discipline on the part of the parent. "Reacting" requires no self-discipline: it is the path of least resistance. Lynn said, "Criticism is definitely related to discipline problems: *As positive statements from parent to child increase, discipline problems decrease.* Approval is as much a part of discipline as punishment. Find good things to say to your child about himself. The more good feelings you can develop in him, the easier your job will become. It is the child who feels that no one cares about him and there's nothing good about him who becomes the behavior problem."

Jean Orgill takes this principle one step further and suggests that positive reinforcement is the most effective teaching or discipline tool we have. She says, "The best reason to try it is: it works! If you say to Michael, 'You are doing very well remembering to put your crayons away', you reinforce a behavior you *want* and Michael is all the more likely to remember to put his crayons away next time." A lesson in Relief Society stressed that the best way to improve behavior is to notice when a child does something *right* and tell him about it!

I Want to be Free!

One father said, "The hardest job of parents is to leave children free to make their own mistakes." Because we dislike seeing our children suffer the consequences of a wrong choice, we sometimes try to force them to do what we think is right. Satan suggested forcing righteousness—and Heavenly Father rejected that plan.

Elwood Peterson, in a B.Y.U. education week class, discussed the problem of using force with children. He commented that parents are inclined to force children because they are so emotionally involved with them. He told a story of when he was a bishop, and was trying to get his teenage son to give a talk in church. After his son had said no, Brother Peterson kept telling him how good it would be for him to give a talk and kept prodding him about it. He even helped his son prepare a talk. In the meeting Brother Peterson announced that the boy would talk. Instead, his son got up and walked out of the church. Elwood said, "It's too easy in the name of righteousness to encroach on the rights of our children. But God himself always respects free agency, regardless of the cost to Him."

Joseph F. Smith said:

> You can't force your boys, nor your girls into heaven. You may force them to hell, by using harsh means in the efforts to make them good, when you yourselves are not as good as you should be. The man that will be angry at his boy and try to correct him while he is in anger, is in the greatest fault; he is more to be pitied and more to be condemned than the child who has done wrong. You can only correct your children by love, in kindness, by love unfeigned, by persuasion, and reason.
>
> (Gospel Doctrine, pp. 316-317)

The age and abilities of a child determines the amount and strength of guidance that is appropriate. Linden Hurst, father of seven and a member of a stake presidency said, "There is a time in a child's life when he is very small when you can almost dictate and say, 'This is the way it's done', like a mother bird feeding her young and getting the right ideas into them when they are little. But there is a time when the young birds must begin to leave the nest, and this is the time for 'shadow leadership' when you have to step back a little bit and leave them on their own. This is the difficult part, drawing away from the older ones and giving them full responsibility for the things they are ready to handle."

Marilyn Skousen said, "I think one of the key things that helped me is that my parents really took a lot of time teaching us when we were smaller, and then when we got to be teenagers they let us on our own, trusting that their teachings would guide us. So when we were ready to make our own decisions, they let us. We didn't have to rebel."

"I feel that discipline is a process," said Rex Stallings, father of five (who was bishop for nine years and is presently a member of a stake presidency). "First, children must be taught what is right or acceptable. (Sometimes spanking, etc., is a schoolmaster in this teaching process.) Then children must be given an opportunity to test out what they have learned, make their own choices, and win or lose. I feel you should compliment children when they win, chat with them when they lose, and try to help them understand the consequences of their own choices. I remember when one of our boys said that he didn't know how we had done it; we never forced them, yet they felt obligated to do what was right." Stallings' son, Alan (recently returned from the Venezuelan mission) joined us as we chatted with his parents. We asked him why he thought his parents had been so successful with their children. "It was their example, coupled with love," he said, "And then, too, instead of telling us what we had to do, they showed us." Sue, their sixteen-year-old daughter added, "Right! You don't like to have parents shake their finger in your face and say, 'Now you do this or that.' Mom and Dad rarely did. They just told us what was right, did what was right, and expected us to follow."

Rex said, "It is such a thrill to do something right when it is your idea to do it—then you can take the credit for it. But if someone else makes you do it, they get the credit and you don't feel any rewards. Because we've left the decision up to them, I think they have felt the rewards of their own right choices. Until a child makes a right choice of his own free will, I don't think a parent has really accomplished anything, no matter how obedient they are to commands."

Helena Evans said, "In teaching my children to take responsibility for their own choices, I used two lists. A "Must" list, which included rules which governed our home, and a "May" list, which included things they could decide for themselves. I started my young children with little choices (from their "May" list) and then gave them bigger and bigger ones. I feel it is very important to a child's personal development to give them choices as much as possible, because choices help them grow and develop and learn to make decisions. If forced, they do not grow. I tried to teach them correct principles, then let them govern themselves according to the principles. I felt that by the time a child was a teenager, the only things on my "Must" list for them was gospel principles. (If they wanted to wear purple pants or dirty cords to school, I let them. Those things didn't affect their salvation. I noticed the mothers who made a big issue over little things like this often lost their children's obedience on the big things that do matter.)

"Even on gospel principles, though, I let them make a choice after I had taught them correctly. Let me give you an example:

"One Sunday after church my son said, 'I don't know why you don't let me go to the show on Sunday. All my friends are going and here I stand by myself and they think I'm a sissy and tied to your apron strings.' 'I'm not keeping you from going to the show,' I said. 'You can go if you want to, but first I want to be sure you know exactly what the Lord has said about Sundays. Let's go home and read about it. I have the responsibility to teach you correct principles. Once you know them, you can choose. If I have taught you what is right, then you will take the consequences of your actions, not me!' We went home and read all the scriptures I could find about the Sabbath, and then I said, 'Now, you can decide for yourself.' He never said another word about Sunday shows and as far as I know he has never gone to one."

Freedom within limits seems to be a concept that most parents *and* children feel comfortable with. In stressing the importance of free agency, we don't want to give the impression that parents should not set limits or be firm. But the most effective kind of firmness is deciding how *we* (the parents) should act, and what we will and will not do, instead of deciding what we are going to *make* the child do. For example, Helena Evans told her granddaughter that she would not give her bread and honey, not that the child *had* to eat what was good for her. The choice of whether to eat or go hungry was left up to the child. If we create an atmosphere of mutual respect and consideration, we will be providing opportunities for our children to comply willingly with necessary demands and learn to live comfortably and happily with others.

Consider Consequences

"One way we need to take stock of our actions as parents is in the area of teaching consequences," said Ross Richins, bishop and father of five. "Heavenly Father rarely steps in and shields us from the consequences of our own acts, and I feel we should follow his example in regard to our own children."

Parents sometimes do not realize they are shielding their children from consequences. An example might be:

"Kevin, it's time to get up!"

"Mmmmmm"

"Kevin, if you don't get up now you won't have time to finish your homework."

"Mmhm. In a minute."

"Kevin, if you miss the bus, I'm going to be so mad at you!"

Kevin drags out of bed at the last minute and then the rush is on! Mom finishes Kevin's homework, combs his hair, pushes him out the door and drives him to school. Kevin's mother chose to suffer the consequences of Kevin's bad choice to stay in bed.

Choices teach responsible behavior only when a child reaps the consequences of his choices—good or bad. Many parents we interviewed recommended the study and use of natural and logical consequences as teaching and discipline tools. Several excellent books are on the market which explain their use in detail. To explain them briefly: If Kathy refuses to eat what is served for supper or stays outside after she is called to a meal, the natural consequence is to let Kathy stay hungry. This consequence alone will probably motivate her to improve her behavior (to come when called or try whatever is on the table). However, if mother provides alternate choices when Kathy doesn't like what is provided, or if Kathy is allowed to eat whenever she feels like coming in, then she hasn't felt any consequences from her choices and will probably continue the undesirable behavior. A natural consequence lets the child feel the results of his own action without parental interference. However, a logical consequence is one which the parent structures. Whenever two-year-old Jason goes into the street, a logical consequence would be that he loses the privilege of playing in the yard and must go into the house. When the parent lets him out again, he reminds him that he may play outside only if he stays in the yard. The moment he forgets and goes into the street again, he is returned to the house. Parents who have used these methods say they are extremely effective and save much frustration and friction.

Discipline and Relationships

Rex and Barbara Stallings said, "Relationships are so important, and we need to find ways to teach and discipline which don't keep parents and children at swords point with each other. A good place to start is by admitting that we are not perfect, either, but we can learn together and strengthen each other. The thing we always try to impress on our children is the need to learn from mistakes. We aren't nearly so interested in punishing for mistakes as in seeing that they learn from them and don't repeat them." Rex continued, "Many times when my children made a mistake I said, 'Did you learn anything from it?' If I was satisfied with their reply and felt they really were wiser, I would say, 'If you learned your lesson, then it shouldn't happen again.' It rarely did, and we were able to solve our differences quickly and feel good toward each other immediately afterwards."

Children are meant to be loved and enjoyed. They can be lots of fun; but when we see discipline as drudgery; when we nag and yell and fight, we deprive ourselves of much of the pleasure of being parents. Certainly we need discipline in the home because there are many things children need to learn. But the basic rule of happy parents seems to be respect for the rights and feelings of each family member. Respect sustains relationships.

We have great power over our children because of their dependency on us, and we need the Lord's help to know how to use that power in a way that will build them and build relationships. A guide for priesthood power is found in D&C 121:41,42. Shouldn't the same principles apply to parental power?

> No power or influence can or ought to be maintained by virtue of the priesthood, only by persuasion, by long-suffering, by gentleness and meekness, and by love unfeigned;
>
> By kindness, and pure knowledge, which shall greatly enlarge the soul without hypocrisy, and without guile—

Not only does this scripture give us accurate guidelines for the use of parental power, but it is also a beautiful summary of the qualities of a parent who is following the Lord's example.

Ten Things to Try

1. Evaluate your respect-ABILITY as a parent. Contemplate the respect shown us by our Heavenly Parents.

2. Analyze the rules in your home with questions such as: What is the rule? Do both parents agree? Do the children clearly understand it? What does Mother do when the rule is broken?

3. Try using the "What is the rule?" technique to enforce rules that are clearly understood.

4. Use questions instead of commands to encourage action. For example, say, "What do you need to do in your bedroom?" not "Go make your bed!"

5. Practice being consistently honest in communicating your feelings and the needs of the situation.

6. Explain, even to very tiny children, what you are doing for and with them, and why.

7, Give "bouquets" of appreciation and recognition at family home evening. Include "bouquets" with necessary requests for improvement.

8. Try to talk with your children as you would your best friends—even when you are correcting them.

9. Explore ways to give each of your children more freedom of choice as they are ready for it. Try a "Must" and a "May" list.

10. Look for an alternate method of discipline when you can see the method you are using is damaging your relationship with your child. Consider first "What am I teaching?"

16

"The Chore and the Challenge"

Getting our children to whistle as they work is a great goal, but in many homes groans are more common than songs, and teaching children to help is a thorn in the parents' side—or at least a prickle, as it was in the Eddington home. Vera Eddington had tried nearly every plan imaginable to enlist the help of her eleven children with household chores. She said, "I used to greet

247

my children after school by saying, 'I'm so glad to see you! Now, I need you to fold the laundry and peel the potatoes for supper.' One day my fifteen-year-old daughter, Barbara, said, 'Mom, I hope when you get to heaven, Heavenly Father opens the door and says, 'I'm so glad to see you. I've got this job for you to do!' I laughed and said, 'I hope so, too. I can't imagine getting up there and not having anything to do!' But this incident made me more determined to find a plan to teach my children responsibility and relieve me of the pressure of constantly having to ask and remind."

Vera found a way that works for them. She exchanged chore charts for "ACCOMPLISHMENT CHARTS". The basic idea is very simple. The children's names are listed on the left-hand side of a chart with space for each child to record all of the jobs he completes each day. The children are free to choose their own jobs and when they will do them. There is only one basic rule: each person must spend one hour per day and two hours on Saturday helping at home. In the evening Vera looks at the charts and anyone who hasn't done their fair share must finish before they go to bed. She can also ask for help when any job needs to be done immediately, and the time spent counts on the hour requirement. The children know the basic jobs which must be done each day, but to give everyone ideas, the extra jobs such as cleaning drawers, washing walls, etc. are listed on a sheet placed next to the accomplishment chart.

The solution to the challenge of chores and children is met in as many different ways as there are families, but parents we interviewed agreed that the method we choose should meet this criteria: it should help the child build responsible habits. Even though many different methods are used, without exception the families we talked to had all taught, and are now teaching, their children to work, and felt this was a basic part of the children's training for life.

"One of the most important ways we can show our love to our children is to give them responsibilities and teach them to manage their own lives," commented Linda Garner. Linda was a senior resident in a university dorm at one time and was disappointed by the number of girls who came to college very unprepared for being on their own. She said, "I had to teach one girl to fry an egg, another how to scrub a floor. The mothers of those girls surely loved them and thought they were doing them a favor in letting them have a care-free life when they were young, but it was so hard on the girls when they got to college."

Some parents view a child's world as separate from their own and chiefly a time for play. They see adult time as one for heavy responsibility. But how do we get to the place where we can take on the heavy responsibilities? We must move gradually from one stage to another and be taught to balance duty and pleasure, work and play.

Sterling Sill has said, "Work is our primary means of both growth and happiness. Strength comes from struggle, whereas weakness comes from ease."

"We like to cause things; to see things happen because of us. That is why work is so important," states Lynn Scoresby, director of Rocky Mountain Family Institute. He adds, "We do our children a grave disservice if we do not give them responsibilities that make them feel a vital part of the family. They *want* to feel needed and that they are a contributing part of the whole family unit." When children learn to help at home, they are learning about the real world, and the skills they will need to cope with this world. They are also making it possible for parents to have time and energy to do things for and with them!

Children need to understand that none of us can be good members of society by doing just what we prefer. Of course, we would rather play than work but few things are more crucial to success and happiness than learning to do what needs to be done—not just that which we feel like doing. One parent said, "We want our children to have all the advantages, and learning to work is one of them!" But *how* to teach children to work is a common concern of most parents. Perhaps the following informal run-down of how other parents solve the dilemma of children, chores, and money may help.

The Younger the Better to Make Helping a Habit

Even a very young child can get a sense of importance and dignity from being able to do something which the family depends on him to do. Families agreed that establishing the helping habit early (so children take it for granted and think of it as a natural part of home life) simplifies the whole teaching process.

In Linda Garner's childhood home, everyone had responsibilities from the time they were very little. Linda says, "We *expected* to help. It never entered our heads to think we should be the only one *not* to help. Now I let my own small children help while they are little and want to. They scrub floors, do dishes, etc. even if I have to do it over, because it gives them a feeling of importance and is teaching them to expect to help. They also have their regular duties, such as taking dirty clothes to the clothes chute, though the oldest is only four."

"Children most often rebel against the unexpected," said Narda Woodford, "but if responsibility around the house is a natural part of their daily routine from the time they are young, they expect it and don't fight it." The five Woodford children have definite jobs to do from the time they are small, and know they are not allowed to play until their work is done. They have three rules about work: 1. Don't fight. 2. Work fast. 3. Tell mother when you are done.

Narda always checks a job to make sure it has been done well and she says, "I'm very fussy about how they do their jobs, but I'm careful not to give them jobs that are too hard for a child their age to do well." Narda feels that if they are encouraged to finish their work quickly and well, then they can feel relaxed and free to play. Her children know they will be expected to help for about a half hour after they get home from school, and Narda keeps a daily list in the kitchen where she jots down things she notices during the day that she would like the children to do when they get home. Narda notes that when there are several children in the family, there seems to be a natural tendency to have the older children do more than their share. The youngest child often just "gets by" and loses the feeling of contributing. So Narda makes it a practice to start thinking of the littlest first when a job needs to be done. "Can Alisa do it? Is she capable?" If not, then she thinks of the next oldest child, etc.

It's our Home—So It's our Work Too!

Helena Evans believes that children feel better when they share the responsibilities of the family and get the concept that it's "our" family. She suggests that the family sit down periodically and plan together what needs to be done. They found weekly home evenings were a good time to do this. "The key to cooperation," Helena said, "is to have the children be part of the whole process so they feel like it is their home, too, and that they are an important part of it!"

"Children need to have the concept that housework is not just 'Mom's work' and they are not just helping Mom with 'her' work," commented Karen Reilley, mother of eight. "If I didn't have the kids, I wouldn't have most of the work; but the work is there, so the only fair way is to cooperate, work together, and share the load. Then we can work together *and* play together, instead of mother doing all the work, while they do all the playing. I often catch myself saying, 'I need you to do' or 'We need such and such done,' and with eight children I'm not kidding—that need is very real. I let my children know that I'm depending on them and that I expect their very best—that we all need them to do their best for the good of the family."

Karen's three oldest children have one major job each week, on a rotating basis. Their rule is that they have to be finished before they can play. Karen says, "I don't clean house all day while the kids are in school so they can come home and play. I do the things they can't do, then supervise them in the housework they can do when they get home. If they don't do a job right, I have them do it over until it is acceptable, even if it cuts into playing time. If they are allowed to play before work, they don't get their priorities straight. We feel they should have school homework, housework, churchwork, and any other family responsibilities caught up first—then they can play. If they are planning on being away from home for a scout overnight campout, or similar activity, they must have their work done in advance where possible or trade jobs with someone else."

We asked Karen how she keeps a good feeling between herself and the children when she is enforcing these work standards and rules in their home. She replied, "The key is for Mom to stay in control and simply be firm but not mean or punitive. I remember reading in a church magazine that punishment hurts, but 'firmness directs, influences, and persuades along desirable paths.' " Karen has noticed that as long as she stays in control, and is "nice" in her firmness, the children usually stay in control, too, and are cheerful about the work.

Pick a Plan to Fit Your Needs

In the Malin and Myreel Lewis family, the first home evening in September is devoted to making up the job schedule for the school year. Each of their twelve children choose the jobs which fit best with his or her schedule (the number of jobs depends on the age of the child). Then Myreel dittos off a chart showing each person's responsibilities and the amount of allowance which will be paid at the end of each week if all jobs are checked off. At the end of the week, each child is responsible to see that his chart is marked and on Myreel's desk by Monday morning, or they will not be paid. Myreel said, "We chose to change chores annually for several reasons. First, it saves arguments. Second, it is easier for mother to keep in mind the chores and check up on them." Malin adds, "If a child's duties are rotated too often, the child does not develop a habit and does not become as proficient, and mother and father cannot keep track of whose turn it is. Children tend to take advantage of this by saying 'It's not my turn!' " Myreel believes that consistency is the most important word to a mother trying to teach responsibility. She says, "Sometimes it may even border on nagging, but I believe it is better to remind than to let them be lazy or irresponsible." Myreel suggests that following through with whatever consequence you give a child is imperative. "If a child doesn't measure up in taking his responsibilities, then see that you measure up and follow through with consequences!" Malin is firm in his belief that "Work is necessary for salvation, and a child must learn to work as soon as he can understand 'Pick it up'."

Most parents agreed that there was no system or method for teaching good work habits which could be used indefinitely, and they felt the need to change methods occasionally to add incentive to their work program. Dean and Claudia Black said, "We have changed our system several times in the past few years." "Right now we are using the *job-card* system," Claudia stated. "We made a list of all the jobs that need to be done each day. Then we listed one job on each card, and asked the children to divide up the cards. They were quite relieved when we redivided the job cards with Dean and I each taking our share, too. We explained that by dividing the work at our house, we can all have the time to fulfill our goals, but this is possible only when each person does his share of the routine chores. For the Job-Card system, the jobs were listed on different colored cards according to the time of day they should be done. The children kept the cards in separate envelopes attached to a chart, with one for the jobs to do, and an envelope to put the card in when the job is completed.

"Five-year-old Adams' favorite job was emptying the dishwasher. He was small for his age, but I placed the dishes, silverware, and pans in low cupboards which are accessible to all the children, so he was able to put everything away without climbing on a chair. This arrangement is also helpful when the children set the table or cook. Since three-year-old Christopher is the youngest, one of his jobs was 'Treasure Hunt' (cleaning under the beds). This job has always been reserved for the smallest member of our household because they can easily climb under the beds. Christopher thinks this is a very important job, and of course it is! We tell the children every job is important because they all need to be done to keep our home neat and clean, and things running smoothly.

"Other methods we have used to train the children have been the *Punch Card System* and the *Black Family Buck Plan.* To initiate the Punch Card method, I listed all the jobs on paper, and then made four charts on poster paper assigning the children a different combination of jobs on each chart. This allows us to rotate jobs every month, and no one has the same set of jobs again for four months, then we start over again. The children really enjoyed this because it kept the work from being too monotonous. There are some jobs on the charts which the child does because he is a part of the family, but certain jobs are worth a pre-determined amount of money, and they are identified by a smiley face. Each child has a 3 x 5 card with numbers around the outside. When he has completed his nonpaying jobs, he can do a job he is paid for and have me punch his card. If he doesn't do the job, I don't nag or scold, I simply do it myself, and punch my own card. Then I write on the back of my card what the punch was for. When a child has his card completely punched, (the young children have fewer numbers on their card than the older ones), he can collect. However, we subtract money for the jobs which mother has done for him.

"The Black Family Buck plan was one of our most successful. We made some "Black Family Bucks" which resemble dollar bills. On them there is a blank for his name, the job he did, and how much he can exchange the Buck for in real money. The Buck is filled out only after mother has inspected the job. Each of the children has two sets of jobs—the paying, and the nonpaying. If a child decides he doesn't want to do one of the nonpaying jobs, he can hire one of the other children to do it, and allow him to earn the Buck. Every Monday night as part of our family night, we would read through each child's Family Bucks (which they kept in special envelopes), and comment on the good help he or she had given. Then my husband would ceremoniously give each child his money for his Bucks. This system gave us the chance to let the child know what positive contributions he had made to our family and give him a pat on the back for it, as well as giving them some money to learn to manage."

Some parents felt that work can and should be fun (at least in part). Many families had ideas to help. They suggested such things as music to work by, stories, songs, riddles, and heart to heart talks while doing dishes (or any job where two or more work together). Pretend games work well for smaller children. The boys can pretend to be the cleaning man, the grocery man, mailman, Daddy, waiters, or laundry man. The girls can be the cleaning lady, laundress, waitress, Mom, cook, maid, etc., and sometimes even using appropriate costumes.

Check up on Chores with Charts

Jean Porcaro believes that job boxes, or charts of some kind help make the work in a home run more smoothly. She has used various methods such as a printed floor plan which had the jobs written on the square representing a room along with the name of the person responsible to do them, and job cards for each child.

Snapshots of their children doing each of the jobs they are assigned in the home is the creative chart arrangement of the Krzymowski family. These snapshots make it possible for even the children who cannot read to tell at a glance what they are supposed to do that day.

Betty Ellsworth also feels that charts have been her saving grace. She adds, "A house must be cleaned, and there is no way a mother can do everything. (Of course, she wouldn't want to, because then she would not be teaching her children responsibility.) But a chart helps a mother delegate all the small tasks that children can help with. When my children were little, I ran off on a ditto a chart with pictures of the things they were supposed to do. There was a picture of the vacuum, and the sink, and the dishes, and their beds. Then each child would write their own name by the picture of what they would do to help that week. As they got older, we divided up the entire house either by room, or by job. We talked about their jobs as opportunities to learn to work. We felt that too many times young people grow up with the idea that work is for somebody else, and we wanted to help them understand and feel how important work is in their own lives."

Mary Safsten tells her eleven children, "It is not because I am lazy that you do whatever you are able. Dad and I feel strongly that the way to learn is to do, and satisfaction comes from being independent. Learning to work will bring satisfaction and independence." Mary's general philosophy is: "If they can do it—let them do it. That's the way they learn and that is the way they gradually take on responsibility. One-year-old Sherna can now put on her socks, so I let her do that while I do something for her which she cannot do for herself. If twelve-year-old Mark volunteers to bring some cookies for a scout meeting, that's fine; but he will make them himself, because I don't feel I should make them when he knows how to fulfill the obligation himself. As for methods, we've had several different charts, each listing daily jobs and Saturday jobs, which the children have to check off before they go play. I found I can't use the same method for very long because the children tire of it. The one we are using now has three wheels. One is for jobs which the younger children can do (such as empty the garbage and help with dishes and care for pets). One is for jobs which the middle children can do (such as clean bathrooms, vacuuming, and outside jobs). The third is for jobs which the older girls do (such as the total dish responsibility, cleaning the family room, and helping with laundry). Each wheel has the jobs listed around the edge, and the names of who will do the jobs are on a separate piece of paper attached under the wheel so that they show through slots cut in the wheel. The wheel is rotated each week to change the name of the child who is responsible for each job."

YOUNGER CHILDREN **MIDDLE CHILDREN** **OLDER CHILDREN**

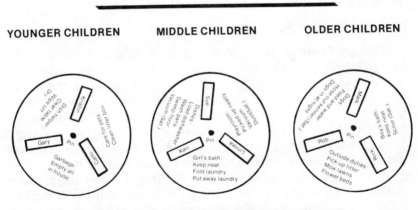

Hustle not Hassle

Carol Davis says she just cannot be happy if she has to hassle her six children about doing their work. So she said, "We have tried lots of little things, and we have to keep changing. We find there are many things that can give the children incentives. At one time when they were smaller, we decided to give them fifty pennies a week if they did their work. When they are young, those pennies look like a million dollars. Their Daddy would come home with a few rolls of pennies, and then we would look at the chart. They were responsible to check their own charts so I didn't have to worry about that." Carol adds, "Lots of people feel this type of thing is just too much work, but it is more than worth it to me not to have to hassle the children. And I *don't* hassle them about their work. If they come and say, 'Can I play?' I may say, 'Have you done your work?' and that is all I say. At the end of the week—if they don't get paid, they feel the results of not doing what they are expected to do. All it usually takes is one week. I feel it is the best way to learn responsibility when we suffer the consequences of our own actions."

Janice Burton found that charts were helpful for a time in order to establish good habits, but were not essential indefinitely. The Burtons had a detailed check-chart for about a year which was a lot of bother for everyone, but which accomplished the purpose of helping the children get in the habit of doing all their regular jobs. Janice says, "Now they do those jobs on their own, and it only takes me about five minutes in the morning to walk through the house and check to make sure everything has been done before anyone leaves for school."

Work Has Its Own Rewards

Melba Flandro said, "We've always told our children 'No matter where you live you are going to have responsibilities (whether it is in the mission field with companions, in the dormitory with roommates, or in your own home). So you might as well learn responsibility in our home right now.' Some people have the idea that you should make all this fun, like making a game out of carrying out the garbage. But I believe people should learn how to work for the satisfaction of working. It doesn't have to be drudgery, but I believe they should feel the basic satisfaction of doing the job and having it done." Lillian Bradshaw said in the June, 1968 Relief Society magazine, "Whether or not our children like to work has never been our main concern. There will be work to do all their lives, and some work is just plain work no matter how you look at it.

"That they learn how to work in as many varied experiences as possible is our first objective, but my ultimate aim as a mother is to teach my children the *joy* of work."

"As they learn to dig in and really help, they learn there are satisfactions involved," stated Karen Reilley. "I think of the time

I taught my thirteen-year-old to organize and clean the basement. He was restless at first and said, 'Gee, Mom, how long will this take?' But he stuck with it and a few days later he used the same ideas I had taught him, to clean and organize the shed. He came running in and said, 'Mom, come and see! Just look what I did with this shed!' He had done a very good job without any super-vision, and I asked, 'How does that make you feel to make such an improvement in the way that shed looks?' He said, 'I feel so good, I'd like to clean it all over again!' Of course, we can't expect that our children will always be that enthusiastic, but they *can* learn to feel the satisfactions of a job well done."

Give Them a Broader View

We laughed with one mother who said, "My secret to get my small children to love work is to be ineffecient, inconsistent, but enthusiastic! I tried assigned chores and kept charts, but I still did most of the work. Now instead of having them do the chores, I have them keep house. I have them work *with* me, not *for* me, and we all have more fun while the work gets done! For example, when I mop the floor, they clean the baseboards; when I am vacuuming a room, they dust it."

"I want my girls to enjoy their home," Helen Sharp comment-ed, "and that is why I don't give them jobs to do, as such, but instead of saying, 'Here are your jobs for today', I will say, 'This is your list to help you learn how to be good mothers.' If they are trained from the time they are little that learning to work helps to make them better wives and mothers, then it puts work in a whole new light. I also really stress how it makes you feel when the work is all done, and the feeling of accomplishment you get afterwards. A wider perspective helps me, too. Instead of saying, 'I have all these things to do today', I can say, 'I'm doing these things in order to be an example because I've got the bigger job of training my children to live successfully'."

Gayla Wise recalls, "One night as I went in to kiss my six-year-old goodnight, I tripped over the slacks he'd worn that day. I said to him, 'What are you going to do when you go on your mission? I won't be there to pick up your clothes, you know.' 'You won't?' he questioned, his eyes growing big. It was obvious he had never thought of that before. 'No, I won't, and when it's time to go teach people, what would you do if your clothes were in a wrinkled heap on the floor?' He instantly understood in a new frame of reference why he should learn to pick up his own clothes."

Giving children a "broader view" can be helpful in many different ways. When they realize they need to know how to cook and clean house and take care of their clothes in order to be successful missionaries, roommates, or husbands and wives, rather than just because Mom doesn't want to do it for them, their motivation to learn will be far greater.

More Motivations to Keep Them Moving

Joye Billings, one of fifteen children, said, "Many times my mom's methods were simple in motivating us to work. She used no charts, and no rewards other than letting us do as we pleased when the work was done. But she made work pleasant because we did it together. She might say that if five of us would come and clean up the kitchen, we could have it done in five minutes. And we would. On days when all of us were going to be home from school, she would plan a big project—such as tying or piecing a quilt, canning or cleaning; then she would say, 'Let's all work together for an hour today on this project, then you may do whatever you wish.' An hour out of the day didn't sound like too great a sacrifice, and we would all pitch in." Joye said it was astounding how much they could get done in an hour with that many willing hands, and the children learned to enjoy working together.

This principle can work with any number of willing hands. When the entire family pitches in, it helps youngsters associate work with pleasure. Pitching in as a family to share the routine encourages a cooperative attitude and gives a sense of family solidarity. Darla tells us, "I remember as a child, when I was helping and cooperating, I felt great." Arlene adds, "Some of my best memories are memories when we were all working together as a family. Everybody had specific things to do, and we all had that feeling of unity and accomplishment." Darla said, "For instance, when we were canning corn, we knew that each of us was needed because it was such a big job. Those were sharing times, which I remember gave me a feeling of importance."

Katherine Gifford uses the kitchen timer to good advantage in motivating her children to do their tasks quickly. She feels that it helps to give them a time goal to work for. She might say, "How long do you think it should take you to clear the table?" Then when they tell her, she sets the timer and says, "Now let's see if you can beat the timer and finish before it rings." She also uses the system of "Everybody pick up ten things and let's see how quickly we can straighten the house." She believes if children have a clear, definable task, they do not feel overwhelmed and are more willing to help.

Appreciation was the best motivation used by Elaine Christiansen. She said, "The minute I went out of the house, my daughter would get out the vacuum and scrub brush, and clean the house. Nothing delighted her more than to have us come home and say, 'Wow! Who cleaned this house? It looks great!' and I would generously praise her for her thoughtfulness and ability to make the house look so good. I think my children continued to do this sort of thing because I always let them know how much I appreciated it."

One mother used hidden pennies as motivators; as the children cleaned, they could keep any pennies they found. Another gave a "Clean Bedroom" award each week.

Some years ago, the Robert Porcaros began to give their children a super incentive to get their work done, and they call it Super Saturday! Every Saturday when the children finish all their work and the weather is nice, they go on an outing together. They have enjoyed swimming, hiking, bike riding, and playing games at the park or soccer and baseball at the school playground. They have also visited the zoo, the boat harbor, church history sites, and many other places of interest. Several other parents mentioned using this type of incentive. One mother remembers, "Saturday was our big working day—but we always had a great motivation to finish because when we were through with our work, we had family activities and we knew we couldn't get started with the fun until the work was done." Betty Ellsworth mentioned that when her children were little, they would all go for an ice cream cone when everyone had their Saturday work done, which gave the bigger children a reason to help the little ones so that they could all go together.

Give Children a Choice

Helena Evans feels that it is of utmost importance to let the children choose their own jobs periodically, so they feel personally responsible for them. She said, "It worked for us to start with the smallest child and say, 'Now what can little Susy do to help?' Then we would proceed on up to the oldest, letting the children choose their jobs and write them down on lists or little cards to remind them during the week what their jobs were to be."

Lillian Bradshaw told her children something like "You must work, but your free agency lies in whether or not you choose to be happy working." She also feels that we can respect the children's need for independence by giving choices as to the work they do. In her previously quoted article in the 1968 Relief Society magazine, Lillian said, "Our daily work schedule is rather rigid, each knowing his duties on Monday for the following week. But on Saturday, I list all the work to be accomplished, including outside work, and then I sprinkle in work that is more fun, like arranging flowers in the house, or making jello salad for Sunday. The list is long and fairly well broken down. Then they go round-robin. Each selects his first choice which is always the easy one, then the second choice, ending usually with the harder third choices, thereby each sharing in what they choose to call the 'icky' jobs. Making their *own choices* keeps them from complaining that I gave one hard work and the other the easy work."

Sometimes we can't give children a choice, but we can allow children the freedom to complain. Janice Burton believes children have a right to complain sometimes. She says, "It is unreasonable to expect children to be cheerful about everything we ask them to do. First we make demands, then we demand that they be cheerful about our demands, and that's really not fair." She believes the important thing is not to react to their complaints, and never say, "I wish you wouldn't grumble" or "Why can't you just do what you are told to do without complaining", etc. She calls that "counter-grumbling" and believes this gets you involved at their level, and sometimes makes them feel you might change your mind about the request. But if you say nothing, and let them talk, they soon talk themselves out and they go do what they were asked to do.

To Pay or not to Pay?

You may have noticed that money was part of the plan of several of the families we have just mentioned. There seemed to be three distinct opinions about this subject. There were parents who were unequivocally against payment for chores. They said things like: "Children who are paid for routine help are cheated because the emphasis is put on earning money rather than on being helpful", or "It is their home as much as it is ours." The second group of parents believe in paying only for special or extra jobs such as heavy cleaning jobs, and babysitting. These parents said it made sense to them, and to the children, to separate the jobs which must be done routinely, and those not usually required into nonpaying and paying categories. The last group of parents has the practice of paying for most chores done in the home, (excluding care of their own room and clothing) then requiring the older children to buy their own clothing and pay most of their own expenses. They felt that this system can teach the children not only how to work, but how to manage their own money as well.

Ian and Floy Dawn Mackay told us their plan in detail: "Levi Strauss was the inspiration for our family's financial arrangements with the children. He charged fifteen dollars for a pair of pants, while an 'unknown' brand of similar style was eight dollars. Our two teenage boys preferred worn out, patched Levis to the eight dollar brand. Having come from a family where thrift was considered both a necessity and a true art, I found myself on an endless campaign to promote the virtues of eight dollar pants (always returning to the most obvious one, that you could get two pair for the price of one of Levis!) The boys were not rebellious. They understood the logic. But they were firm in their loyalty to Strauss. This and several other circumstances caused us to take a hard look at our "money as you need it" plan and prompted us to change. We wanted a plan which would teach responsibility and the value of long-range planning. So we set up the following plan based on the premise that we are placed on earth to learn and that learning is enhanced and fortified by actual doing—making your own choices and being responsible for, and taking, the consequences of those choices.

"*First,* the children are responsible for cleaning their own rooms without pay, and it must be done on Saturday before anyone (individually) is allowed to leave—even to an important baseball game. If they've been especially busy with homework, I help them.

"*Second,* they get NO money as an allowance. They simply have the opportunity to earn what they need. All the jobs are listed on a worksheet at the rates we pay. As they do the job, they make a check on their own sheet.

"*Third,* each child has three or four meals they must provide kitchen help for. We take care in assigning fairly permanent times that are convenient for each person. If they cannot do the job, they must negotiate with another child for a trade. They do get paid for these tasks, but this is primarily for the benefit of the younger children who would have no money if not paid for rather routine tasks. The two teenagers rarely mark this on their charts. They consider it an assistance to me, and of small monetary value. They keep track only when they need money badly. Our pay scale is fairly generous for larger tasks (about what it would cost if we hired the work to be done), and they are paid twice a month—the day after we get our paycheck. When they have the money in one sum, they know how much they have to work with, and they are learning to manage it well.

"*Fourth,* if they run out of money, there is credit ONLY in the most unusual circumstances. They are reminded that having money for what you want takes planning and they must plan ahead (trying to earn four dollars in an hour just won't make it!) The children are required to pay for shoes, school supplies, movies, birthday presents, etc., and the teens also must buy all outer clothing.

"The benefits have been: the children have their own savings accounts, and they like to save. They try to save at least part of everything they make. There is much greater incentive to work than existed before because the children can now see the relationship between work and satisfying their needs and wants. The children have learned how to work. (Recently, one boy got a job cleaning up an old house, and the employer said he worked like a grown man.) Mother is learning, too—sometimes fifteen dollar pants *are* better than eight dollar pants. The fifteen dollar pants lasted twice as long, looked better all the time, and did not shrink nearly as much as the less expensive ones! Finally, the children LIKE making their own choices. There is a better attitude about listening to Mom and Dad's advice, because that is what it is—advice, not demands.

"The disadvantage to our plan is that it takes time for the bookkeeping, and the children don't like that part (although it certainly helps their math!) Also, I have to take time to help the younger ones. This plan will not work unless you can say 'no' when they don't have money and need something they haven't planned for. But we found we could do that if we reminded ourselves that was the only way they were going to learn."

Willis and Lynnette Brimhall also have the philosophy that learning to manage money is part of learning to be responsible, and each month they give their children a "Requirement Budget" (money for the main essentials they require). Willis talks over with them their needs for the month, and they agree on a certain amount. Each child has a three column budget book where they list their income, expenses, and balance. They keep this record current and Willis reviews the record with them before he gives them the money for the new month. The Brimhalls believe that having the experience of buying their own things, and keeping track of their expenses is excellent training, and has helped the children learn to make wiser choices. Lynnette says, "It's interesting how some of the things they thought were essentials when we were buying are not so important anymore when they have to put out their own money for them!" Willis adds, "I believe that we have the responsibility to help the children learn how to manage their money because learning good money management is fundamental in order to have a successful marriage."

Ten Things to Try

1. Analyze the "Accomplishment Chart" idea. Would it work in your family?
2. Try to think of the youngest child in your family first when a job needs to be done (in order to give the younger ones a feeling of contributing and being important, too!)
3. Decide if choosing and keeping the same chores for the whole school year could be practical for your family.
4. Try making jobs easier for younger children by trying ideas such as placing dishes, etc., in low cupboards so small children can help more easily.
5. Try making work fun by using music to work by or using pretend games with young children.
6. If you aren't presently using a chart to help you keep track of chores, check the ideas in the chart section to see if any of them would fill the bill for your family.
7. Consider using money as a reward to motivate children to work and give you an opportunity to help children learn good money management.
8. Work together as a family to help children feel part of a team and learn the fun of joint effort.
9. Give children time goals and deadlines to motivate them to finish their work quickly.
10. Try hidden pennies, "Clean Bedroom" awards, "Super Saturday Outing", and choices for additional incentives.

17

Skills for Turning Mountains Into Molehills

"When I was a young boy, I was out playing on my bike," said Rex Stallings. I hit a rock with my front tire and went flying over the handlebars and landed on my elbow. It started to bleed and it hurt like crazy! I wanted my mother and started running for home as fast as I could! I found Mom busy in the kitchen; but she stopped what she was doing, picked me up and said, 'Well now, we'll have to see what we can do to make it better.' I re-member the warm feeling of being held in her arms. She washed the wound and put iodine on it (and the iodine hurt even worse than the scrape!) But somehow the hurt didn't matter anymore because inside I had a special warm feeling that said, 'Everything is going to be all right.'

"That inner peace (knowing that everything will ultimately be all right, and that we will be taken care of) is what the Lord has promised if we keep His commandments. Righteousness does not bring exemption from problems or adversity; but it does give us the courage to meet them and be strengthened by them; to feel in the midst of the hurt that everything will turn out for the best."

Life is a series of problems to be solved, and problem solving is one of the most valuable skills we can teach our children. Many families we interviewed contributed ideas that can help us and our children become better problem solvers.

Learn to Foresee and Prevent

Some felt the most effective way of handling problems is to foresee and prevent them! Lucene Hougaard said one of her favorite methods of preventing problems with her six children is the "What would you do if?" game. She suggests a variety of situations her children may have to face and says things like, "If someone asks you to let them copy your answers, what would you do?" She feels that to get a right choice firmly established in a child's mind *before* the situation comes up gives him an ad-vantage and real leverage if he is faced with the actual situation.

A technique Faye McFarland uses for problem prevention is taking time to explain new experiences before they happen. For example, before her children go to the dentist she tells them what will probably happen, how it will feel, and how they will be expected to act. When her little girl started kindergarten, Faye explained to her what kinds of things she would be doing there, and prepared her for the fact that many of the other chil-dren wouldn't know how to read as she did (but they might know a lot of other things she didn't know, and she must be patient and kind). Faye feels this type of explanation has helped enor-mously in avoiding problems and helping her children enjoy new experiences.

Karen Reilley said, "Certain rules in our home help us to avoid problems. For instance, we have the rule that the older children keep their hands off each other. When they are angry, they may say how they feel, but may not attack the other person. We have found that just being able to verbalize feelings is like a pressure valve that releases the pressure of bad feelings, but that physical hurting just isn't necessary or beneficial."

Many times children do not profit from making mistakes or prolonging a conflict. To keep many problems from happening and to keep small problems from getting big, try:

1. Arbitrating *before* two boys come to blows over a wagon.

2. Suggesting a new activity *before* children grow tired and irritable.

3. Preparing children *before* a new experience through positive teaching.

4. Planning in advance the activities you *do* want children to do.

Elvin Christiansen believes that when you build a strong foundation when children are young, it is like preventative medicine that can help them avoid most of the problems later on. What you have taught them in these formative years stays with them and continues to guide them when they are not so willing to accept direct counsel.

Listen, Listen!

Since we as parents cannot possibly prevent or avoid all problems, we need to learn an effective process for helping children talk through problems and find solutions. One method might be illustrated by a triangle:

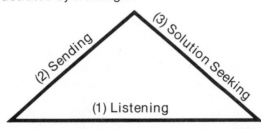

The base of the triangle is always *listening.* By encouraging a child to talk about a problem, he can often clarify it in his own mind, and find his own solution. Talking freely can help him sort and identify his feelings so he can begin to understand himself and the problem better.

Problems are often accompanied by strong feelings which do not vanish by being banished. (Now, Johnny, you mustn't feel that way!) However, they almost always diminish in intensity and lose their sharp edges when a kind listener accepts them with sympathy and understanding.

Many times children get very upset about things which seem like trivialities to adults. At such times, it will help to remind ourselves that it is the child's feelings that should be taken seriously, not the cause (which may not be serious at all).

We also need to remember that when a child is in the midst of strong emotions he himself cannot listen. This is not the time to counsel, advise, point out responsibility, etc. Emotion might be compared with a fire. If a parent criticizes, counter-attacks, or becomes emotional about his child's negative emotions, it is like pouring gasoline on the fire; it is sure to burn hotter and it might explode. But if the parent listens; (just listens) it is like pouring water on the fire. Nothing burns without fuel, and before long the fire will burn itself out and the child will feel more calm again.

This is true for adults as well as children. For example, if a wife has had a terrible day with the kids and everything has gone wrong, if her husband listens to her problems sympathetically (even if she becomes very emotional) and says something like, "It has been a tough day for you, hasn't it?" her problem and her negative emotions may disappear. But if he says, "For Pete's sake, can't you see your problem is that you need to get better organized?" or "When will you learn to handle the kids without getting so upset?", her problem (and her bad feelings) will probably double.

Similarly, if we begin pointing out how a child brought the problem on himself, or that it is an indication of what he needs to learn in some area, or if we say, "You're old enough to know better than to get yourself in such a situation", we invariably compound his problem (and lose the possibility of having the child listen responsively to advice or counsel we might be able to give him). But a sympathetic response creates intimacy; love is deepened when we feel understood. One counselor summed it this way, "Let our communications with our children be bathed in warmth and caring."

Keep Them Talking

Bernice Ursenbach said, "I have learned that you can sometimes really help children solve their own problems by just letting them talk; but the key is to keep them talking. If one of my children says, 'Mom, George is mad at me!' and I say 'What did you do to him?' the conversation might end right there. But if I say, 'It really does bother you when someone is mad at you', then he keeps talking, and I just listen, and through being able to share feelings without being condemned or lectured to he might find out his problem is not so bad after all and go his way feeling fine again."

Bernice's way of keeping her child talking is an example of "Reflective Listening", a technique which has been widely discussed in recent years. "Reflective Listening" involves stating in our own words what we think the other person has said or what he is feeling, and encouraging him to continue. By doing this we test the accuracy of our listening and show our interest and desire to understand the other person. One authority called this "The Healing Dialogue."

Thelma Jones mentioned that when her four older children were little, she had never heard of reflective listening. But when her youngest son was a teenager, she learned about it in Relief Society and decided to try it. She said, "Previously, when my son started talking about a problem I might have pointed out what he'd done wrong or what he could do better and he would immediately turn me off and wouldn't talk anymore. But after I heard this lesson, when my son came to me and told me about a problem he had at school I said, 'That was really hard for you, wasn't it?' He looked at me a little strangely, then said, 'Yes, Mom, and do you know what happened?' and he talked and talked. I became very converted and really tried to use reflective listening from then on."

However, we must adjust our responses to each child's needs. Annette Capener said, "I have two daughters who are so different it is almost funny. They require entirely different "listening skills" from me. One *wants* me to get excited when she gets excited, and if I 'play it cool' she says, 'Oh Mom, you don't even care!' My other daughter, if I respond a bit emotionally says, "Oh Mom, don't get all excited. I just want you to listen!"

"One thing I believe," said Helena Evans, "is that if a child is allowed to express himself freely and the parent is secure enough himself not to feel threatened, it is much better for the child, and makes problem solving much easier." If we listen, and respond with understanding, not criticism, our children will probably feel they can tell us anything—then *we* will be in a position to know what their problems really are and *they* will be in a frame of mind to listen to our counsel and guidance.

The Right Time for a Parent to Talk

Once you are sure your child has talked his problem out and has calmed down, then a parent can often move tactfully to the "sending" part of the triangle illustration (on page 267). If you "send" too soon, however, he *won't* listen: he will still be "Hung up" on his own feelings. But if you have really listened, and he gets to the point where he is through talking and hasn't solved his own problem, then he will probably be ready to listen to your view of the situation.

Two mothers gave examples of effective "sending" a parent might do after a problem has been talked through and the feeling tone is calm.

Connie Maughan had a deacon-age son who was asked to go to the local Rest Home and help pass the sacrament to the old people. He refused without any explanation. Connie couldn't understand why, and since her husband was in the bishopric, she felt strongly that her son should help out. But she didn't demand, or accuse him of being thoughtless, or tell him that he would be grounded if he didn't go. Instead, she sat down and talked with him in an understanding way. She said something like, "Son, I really would like to know what is troubling you. It just isn't like you not to be willing to help out when you are needed. Is there something special you would like to talk over with me about not wanting to go to the old folk's home?" The boy broke down into tears, and admitted reluctantly that he was afraid of the old people and didn't know how to act around them. She listened quietly until he was all through talking about it. Then Connie talked to him about old people. She told him about his grandpa and how they had to care for him, dress him, and feed him before he died. She told him about the aging process and reminded him that someday his own parents could be the ones that wanted the sacrament, and if he thought about that, maybe it would be a little easier. After their talk, he went gladly to help at the Rest Home. His mind was changed because his attitude was changed through concern and understanding. She cared enough to listen and not judge, then shared her own perspective.

Bernice Ursenbach said that after she listened to a child's full account of a problem, she would try to help them find some redeeming thing about the situation or at least help them see it wouldn't last forever. She would sometimes remind them of other times when they felt they had a huge problem, and how well they handled it (and how quickly the problem had faded into insignificance). For instance, she would say, "Remember last Christmas when you didn't have enough money to get just the sweater you wanted for Karen. You thought at the time that the world was going to fall apart because that seemed so important to you. But you worked it out and found a good solution (and found out that life went on without the expensive sweater). I'm sure you are just as capable of handling this problem and that you will soon see it isn't as devastating as it may look to you."

How to Help Them Seek Solutions

Many times problems will be solved through the listening or sending steps of the triangle, but some problems require solutions reached only through proceeding to the third side of the triangle illustrated on page 267 (solution seeking and analyzing). Learning to help children help themselves in this solution-seeking step is a skill worth working for. Karen Reilley said, "I try to get my children to do their own thinking and solve their own problems as much as possible. (If I tried to solve them all, I would not get anything else done!) I say things to the children like, 'What do *you* think would work best?' or 'What do *you* think will happen if you do such and such' or 'Let's see how many alternatives we can think of, then you can decide which you would rather do.' For each alternative they write down, I have them try to visualize the end result. I try to teach them that we can learn to think through our own problems and see which solution is best because of the results it would probably bring. When a child makes a decision that I can see is going to be a mistake, if it isn't serious I let him follow through and learn from the experience. For instance, Franky was going to work on a science project with a certain child. I knew that this combination wouldn't work and they wouldn't get a thing done. But I let him go ahead, and then talked with him afterwards and had him analyze why the day had been wasted."

Most parents feel that children learn more through helping find solutions to their own problems than if the parent imposes a solution. We can help the process along by asking questions like "How do you think this problem should be handled?" or "What do you think should be done about it?" When inviting solutions we should listen to *all* possibilities and not judge or evaluate. To keep children thinking, we might say, "That's one way we can consider; can you think of any other ways?" When they run out of ideas, and have visualized the possible results of each, we can help them choose the solution that looks best and commit to whatever action or change is necessary to carry it out. We might also set a time to get back together and discuss how well the solution is working. (Children should be guided to choose an alternate solution if the original one isn't getting the desired results!)

Problem Solving Pointers

Several parents mentioned miscellaneous pointers.

1. *Stay Calm.* Julia Moore, who has eight children and a Lamanite foster son, said her formula for problem solving is simple—stay calm. "If Mom stays calm, then things even out quickly," Julia said, "but if she doesn't, a small problem can become a real disaster."

2. *Try Interviews.* One family has started having weekly interviews with each of their children where the problem solving process unfolds naturally. They report they can hardly believe the improvement they have seen in their family since they started this plan.

3. *Play-Acting can Solve Problems.* Faye McFarland uses play-acting as a problem solving technique. For example, her oldest daughter, Kathleen, was slower to make friends than her second daughter, Rosalie, and Kathleen felt badly about this. One day Faye said, "Kathleen, let's pretend we are going to a new school and I'll play I'm a girl coming along the hall and you practice what to say." "Hello, my name is Faye. What's your name?" they began. By playing this "game" with both girls, she discovered the difference was that Rosalie always countered with a question which kept the conversation going and helped her learn more about the other person, while Kathleen just gave a short answer or said, "Oh". By getting better perspective of the problem, she was able to help Kathleen practice at home to be a better conversationalist and question-asker which helped her make friends more easily. Faye has used this same procedure to solve other problems.

4. *Remember when you were Young.* One author said that a good way to help a child get his problems into perspective is to tell him about some of the troublesome episodes in our own

childhoods. Recounting a time when we brought home a bad grade on our report card or told a white lie that got us into trouble can "humanize" us to our children and help them see that growing up wasn't all fun for us, either. If we are open and honest about admitting some of our past weaknesses and problems, a child will feel less need to wear a mask of bravado or indifference. It's the moral support that counts—the realization that "I'm not the only one."

5. *Try the "Book-Worm" Approach.* Books were always very important in the Calvin Heiner home, and whenever one of the children wanted to know something, Calvin would help them find the answer in a book. So it was only natural to turn to books for problem solving as well. When there was controversy in the family concerning a news item, or any specific subject, they would go to the library and get all available material pro and con and study it out together. When one of the children had a religious problem, question on a gospel topic or how the gospel related to some specific problem, Calvin would look up scriptures, information in church books, church magazines, etc., and help the children see the problem clearly in relation to revealed truth. He never simply passed out pat solutions based on his own opinion, but would say, "Let's look it up." His daughter, Linda, said, "Teenage resistance is much lower to the 'Let's look it up' approach than to the 'I'll tell you what you should do and think' approach."

Of course, the scriptures are one of the best sources we can turn to for solving problems. "When we had our first Indian student in our home," said Rex Stallings, "he was the same age as our oldest boy, and it seems like when you have someone strange come into your house, you have a tendency to pay more attention to them than you do your own. And of course, we were concerned about the Indian student and how he was doing, and he was giving us some problems. My oldest boy said to me one day, 'Dad, do you love Leonard more than you love me?' Well, that brought me to my senses, and in a quick flash I thought of just what I needed to do (it had to be inspiration). We spent a few moments together, just he and I, and I told him the story of the prodigal son and the part I think carried the greatest message where the faithful son said to his father, 'You've never killed a fatted calf for me or had music or dancing,' and the father said, 'All that I have is yours,' and I said to my son, 'Even though we have shown all this special attention to Leonard, all that I have is yours' and I expressed my love to this son of mine. It really solved the problem. It didn't bother him anymore, and whatever we had to do to help Leonard after that, he cooperated and didn't feel left out."

Humor Helps

"I think another thing that has really helped our family solve problems and get through a lot of tough times is a healthy sense of humor," Rex Stallings commented. "We've kind of kept a thread of humor running through the whole family. I remember one time when we sat down to eat and one of the kids spilled a full glass of milk all over the table. Well, I was irritated, and very adamant about telling them that if they would quit fooling around they wouldn't spill their milk. As I brought my arm back from shaking a finger at them, I spilled my milk! We were all quiet for a minute, and then everyone just burst out laughing. Nobody in our house has been scolded for spilling milk since!

"We also have some stories in our family that we often use as a common ground in problem solving. They give us phrases that carry a whole wealth of meaning and give us a chance to laugh together and point out a problem in a noncritical way.

"One of our favorites is the 'fish poem'." (It is actually called 'Man Portrait' and is from a book called *The American Album of Poetry* by Ted Malone.)

> "Look out!" She exclaimed, "There's a bone in your fish!"
> D'ye think he said thanks, Laid it back on the dish!
>
> "Mind your own business, I'll manage alone!"
> And to show independence, he swallowed the bone.
> by Marion Judd

Rex and his wife Barbara laughingly admitted they have often used this poem to remind each other (as well as the children) in a kind way not to resent suggestions, etc.

Annis Duff, in her book *Bequest of Wings* suggests reading humerous books together as a family so that when difficult situations come up we can refer to funny quotes and situations we've laughed about together to ease the tensions and get us over the rough spots.

When your Kids are in Conflict

One problem most parents are faced with is handling conflict between their children. Many of the parents we interviewed had helpful suggestions.

Helen Sharp said, "When my girls were small, whenever they would have a disagreement I could tell them a little story relating to their problem which would quickly end the conflict. I collected good stories from books and from the lives of my own parents and built on these. I have found telling a story so much easier and more effective than scolding and blaming."

LaDawn Jacob also uses the story-telling approach with her six little children. She tells them funny stories such as "Sarah Sourface" and "Tommy the Pig." Later she uses the stories for solving problems. Instead of saying, "Amy, you sure are a grouch today! Why don't you cheer up and quit causing bad feelings?" she will say, "When did Sarah Sourface get in here? Richard did you let her in? I like my sweet Amy so much better—I wish she'd come back." This approach usually results in laughter, good feelings, and improved behavior.

One mother has found it effective to start a story tape or record, or start reading a story when the children are beginning to squabble. They will often become so interested in the story they forget what they were arguing about.

Joella Wolfgramm, mother of four pre-schoolers, said she tries to help her little ones learn from and decrease conflicts by talking to them about it later. She says things like, "It doesn't feel good to be unkind to each other, does it? What else could you have done to solve the problem? Louie, what do you think would have been a better thing to do?"

Helena Evans said, "When my children fought a lot, I tried to determine if maybe they were vying for the chance to fill one of their basic needs (love, security, a feeling of importance, or varied experiences). If I could continually help them fill their needs, the conflict between them seemed to decrease. We have to realize that from age two up a child has to make an enormous transition from thinking they *are* the world, to realizing they are just a speck in the world (even if they *are* an important speck). It's hard for them to make this transition and keep feeling good about themselves all the time.

"We have noticed that another reason for conflict is just the sheer strength of personality in the children. If you get four leaders together and they all want to lead, and no one wants to follow, there is bound to be conflict. So sometimes when our boys were locking horns, my husband would say, 'Now, Mother, that's the Ephraim in them, and you wouldn't want them to belong to any other tribe, now would you?' "

In a B.Y.U. Education Week class on children's quarreling, Lynn Scoresby suggested that blame is an illusion. To say "Who started this fight?" rarely helps determine the cause of the problem (and to think only one person is the cause is usually a myth anyway). It's as though we all have a string around our waists and are hooked to every other family member. There is really no "starting" of any given situation; we are on a continuum, and the relationships and the context have tremendous influence on our behavior. Lynn suggested rather than trying to fix blame when conflict reoccurs, it might be more helpful to analyze:

1. What time of the day does quarreling most often happen?
2. Who is present?
3. What is there about the circumstance that doesn't satisfy the needs of those involved?

If we can see that a child might be causing difficulties because he is feeling "lost in the shuffle" we might give him some special assignment or time for a private chat to make him feel more important and less conflict-prone.

Helping children learn to express their own problems and needs is also likely to decrease family conflicts. The better we can talk and really communicate with each family member, the better the harmony level is likely to be in the home.

Many times when children have a hard time communicating with each other, parents can help them. Lynn Scoresby suggested a parent could say, "There seems to be a problem of communication here; let's see if I can help. Now what is it you are trying to say." And the parent becomes the moderator.

Darlene Gregersen mentioned using a similar approach. She said, "If your children are saying 'He did this!' 'No! he did such and such!' and there is obviously no communication going on between them, the parent can do the talking for both. For instance, he could say, 'Marvin, Kent says you took his basketball and used it in the mud. Is that right?' Then listen. After both have aired their feelings and view of the situation, you could say, 'What would you both like to do about it?' Listen, then repeat back, 'Kent says he would feel good if you cleaned his ball and let him use yours until it's dry. Would you be happy about that?' 'Kent, Marvin says he will clean and let you use his ball, but he feels that he doesn't want you to take his outside now, or he will have the same problem you do.' The parent does not side with either child or pass judgment, just tries to uncover the facts. After children have gone through this process with you a few times, it is very likely they will begin to use the same line of communication on their own."

Lynn Scoresby points out that when a parent is the moderator, the end of the conflict must be negotiated, not imposed; and must be a solution to both. There should not be a victor and a loser. Some of the things he suggested a parent could say to help the negotiation would be "What would you be willing to do to make it better? What will you be willing to do to solve this? What do you think needs to be done, etc.?" He says it is important to get both children to contribute suggestions and tell how they feel about it, and both must agree to change and to work for a better situation.

Two Together Seeking Solutions

Bob and Carolyn Larsen have found creative ways to talk through problems and find solutions. Because they often see the problem differently, Bob asks Carolyn, "What do you see the problem to be?" and they both talk freely about how they see the problem and possible solutions. Then if a solution does not come by talking it over, they try brainstorming. With a creative atmosphere where no one criticizes, they often come up with a solution acceptable to both.

For example, when Bob began working at a job which involved a great deal of paperwork, he worked with it for several months and spent almost every night at his office. But it became apparent he needed help. Since Carolyn is an experienced secretary, she was the obvious one to help him, but she had six children and a home to care for, and was the Relief Society President as well. They talked it over and decided Bob would stay home after dinner and help get the children to bed and then they would both go to his office from 9:00 to 11:00 (leaving their oldest in charge). But neither felt good about being gone from home every night; so they decided to have Bob's office at home. The whole family helped fix up an office so Dad could be at home more and everyone was excited! Now Bob and Carolyn cooperate to get the children to bed; then both work together as before, but they are available if they are needed.

Problem Solving as a Family Affair

Frank and Karen Reilley said, "We solve many problems with impromptu family councils. We simply call the children together, present the problem, and talk until we come up with a solution that all can live with. We did this about the T.V. problem in our home. We called a family council and told the children our objections to certain T.V. shows. 'We want to choose the very best in life,' we explained, 'The best of everything—food, recreation, books, people—and T.V. shows. If something is not uplifting, we don't have to watch it; we can choose to do something else and wait for a good show to come on.' We also explained that the real values of life aren't those they show on many T.V. shows. 'We don't live or believe that way and we shouldn't watch those who do,' we continued. Then we had the whole family make up a 'Family T.V. Code' spelling out our standards and the rules we agreed to follow. It has really helped!"

The Reilley family is typical of many families who told of finding family council a good place for solving mutual problems. (Most families don't try to solve problems with individual children in family council, but talk together about these and then find an appropriate time to counsel privately with the child who has the problem—or who *is* the problem.)

There are several ways to structure a family council according to the needs of the particular family. Some families hold a patriarchal family council where the father always conducts and makes the final decisions. This pattern works especially well for young families. Another pattern is a "family forum" where unanimous decisions are worked for, but majority rules except when parents feel the need to exercise veto power for the best interest of the family.

One family described their democratic approach to family council which is especially tailored for a family of teenagers. They hold it weekly, attendance is voluntary, and a rotating chairmanship gives each member a turn to be in charge. Robert's Rules of Order are followed and the chairman introduces a subject for discussion. Each member must raise his hand to speak, and each has equal voice. After a discussion has been completed, the subject is put to a vote, and the majority rules. This family believes in accentuating *solutions* to problems and therefore they have a rule that any person stating a problem must also have thought of one possible solution. (This avoids gripe sessions with nothing constructive being accomplished.) A secretary keeps minutes of each meeting, and reads them at the first of the next meeting. (This is also a rotating job.) They feel minutes are important to avoid disagreements about decisions made at previous meetings.

The Giles family suggested the following problem-solving guidelines for family councils:

1. *Isolate the Problem.* To keep from getting bogged down in trivia, give everyone a clear idea to begin with of the specific, central issues you will discuss.

2. *Encourage everyone to contribute ideas* and possible solutions to problems. The more ideas you have, the greater your chance of hitting on one that will be really effective. (However, don't insist on complete seriousness—crazy ideas sometimes lead to practical solutions; besides the council should be fun.)

3. *Ask open-ended questions* like "What kinds of things do you think might happen if we tried this idea?" instead of "Do you like this idea?"

4. *Encourage evaluation* after all possible solutions are listed. Help children look at each suggestion with the criteria of whether it would meet the needs of the situation. It is valuable to learn to give and accept constructive criticism and see how ideas can be improved.

5. *Talk About Goals and Alternatives.* Specify and try to agree on what you want to accomplish through the solution to the problem—what is your goal? Then help the children recognize that there are always many ways to reach a goal, and there is almost certain to be one way that will please most of the family members. To identify the alternatives which are most acceptable and consistent with family goals is one of the big tasks of problem solving in family council.

Cynthia Giles concluded, "If your experience is like ours, your children will come to value the open, honest communication a family council promotes. You'll find yourself happier, too, knowing that you're in touch with the way your youngsters' feelings and thoughts are developing." Many families shared the conviction that a council can give each family member a greater feeling of importance as they take part in the family problem solving process, and that the benefits are numerous and far-reaching.

The Spiritual Center of Problem Solving

Many parents talked of a spiritual focus in their approach to their own problems and their children's problems. Carolyn Plain said, "My best problem solving technique is to pray a lot. I find I am often hurt more by my children's problems than they are, and the only way I can help is by praying for them. We had one son who was keeping company with a friend who was not a good influence on him. We talked and talked to him about it but just couldn't get through to him, and for two years we struggled with the problem. But after much praying, one day he could finally see what we were talking about; it was just like a book opening up to him and he accepted what we were saying."

LaDawn Jacob said, "When my children get in conflicts, I often stop them and ask them to all kneel down and have prayer with me. To encourage cooperation and kindness, I tell them, 'You chose each other as brothers and sisters because you loved each other in heaven. Heavenly Father let you live together in our family so you could help each other.'"

Mary Wright, mother of fifteen, said she always tried to teach her children the philosophy that problem-solving is a strengthening process that we can learn and grow from. She made it a practice to sit down with any child who had a problem and talk it over with him, discussing pros and cons, and possible solutions. She shared the philosophy that "any problem can be solved with the help of the Lord", and always advised the children to pray about problems.

"It's frustrating when our children have problems," said Helen Sharp, "because we want so much to help them; yet we are so limited in what we can do. But I've noticed that if I can keep still and listen and have a prayer in my heart (that the Lord will bless me to know what to say and how to act) things go much better. I don't think you can do more than rely on the Lord for His help."

Problems can defeat instead of strengthen us only when we are out of touch with spiritual help. George Pace, associate professor of religion at B.Y.U. said, "In the gospel of Jesus Christ we have the answer to all problems. And the gospel means finding the Lord."

Ten Things to Try

1. Play the "What would you do if?" game with your children, to help them make right choices mentally before they are confronted with an actual decision.

2. Analyze what time of day is most "problem prone" at your house and plan some positive activities for the children during that time.

3. For one week keep a record of how many times you stop a conversation by judging, criticizing, etc. Try to practice just *listening* and watch for results.

4. Encourage your children to brainstorm for solutions to their problems and visualize the possible results of each solution. Then have them choose the solution that seems best to them, carry it out and analyze its effectiveness.

5. Look up appropriate stories beforehand, and when your kids get in conflicts, try the story-telling approach. Or simply distract them from a squabble by starting a story tape or record or reading them a story.

6. Read humorous stories or books together as a family and memorize favorite poems and phrases to "smooth over the rough spots" when problems arise.

7. Be a moderator when children are not communicating well in a conflict. Don't take sides or pass judgment; just have each child state the facts and what they would be willing to do to make the situation better.

8. Try creative problem solving with your mate. Ask each other, "What do you see the problem to be? and brainstorm for solutions. Involve the whole family in the solution when appropriate.

9. Call an impromptu family council the next time you have a family problem that needs to be dealt with immediately.

10. Don't forget to pray.

18

Happily Ever After?

This fictionalized account of one marriage is actually a composite of many true experiences which were shared with us in confidence. It is included in this book to encourage improvement in the marriage relationship because happy marriages contribute richly to family success.

Ann Starks and Tina Johnson have two things in common. They were married the same day ten years ago, and they each have four children. There the similarity ends. For Ann is now a divorcee, and Tina is happy in her marriage. Tina, who knows Ann and her story, believes that Ann could also be happily married. She feels sad that Ann did not find answers to her problems as she has, for Tina has not always been happy. She married with the popular misconception that we "live happily ever after." In fact, she admits her attitude was, "Here I am— now make me happy."

The disillusionment began immediately. Even though they had enjoyed what she describes as a "storybook romance", Tina now found that her husband rarely took time to be with her anymore. He had three major interests: television, sports, and cars. It seemed the only thing they had in common was their interest in the church. Since they were not interested in the same things, even when Ron was at home, they didn't spend much time together. Also, he now seemed anxious to maintain a distance between them, and avoided talking about feelings, even though Tina often tried to discuss her own feelings with him. Tina confesses that after only a few months she was ready to give up and call her marriage a failure. Then she found she was pregnant, and made a decision to stay with Ron and try to make the best of her situation. By the time their second child was born, the situation had not improved, and Tina was desperate. What could she do?

She remembers reading many books in her search for an answer to her problems. Mrs. Norman Vincent Peale, in her book *The Adventures of Being a Wife* described the complete and joyous relationship she and her husband had developed. Mrs. Peale said, "My husband and I have not achieved the relationship we have just by thinking happy thoughts or waving a wand. We fought for this relationship! We hammered it out on the anvil of joy and sorrow, of pain and problems—yes, at times, of discouragement and disagreement. But we never thought of marriage as a trap. We thought of it as a privilege. And there's quite a difference!"

This made Tina think, and she concluded that she had a lot of work to do. Later she said, "I think our culture leads us to believe that a good marriage is something you either have or don't have, and this discourages the idea of working at marriage to make it good. I was under the illusion that there must be an easier way to solve my problems than the hard work of facing up to them, finding solutions, and making the needed changes."

Making Marriage Work Takes Work!

One day when Tina was feeling sorry for herself, one of her friends said to her, "Tina, life was never meant to be easy. The Lord knew it wouldn't be easy for us to make a marriage work, but He knew that we grow through opposition, if we meet it right. The opposition which comes from having two separate individuals trying to become as one is a real challenge. Remember that the satisfactions of life come from meeting and coping with the challenges. You will always have problems; it is what you do about them that counts!"

Even though Tina wanted to believe this philosophy she still struggled with conflicting feelings. She rationalized her resentment and critical attitudes toward her husband by saying, "If only Ron would...then I could change." His procrastination nearly drove her crazy, and his lack of expressed affection constantly hurt her. Also, Tina discovered that much of the trouble in marriage is caused not by any one big thing, but by our attitudes about all the little annoying, irritating habits and idiosyncrasies, and the small demands we make on each other to change and be more like the other (or more like what we expect in a mate). Tina noticed that many couples seem to love their mates not for what they were, but only as they become more like what they want; while other couples learn to enjoy their differences and to laugh at the idiosyncrasies.

She could see it is relatively easy to tolerate weaknesses of friends and neighbors because our lives are affected only indirectly by them, but the weaknesses of our mates may cause us disappointment, delay, and inconvenience. And so, even though we believe in the principle of loving others as ourselves, and not judging them, we may become judgmental, critical, even condemning. Tina realized her own critical attitudes were the reason for her inner conflict; her attitudes were at odds with her beliefs.

Mutual Agreement to Change

Tina went to talk to her bishop about her unhappiness, and he recommended a counselor. She and Ron went, and during their first visit, the counselor suggested they make a list of all the good qualities they saw in each other at the time they were married. He asked them to frame these lists and hang them on their bedroom wall and look at them every day to focus their thoughts on the things they liked about each other. Later, he told them it almost never helped to try to change things we don't

like about our mates in a direct attack, but suggested if something was bothering them they might try drawing up a contract
where each agreed to try to change one thing which irritated
the other person. To add to the incentive to honor the contract,
they could add shared rewards and consequences to the contract!

They followed the counselor's suggestion, and each week
Tina and Ron drew up a new contract. If they had not felt progress on the past contract, they kept it in force until they did.
One week Tina agreed to watch television with Ron on Friday
nights rather than spending the evening sewing by herself in
the bedroom, if Ron would spend part of each Saturday morning
doing one home improvement job he had been putting off until
he "had time". If they both carried through their agreement for
a month, they decided they would go out to eat at a nice restaurant, but if they did not, the consequence was that they would
have to put in two hours of hard labor in the yard!

Next, Ron agreed to take Tina on a date once a week, if she
would keep his clothing mended and well-taken care of (part of
Ron's expectations of a wife was that she keep his clothes in
good repair, and Tina disliked mending and was often guilty of
procrastination in this task). Another time, Tina agreed to put
the cap back on the toothpaste and roll it up neatly and Ron
agreed to kiss her goodbye before he left for work, and they spent
half the week laughing with each other over the difficulty they
had in remembering such small things. Tina and Ron found
humor to be a practical aid to solving problems; besides relieving
anxiety, this lighter approach (especially a sense of humor about
their own imperfections) opened the way to a clearer understanding of themselves.

Marriage is not a Reform School!

Tina began to realize that sometimes she had focused on
understanding Ron, when it was even more important to be able
to evaluate her own feelings. She found that a clear look at her
own reactions and their causes helped her to see when she was
over reacting. (The amount of importance we attach to insignificant things can make a difference in how we react to them.)
Tina noticed that when she attached too much importance to
any specific type of problem, it became a source of stress (over
and over again). Ron and Tina both discovered to their surprise
that they could bring these behaviors down in their scale of sig-

nificance by being aware of what bothered the other person and laughing together over these little nuisance-type traits (and their idiosyncrasies could become a source of closeness rather than conflict and distance when handled this way). Ron asked himself, "Is Tina's lateness reason enough to throw me into a fit of anger? It's a nuisance, and nothing more." Tina reminded herself that Ron's forgetfulness about the little things was not cataclysmic—just an irritation. After this new insight, when Ron said he would meet Tina at 6:00, she might retort, "See you at 6:30", or if Tina asked Ron to fix the sink, Ron might say, "How about next month?", and they would both laugh.

As they tried to work on and remove these small areas of friction, they began to notice their concern for the other's happiness increasing, and Tina's resentment concerning Ron's faults also began to diminish. She had laughed when one of her neighbors had told her she thought some women must feel that marriage is a reform school for husbands, but now she gave some thought to how many things she had expected Ron to change. She began to realize that she couldn't offer perfection to Ron, and therefore she was unreasonable to expect it from him.

Acquire the Acceptance Attitude

In a Relief Society lesson Tina learned that the only real power we possess in helping others change, grow, and improve is to accept them as they are, look for good and seek to bring it out. The lesson pointed out that telling your husband he is thoughtless and unloving will not make him thoughtful and loving. However, if we develop a real acceptance of the mate (including their failings and objectionable behavior patterns), our acceptance gives them the freedom which may even encourage them to change the things we dislike. Tina observed that few of us can resist love and approval; and when we feel accepted (rather than criticized or condemned) we often give up our need to cling to an objectionable habit which we may have kept out of self defense when we were criticized. She concluded that acceptance gives a person a sense of well-being which helps him to be free to change and improve; and that when we accept things the way they are, we are not giving up the desire for improvement, but making it possible!

Tina decided she would honestly try to accept Ron in every way. She began by praying with sincere and earnest pleading that the Lord would help her be more accepting and loving, and less critical of her husband. She made herself a chart on which she kept track of any time she resisted an unkind or hurtful remark (trying to improve each week). When she found herself thinking, "Oh, if only Ron would..." she would catch herself and think, "Now what is it that Ron is wishing I would do for him?" and then she would do it.

The Only One you can Change is Yourself

Their counselor had reminded them that one of the basic principles of improving and building a relationship is "The only one you can change is yourself."

Later, Tina read a story of a woman who went to the lawyer to get a divorce and she told him she really wanted to hurt her husband. The lawyer advised her that if she really wanted to hurt him she should go home and make herself indispensable to him by always thinking what she could do for him instead of what he could do for her...and then come back for the divorce. The woman went home fully intent on hurting her husband, but she never came back for the divorce. When she met the lawyer on the street, she said, "Oh, I don't need to get a divorce. My husband is a completely changed man!" Since marriage is an interaction, one person can't change without changing the other person, and Tina found this to be true. As she started overlooking Ron's faults and trying to put his needs ahead of her own, he started reciprocating with acts of thoughtfulness. One morning when the children had kept her up half the night, she was tired and discouraged. After Ron had gone to work she found little notes all over the house which expressed his love and encouragement. One said, "It's all worth it. Thank you for taking such good care of our children." Tina remembered that her mother had said, "If a woman feels her husband should meet all her needs first, it will never happen. But if she honestly tries to meet his needs, it makes it possible for him to meet hers." *Now* Tina knew the meaning of the words, and she doubled her efforts to notice the good and overlook the negative in her husband.

Whenever she found herself feeling angry with Ron, she would go into her bedroom, close the door and sit down and write every reason she could think of that she had married him, and everything good that he had done in the past week, and then she found that the things she was angry about didn't look very big anymore.

One night Tina fixed her hair especially nice and put on a fresh outfit before her husband came home. She had noticed he had been a little depressed the night before, and she was hoping to lift his spirits. But when he came home, he seemed too pre-occupied to notice and hardly talked to her all evening. That night, he acted upset, and when she asked what was wrong he said, "Oh, I'm not doing anything right." He stomped out of the bedroom, and went downstairs for awhile. When he came back up, he said, "I'm sorry I'm so insensitive. I feel like I've stifled a lot of the feeling you used to have for me. You got dressed up and fixed your hair tonight, and I didn't even say a word about it. No wonder you never meet me at the door anymore the way you used to."

This started a time of honest communication. Tina explained to Ron that she still had the same feelings, but she had stopped meeting him at the door because it seemed to make him un-comfortable to have her be so expressive. He was relieved to know it wasn't because she didn't feel the same about him, and told her he wanted her to start doing it again. Even though he hadn't shown it, he really liked her to meet him at the door.

Different Roles, Different Needs

When the communication lines were more open, Tina found it easier to help Ron understand some of the differences in their needs. Tina said, "Many times I could feel Ron's impatience with my need to talk about my feelings, and he would say things like, 'Tina, I just don't understand you.' One day I replied, 'Ron, it's not important that you understand me. You are not a woman, and you may never feel the way I feel, or see things the way I see them. But the important thing is that I need to feel free to express my feelings to someone. Do you want me to go to my mother, or my friend? I have to have someone to talk to, and I want you to be the one. I want to know that you will just listen and accept my typically feminine need to share feelings.' " This discussion helped Ron learn to listen patiently, and let Tina talk even when she got emotional. He saw that she soon got everything out of her system, and it was very good therapy for her.

Tina tells of another experience which helped Ron under-stand her viewpoint, and the problems of her role as a mother. When they had two children and she was expecting their third baby, they were getting ready to move. She said, "The day I need-ed to do most of the packing so we would be ready to move, my two little ones were not feeling up to par, and were grumpy and whiny all day long. By late afternoon I felt I couldn't stand it any-more, and I made a sudden decision. Rather than stay home and fall apart at the seams, which wouldn't help anyone, I would go out. I called the florist, and ordered a pink rosebud corsage for myself, locked myself in the bathroom and took a leisurely bath, did my hair and make-up, and put on my prettiest dress. My hus-band came home just as the florist arrived. I signed for the cor-sage while he stood there with his mouth open. 'Where are you going?' he asked. 'I don't know, but I'm going,' I replied. And I left. (It was the first night since we were married that I hadn't had dinner ready for him when he got home.) I love to read more than anything in the world. So I went to the library and read for a cou-ple of hours, enjoying the soothing effect of the words and the quiet atmosphere. When I went home I was scared to death to go in the house. I had no idea how Ron would react. But when I walked in, Ron grabbed me and pulled me onto his lap and said, 'I want you to know, when you first walked out of this house I was soooo angry with you. But after I listened to these kids for fifteen minutes, I began to understand. I'm sure I couldn't cope with them for half a day!' " That night Tina was also able to explain to Ron a basic difference in their daily challenges. He could get up and go somewhere each day and experience tangible progress—finish some things, and start new things. But in her role at home, progress wasn't as easy to see because almost everything she did soon needed to be done again, and perspective was easy to lose.

The Need for Appreciation and Admiration

She helped him understand why she needed his appreciation to make it seem worthwhile, and to keep her mind on how im-portant her work really was. Since then Ron has shown her more appreciation and has never said anything like "Why should you be tired? You get to stay home all day!"

Later Tina began to wonder if she had let Ron know that she appreciated the way he fulfilled his role. She told him that night how very happy she was with him as a provider. He seemed sur-prised and told her he had felt that she wasn't satisfied with the way he was providing, and he was noticeably pleased.

Because her remark had pleased him so much, it encouraged her to notice other things that she had been overlooking, and to express her feelings about him. "I found that letting him know the things I admired communicated love better than just saying, 'I love you.' He really thrives on admiration...and I think most men are like that. Now I try to let him know I admire anything from his strong arms to his ability to balance the checkbook. There are so many things to admire; it is just a matter of remembering to comment on them. I really saw that my expressions of admiration and acceptance made a difference in his attitude toward me. I believe that how a husband feels about a wife depends a great deal upon how she makes him feel about himself."

"Wives Submit Yourselves Unto Your Own Husbands"

Tina remembers clearly the day another significant thing happened to influence her and help make her marriage a happy, strong one. She was reading the scriptures one morning and in Ephesians 5:22-24 she read,

Wives, submit yourselves unto your own husbands, as unto the Lord.

For the husband is the head of the wife, even as Christ is the head of the church: and he is the saviour of the body.

Therefore as the church is subject unto Christ, so let the wives be to their own husbands in every thing.

Tina was stunned. Right there it said submit yourselves to your husbands in *everything.* Could she do that?

Tina began rising early to study and pray for help to truly submit herself and her life into her husband's hands...and as she prayed she began to have a new understanding of what this meant. She realized that if she truly put Ron at the head of their home, she would pray not for solutions and answers to problems herself, but that her husband would receive them. She began to understand that as the Lord inspires and influences the husband, then the solution comes from the Lord through the priesthood channel, and the husband maintains his rightful position as decision-maker and head of the house. When she had a concern, she should put her trust in the Lord, and pray mightily that he would inspire her husband to see what needed to be done, to have a change of attitude if it was needed, or to see the situation with a new perspective. Then, recognizing the tremendous power of prayer, she should trust her husband to give her the right direction, counsel and help.

Spiritual Leadership in Action

Tina's best friend influenced her a great deal at this point in her marriage because she helped Tina see how this principle works in actual practice. Her friend said, "I don't believe a woman can be truly happy unless she is helping her husband exercise his role as leader in the family. One of the best ways to do this, I believe, is through your prayers. When I was worried about getting our life histories written, Jim seemed completely uninterested. I began praying that my husband would see the importance of this, and one day Jim came in and said, 'I think we should start writing our life stories. Early Sunday morning is a good time for me, could you do it then?' This has happened many times since. Instead of nagging him or attempting to lead him, or push him, I just leave it up to the Lord to influence him." She added a caution to Tina saying, "Of course your husband doesn't need to know that you are asking. When he comes up with an inspired solution or decision even if it is a temptation, don't tell him he thought of it because you've been praying for him to! That would indicate that you are trying to manipulate him, but you are not. You are only asking that he be righteously influenced. I believe it is one way the Lord intends us to work with our husbands to help them be the leader."

Financial Leadership

Tina believes that there are many things a wife can do to help her husband sense his leadership in the home—and in fact take over that responsibility (and she believes this is the most important lesson she learned). Tina had always handled the finances in their home, paid the bills, balanced the budget and the checkbook, and handed out the money to all the family members (including her husband) when they had special needs. But Tina began taking a class concerning husband-wife relationships, and one day the teacher suggested that a man should have total control of the finances in order to feel his true leadership; that it was *his* responsibility to pay the bills and portion out the money. She intimated that while men often think they are happy to be relieved of these tasks that they nearly always resent this usurping of their rightful responsibilities. It makes them feel less the provider, less the decision-maker, less the head of the house. The teacher also suggested that the wife should not have a checkbook but should give her husband the special feeling of putting the money she needed for her household budget and personal needs right from his hand to her hand; reinforcing his feeling of caring for her and providing for the needs of the family. At first Tina fumed and fretted and refused to accept the validity of such ideas. She enjoyed the freedom she felt she had to buy what she wanted when she wanted, and didn't think it could make that much difference to her husband. Then she began noticing that many of the bad feelings that crept up from time to time were about what she had spent, and why there wasn't money left, or why this bill didn't get paid when Ron thought it should have. Tina finally decided it was worth a try, and when she made a mistake in the checkbook and couldn't make it balance, she decided to ask her husband to take over the finances. Tina said, "Ron, I really am having a hard time with the bills and the checkbook. I think you could do much better. I'd really appreciate it if you could start handling them." Ron was reluctant at first, but when he did it they were both surprised at the difference it made! Tina felt an enormous relief and Ron felt much more "in control" (although he had said, 'What difference could it possibly make who writes out the checks?') It did make a difference, and they both enjoyed it when he brought her household money and personal expense money home in cash every pay day. Tina found that the freedom she felt in being able to spend this money which was especially allotted to her (without fear of slighting other things or facing Ron's displeasure) was much greater than the freedom she thought she had had in having free acess to the whole paycheck. But most important: in some very real, tangible way, this change helped establish Ron as the head of their house.

Get Away Together

Tina recalls one more incident which made a decided difference in their marriage. "When we had four small children, our very wise Bishop sat us down and said, 'You two need to take a trip together.' And we said, 'But Bishop we can't afford it!' He told us we didn't have to take an expensive trip, just a weekend away somewhere together without the kids. We decided his advice was good, but we wondered where we could go, and who would tend the children for us. Luckily, I had a cousin going to college nearby, and she was willing to come and stay over the weekend to help out. We put a mattress in the back of the station wagon to make a good bed, and toured the nearby Canyonlands. When we got away from all the routine and pressures, it was easier to see everything in perspective, and there was time to talk and plan and talk some more. To be able to talk things out without interruptions was a marvelous thing for our marriage. We came back 'whole' people again and found we could cope with our family problems better because we had become a team, and we continued to really communicate."

Communicating and Co-operating

Although earlier Ron and Tina had each had their own "private" goals; as they talked and prayed about it, they were somewhat surprised to learn that their basic goals were the same, but they had been going in different directions to reach them because they hadn't been communicating or cooperating. She says, "Life was really exciting once we started communicating and working on our goals together. We found that when we had problems, if we knelt together seeking the Lord's help and guidance and wanting to do His will, there was nothing we couldn't overcome. It was like we were making a hard, hard climb up a ladder, but we were making it. We felt good; we felt satisfactions and joy because we were learning by each experience."

Over the years Ron and Tina have learned that planning together takes time, and that they have to have the desire to arrange for the time. They established a weekly appointment with each other and each Sunday evening they meet to talk about and plan the coming week. They also discuss their feelings about how they want their children raised...and what they want the children to learn and to accomplish. They actually find that it is fun to make and implement plans to make their shared desires and goals a reality. During some of these planning sessions Ron and Tina worked out a list of "Celestial Goals" which deal with everything they felt might be significant to achieve if they were to reach the Celestial Kingdom. It included spiritual, emotional, intellectual and physical goals—even such simple things as helping the children develop habits of orderliness (a place for everything, and everything in its place).

Tina says, "As we began to work together as a team we sensed more and more the importance of teaching and training our children and striving together to bring them back to live with their Father in Heaven. Sharing, planning and working together made us feel we were working toward this lofty goal. When we take time to plan special ways to develop desirable character traits in our children and work out methods to help them overcome weaknesses and problems, it draws us closer as husband and wife, and is one of our most rewarding team efforts. We still have a long way to go to reach most of the goals we set, but they have helped us in all the decisions we've made along the way."

Marriage, as Tina and Ron learned and Ann and her husband did not, is a learning and growing process—not a packaged product. We can take marriage day by day as it comes and do nothing to improve it, or we can decide to make it better—always growing and maturing together in a dynamic process that is part of eternal progression.

Ten Things to Try

1. Make a list of all the good qualities you saw in your mate at the time you were married. Frame these lists and hang them on your bedroom wall to remind you to focus your thoughts on the things you like.

2. Draw up a contract where each of you agree to try to change one thing which irritates the other. Add rewards and consequences if you need more incentive.

3. Give yourself a "Practice What You Preach" Test. List the principles of the gospel and analyze how well you are putting them into practice with your mate.

4. Try looking for the humorous in your reactions to each other. Bring irritations down in their scale of significance by laughing at them together.

5. Remember that "The only one you can change is yourself" and try asking yourself "What is it my husband (or wife) would like *me* to do?" rather than thinking, "Oh if only he or she would...."

6. Pray for help in overlooking faults and weaknesses and to be able to truly accept your mate for what he or she is...right now.

7. Find ways to express your love and respect to each other. (Men need approval and admiration most, women need affection and attention.)

8. Try to talk over and understand your different needs because of the differences in your roles and sex. (Women need to talk about feelings, men need to talk about accomplishments, etc.)

9. When you are tempted to criticize or if you are angry with your spouse, try writing down their good qualities and the good things they have done that week.

10. Take a weekend away together occasionally to renew the spark in your marriage and give time for in-depth planning. Make an appointment with each other to meet together weekly to make plans to improve your marriage and family life.

19

Get Ready, Goal-Set and Go!

In Granada Hills, California, a thirteen-year-old young man named Bob Nisson sets a goal to earn the money for his airfare so he may accompany his parents to Australia to meet his brother at the conclusion of his mission. Bob's parents spend two home evenings exploring with him the possible ways he can reach his goal. He cuts wood and sells it, paints a garage, puts a new roof on a cabana, installs a sprinkling system for a neighbor, and does many odd jobs to earn money. At the conclusion of the two years, he has raised the money to go to Australia.

In Salt Lake City, Utah, a father and several children measure their basement area. They lay out the dimensions of the rooms they want to finish, and then stand back to visualize what the basement will look like when completed. They have a goal which is important to all of them; to finish two bedrooms, a bathroom, and a family room to double the usable space in their home. In the evenings and on weekends the whole family sacrifices other activities to find the time to work together to put up sheet rock, paneling and ceiling tile. Six months later they admire and are ready to enjoy their finished basement.

In Washington, D.C., a young mother of four pre-schoolers finds children's bedtime extremely trying. As she responds for the fourth time to a child's cry for a drink of water, she makes a mental note that her most important goal in the next month must be to find a solution to the dilemma of getting the children to go to bed and stay in bed. Talking to other mothers, and reading from "how-to" books helps her realize that her problem is lack of a routine. After deciding on a routine which the children are happy with, and staying with it for a month, she is well on the way to reaching her goal of solving the bedtime problem.

These are just three examples of an upsurge in what could be called the "Great Goal Rush." People everywhere are discovering what behavioral scientists have told us for years—that setting goals is like putting rungs in our ladder of progress.

Since progress is fundamental to individual and family happiness, any principle is valuable which helps us make progress. Because of the law of eternal progression, none of us will ever move to the point where further progress is unneeded. It is the sense of progress, the moving forward in the right direction which makes life exciting and worthwhile.

The same principles which bring success in other areas of life also apply to being successful in our homes; yet we may overlook them. Goal-setting is one of the principles which is as important to running a family as it is to running a business. When we set specific goals, we gain perspective which motivates wise time use to bring our goals into reality.

We Could All Use a "Goal Rush"

For more than twenty years of married life, a mother we shall call Jeanine had struggled to overcome her feelings of inadequacy. Last summer Jeanine read a book which taught her the three steps of effective goal-setting, and decided to try them. First she analyzed why she felt inadequate: her lack of skill as a homemaker, her problems in her role as a wife, and her lack of closeness to her children constantly overwhelmed her. Then she set the following goals:

1. To organize her housework and learn to stick to a schedule.
2. To do more things for and with her husband.
3. To have firmer routines and special one-to-one time with the children.

She decided on a daily plan of action to help her reach her goals and took the first step. Now, a year later, she has made progress toward each one. Her attitude has changed a great deal and she is happier and more self-confident. She believes she has greatly improved her life through goal-setting. She said, "I was able to set these goals and accomplish them because I was honest with myself about what I really wanted, and why I was unhappy. As soon as I took time to find out why I wasn't getting what I really wanted from life, and took steps to begin to work toward my major desires, I began feeling more satisfaction from my life."

Five Steps to Reach Your Goals

The five steps of goal setting which Jeanine followed were:

1. *Identify your goals and write them down on paper.*
    A. Start by defining your long-range goals. These are general goals such as being a better mother or father, long-term career goals, etc.
    B. Long-range goals must be supported by short-term goals which are much more specific and are the necessary steps to reach your long-term goals. An example might be: I will spend some time alone with each child, each day.
2. *Decide on a time-limit for achieving each goal.* Although some goals take a lifetime to reach, many goals lend themselves to the deadline approach which motivates us to do the things necessary to move toward the goal.
3. *Visualize your goal.* (Form a picture in your mind of what it will be like when you have achieved your goal.)

4. *Commit yourself to achieve the goal by sharing the goal with someone.*

5. *Make daily and weekly plans or blueprints for achieving your goals.* It is this planning phase which changes the goal lists into specific things to do, and times to do them. Next we must work our plan. Success equals 90% perspiration plus 10% inspiration! We must be willing to pay the price in time and energy. We must also take time to evaluate. How is the plan working? What could we eliminate? What additional things do we need to do to reach the goal? If we don't plan and evaluate our plan, it is too easy to spend most of our time on routine matters, thoughtlessly doing whatever seems to be important at the moment only to find at the end of the day, or week, or year that the truly important things never got started. We may have had good intentions to spend more time with the children or write our personal history, or develop a talent, but these things may not get done unless we plan when we will do them. Once we know what we are working toward and what is rewarding to us, we can make definite plans to include time for those activities.

"The Goal Mine"

Financial advisers tell us when we are thinking of investing money, the wise thing to do is to analyze not only how much our investment will cost, but also the alternate choices we might buy for the same amount of money. We can then determine if there is any other investment which will bring a greater return for our money. Becoming goal-oriented helps us do the same thing with our time. We learn to consider alternatives and make time investment choices which will bring us the greatest returns in the eternal values. In other words, we try to use our time to pay the price for achieving the goals which mean the most to us in life.

Would you like a happier home life? A closer relationship with your children? Would you like to develop a talent? Start now to set your goals and make your plans! Remember, a Goal Mine can be your personal Gold Mine!

Getting Together to Set Goals

Many parents believe in letting their children share in family goal-setting and planning. They recognize the potential for training children to manage their own lives and become responsible adults through practicing in a family setting. Many parents mentioned that family home evenings and family councils are good times to give children practice at these skills.

Family home evening is one evening each week set aside for the family to get together for instruction and/or entertainment. Some families have found this to be an ideal time to discuss family business (work assignments, problems, goals, plans, etc.) as well as to present lessons and participate together in their favorite family activities.

Family council is a gathering of the entire family in a meeting where each member who is old enough is encouraged to express his opinions and help make the decisions and plans which affect the whole family. Mark E. Petersen said of a family council, "In such a meeting, parents can win the cooperation of children in attaining the objectives of good family living, inviting them to help plan for it, and making them feel a part both of the plan and of its operation. Children will respond if parents will take the initiative in righteous leadership."

Family council can be part of family home evening or held at a separate time. In family council we can evaluate the affairs of the past week and make specific plans for the coming week. We can also talk about long range plans and goals in order that the family can work together to make them happen.

Dr. Verlan Andersen and his wife, Shirley, have held family council as part of their home evenings for years, and feel it has been a valuable tool for building family unity and reaching family goals. Verlan conducts each week, and they follow a definite format. After an opening song and prayer, they take time to make a brief record (in a special large loose-leaf binder) of the activities of the family which becomes their family history. Next, the family looks at the past week and decides where improvement is needed, and makes specific plans for the next week. Verlan then gives work assignments after which they have their other home evening activities.

At one time the Delbert Eddington family held their family councils in conjunction with family home evening, but felt that the necessary business was usurping the time they wanted to save for family fun. So they began having them on Saturday morning. Another family found a Sunday morning brunch the perfect time to hold family councils when they are on the late church meeting schedule. When they are on the early morning schedule, their family council is held Sunday evening just before bedtime.

Each family can choose the time and type of council which best suits their needs. A patriarchal council, such as the Andersens use, where the father always conducts and makes final decisions can be ideal for families with young children. The democratic method where the chairmanship is rotated and each person's vote is equal is often used by families with teens or young adults.

Rachel McOmber said, "Our family council is very informal, and although my husband, David, is always in charge, he delegates the chairmanship. We believe it is much better if the children decide their own goals and help set family goals. They have a lot of good ideas on their own. We just give them a general guide of what it is we want to accomplish, and let them take it from there."

Whatever form your council takes, one of the strengths of meeting together to set goals, make plans, and evaluate progress is that we all have a tendency to be more highly motivated to accomplish goals which we have helped set.

Organizing to Reach Family Goals

A basic method of organization can help a family achieve their goals. For the purpose of illustration let us suggest two methods which have worked for others. An easy way to get organized is to use a planning calendar with a large square for each day of the month, plus a notebook for each family member for individual goal lists and schedule plans. When you meet in family council, you can decide what needs to be done each day during the week to reach family and individual goals, and write each person's major plans and commitments on the calendar. The Leo and Katherine Gifford family follows this plan. She said, "We have a big calendar, and we go around the circle and ask each person what they have to put on the calendar so we all know ahead of time what to plan for. We plan car arrangements, baby sitters, etc. One of the reasons we feel this plan is beneficial is that it encourages and teaches children to plan ahead, and to avoid infringing on the time or rights of other family members. We feel it has helped them to be more aware of the needs of others."

A compact way to organize family and individual goals and plans is to have one loose-leaf type notebook where goals, plans and schedules are all kept together. A calendar could be one of the pages of this type of notebook, or there could be a calendar page for each month so there would be room to write in the commitments.

New Goals for the New Year

Robert and Jean Porcaro explain that planning with their children helps them organize their home and keep it running smoothly. Their favorite time for goal setting and planning is at their family New Years Eve party, before the party activities begin. Each family member has a folder in which they keep their long-range goal sheets and the first thing they do is read through last year's goals and evaluate how they did. Then the older children write down their goals for the new year while Dad and Mom work with the younger children. Jean says, "We help the little ones set goals we know they can reach, so they will learn the satisfaction of accomplishing." The Porcaro's have used the scripture in Luke 2:52 as a guide for goal-setting. They choose goals in each area this scripture mentions: "And Jesus increased in wisdom (intellectual) and stature, (physical) and in favour with God (spiritual) and man (social and emotional)." She and Robert believe goal-setting helps children learn the value of making decisions and planning their lives so they have a clear idea of where they are going. She quotes, " 'A goal is just a wish unless you write it down.' When we write down a goal it helps us make it happen." Robert believes in following through after goals have been set. He holds interviews with each child every few months to check their progress and give encouragement and counsel. Jean commented on the satisfaction of seeing growth in her children's abilities to plan and take charge of their own lives as a result of goal-setting and follow-through. Kathy, their married daughter said, "Planning and working toward goals is just part of me now. I consistently set goals for myself and try to reach them just like I did at home and it really helps me make progress."

On New Year's Day, Louie and Joella Wolfgramm plan and write out individual and family goals for the coming year. They plan temporal goals (such as food storage and home improvements) and spiritual goals (such as doing more church reading, and having more meaningful prayers). They also set goals for their little boys. The spiritual goal this year for Louie, who is four, is to learn the names of the prophets and to identify them from their pictures. The goal for the youngest is to learn to pray.

Summer Specials

Summer is another time families often have a special need for goal-setting. To help their family have a more profitable summer, Terah and Joye Billings set some goals with their children.

June: Take swimming lessons, and work together so that Mom will have time to read with Zachary. (He had a reading problem, and was excited about getting special help.)

July: Have a family project of making flannel quilts for each child.

August: Work together as a family to do the canning.

All Three Months: Ride bikes together at least three times a week, go swimming twice a week with Daddy as soon as he gets off work, hike together once or twice a week, camp out at least once a month, and work outside together every other day for an hour.

Frank and Karen Reilley encouraged their children to set summer goals and helped them see what was necessary to accomplish them. At the first of the summer, they called the children together and asked, "What do each of you want to do the most this summer?" The children each had a turn to express their desires, which were listed on a big sheet of paper. (Things like picnics, outings, and swimming lessons were mentioned.) Then Karen added things she would like to do with them and things she hoped to teach them, and asked, "What will we have to do to make all these goals possible?" The children recognized they would have to cooperate to help get the work done so things would run smoothly. Frank and Karen then suggested that the children make a list of rules for the summer which they thought would help everyone accomplish their goals. They thought of rules such as:

1. You shouldn't go where Mom can't find you.
2. Don't play until the work is all done.
3. Have friends help clean up messes they help make.

Frank and Karen were interested to find that they didn't have to say hardly a word during the rule-making process, and the children were more willing to keep the rules because they had made them.

Karen posted the rules and the list of summer goals on the kitchen door, and the family checked off the goals as they were accomplished. This kept everyone up to date on their progress, and motivated them to plan time to accomplish their other goals.

Guide Children to Personal Goals

Roy and Deanne Despain had become concerned about problems each of their children had and decided to try goal-setting to motivate needed changes. They purchased notebooks and told the children the notebooks were part of a special surprise project. They introduced the project in family home evening by asking everyone to take turns saying something they liked about everyone else in the family. Then Roy and Deanne told the children, "You can see by the nice things everyone has just said that there is a lot about you to love. Mom and Dad love you so much that when we are alone, we often talk about cute things you do and also the things you do that make you unhappy." (The children were unusually quiet and attentive.)

"Brenda, what do you think we would talk about that is making you unhappy?" (Brenda was seven years old.)

"Well, when I come home I say unhappy things, and sometimes I only think of bad about other people and not good." (Roy and Deanne were pleased she recognized what her main problem was without coaching.)

Deanne continued, "Brenda, what do you think you could do about this problem?" Brenda replied, "Maybe I can try to find good things to talk about." Deanne said, "Good! We will decide each time we think you have really made some progress, and help you write about it in your notebook. We will give you a star for your special accomplishments, and when you have ten stars, your reward will be to have a date with Daddy, just the two of you!"

They continued this process with each child, and each chose a goal to work on after he himself had described his own problem. Brandon's goal was "Do the very best I can on everything I do." Derrick's goal was "I will cooperate with other people when they need me to."

Each child took the challenge seriously and really worked on it. Over a period of weeks, Brenda became a happier girl. Her school teacher even noticed, and called Deanne to comment on the change. Derrick and Brandon had similiar success experiences and the family learned that goal-setting does work—for children as well as for adults.

When James and Colleen Pinegar had all their children at home, they had a very simple but effective goal-setting plan. They had their children write on 3 x 5 cards specific things they wanted to do and be, and then periodically during home evening had them take the cards out and look at them and plan what they needed to do during the next month. Colleen said, "This seemed to really spark us on to reach our goals."

Satisfaction or Regret?

Every few months we need to evaluate our plans to see if they are getting us where we want to go. We need to take off the blinders of present pressures, stand back, and take a good look at our goals, our schedules, and our lives. Bob and Carolyn Larsen said, "We often analyze which goals we need to work on and what plans we are forgetting or letting slide. We have learned that goal setting and planning has to include more than sitting down and making lists. The challenge comes in making the plans become reality—in finding the time (and the funds) to incorporate the plans into our family life. For instance, during our planning times, Bob and I made lists of experiences we wanted our children to have before they leave our home and lists of things we want them to be able to do. One successful plan we have carried out which came from our evaluating these lists is our Family Outing Day. One Saturday a month we try to go on an outing together as a family. We have visited the zoo, a ghost town, museums, a planetarium, many historical spots and (the children's favorite place!) a copper mine. These excursions have provided the method we were looking for to give our children the opportunity for many types of experiences, and the kids love it! But these experiences take planning and follow-through to make them happen."

Perhaps it would be helpful as we evaluate our plans to ask ourselves, "If we continue to use our time as we are now doing, will we look back with satisfaction or regret?"

Majorie Todd Graham, a mother, a writer, and a person who "gets things done" tells how at one point in her life she suddenly realized that when she looked back she felt not pleasure, but remorse. She asked herself what was the point of all her effort if she couldn't look back on it with satisfaction. She set a goal to be more aware of what was truly important in her life. She confides that as she watched for opportunities to make happy memories, she found that habits of a lifetime cannot be changed overnight, but with sincere intentions to put first things first she did make progress. She found many opportunities, among the most important of which was getting to know her children better. For example, when her son excitedly called to her to come outside right away because he had something to show her, she remembered her goal, and left the meatloaf she was mixing and joined him. She says, "The sense of wonder that my son and

I shared that afternoon is still one of my most treasured memories. And the fact that dinner was a little late that night wasn't even noticed."

A high percentage of the families we interviewed were goal-setters. One family said, "Before we learned the importance of goal-setting, we had the feeling of just drifting, and family responsibilites were often just big chores. But since we have begun to set goals individually and as a group, we have a great feeling of progress, of being in control, and moving ahead in the right direction. Every day isn't one big round of accomplishment or anything like that, but we know now where we want to go and have specific plans to get us there. The excitement of working toward our goals carries us over the rough spots."

Ten Things to Try

1. Write down your long-range goals. Consider the alternatives and make choices which will mean the most to you. This is your personal "Goal Mine."

2. *Get-Ready.* From your long-range set of goals, decide the short-term (yearly, monthly, weekly) goals you will need to have to reach the long-term goals. Be specific.

3. *Get-Set.* Decide on a time limit for each goal.

4. *Go!* Make a plan for achieving each goal. (Change the goal lists into specific things to do, and times to do them.)

5. Hold a New Years Eve family planning and goal-setting party. Evaluate the past year and make family plans for the new.

6. Help the children set their own goals for the new year. Be sure they are realistic goals so they can reach them and feel a sense of accomplishment.

7. To help your family have a more profitable summer, set goals together for the specific needs of the summer months.

8. Introduce your children to personal improvement goals, and let them keep a record of their progress in a special notebook purchased for that purpose. Try offering them a reward for accomplishing their goal.

9. Let children share in family goal-setting and planning in a family council (with a form and time designed to fit your family situation.)

10. Find a method of organization to achieve your goals which works for your family. Try a family planning calendar, with separate notebooks for each family member's goal lists and schedule plans; or one notebook for the whole family.

20

Growing Toward
Our Goals

Lucille Johnson (who has done a great deal of family counseling and lecturing) tells of a dear friend who was having trouble
with her children. The situation was unique because the children
came to Lucille complaining about their mother and asking what
they could do. "Our mother is a witch at home," they said, "She
never speaks to us except in a screeching, demanding voice,

and she constantly criticizes us and makes us feel like we are worth two cents."

"I was shocked," Lucille said. "Could this be my gracious, delightful friend they are talking about? It was hard for me to imagine that they were talking about this same woman, but I recommended to the children a tape-recording technique. The children started the tape-recorder before dinner one night and left it running all during the dinner hour without the mother's knowledge. Then they played the recording to her saying, 'Mom, we just want you to know how you sound to us.'"

Lucille's friend came to see her soon afterwards and said, "I couldn't believe it, Lucille! Why, I wouldn't talk to my worst enemies the way I heard myself talking to those children. I'm so inconsistent! I try to be kind and courteous to other people, why not with my own children? Are they less deserving of respect because they are children? Lucille, I love those kids with all my heart, and I wouldn't hurt them for anything—and yet look what I've been doing to them without even realizing it." She laid her head on Lucille's desk and sobbed. "What can I do? How can I change?" she asked Lucille.

Perhaps all of us ask such questions at times, and we may wish we could wave a magic wand to bring about instant change and make it easier to overcome the problems that come wrapped up in our family package. But the goal of a "happy family", like every goal or dream, has its price; and every step of progress requires effort and change.

When we set a family goal, such as to begin having family prayer twice daily, we are determining a change we wish to make in our family pattern; a destination we want to reach. When we make a plan (such as to have the prayer before breakfast and before the evening meal), we are making a "road map" to give ourselves positive direction. The next challenge is to move into action; to be "doers of the word" and not planners only! Barbara Stallings said, "We had always had family prayer in the morning, and it wasn't hard because we were in the habit. But when we decided to start having family prayer before supper as well, we found it difficult to remember at first. Finally my husband, Rex, said, 'You all need to help me remember family prayer. Whoever thinks of it, please remind me.' It was so interesting how many times we would sit down and get ready for the blessing; then notice one of the children on their knees! With all of us working together, we remembered more and more of the time until evening prayer became a habit like our morning prayer, and it wasn't a struggle anymore."

Habit can Offer a Helping Hand

Everything we do in a spontaneous way without conscious attention is a result of habits we've formed in the past. Once a pattern is formed and repeated enough times, it automatically continues unless it is consciously changed by decision and effort. We are so familiar with the concept of habit that we sometimes overlook the exciting possibilities habit has for helping us build strong characters—and strong families! We often think of habit as a kind of an enemy—an alien force keeping us chained to actions we wish we could rid ourselves of. But habit can also be our very best aid to reaching our goals. In every growth process there *is* a period of struggle, but the struggle is followed by freedom when the new pattern becomes a good habit! Once we have determined in a specific way what we want to do and use conscious will power to *start,* the force of good habit soon takes over and carries us forward. So change is not as difficult as it may seem at first, and the focus of our attention should be on overcoming bad habit patterns and replacing them with positive ones that will contribute to the foundation of strength in our lives.

One mother who was having difficulty breaking old habits and forming new ones, listed every possible reason she wasn't changing and then decided what she might do to overcome each obstacle. She found that understanding the obstacles to change is like being briefed on the "enemies" moves before the battle: and deciding beforehand how to surmount them is like preparing with the best arms and ammunition so that when the enemy appears, instead of being frightened and running, she could fight and be victorious!

One Step at a Time: Where to Start

There is a picture of a whale with a riddle beneath that says, "How would you eat a whale?" The answer? "One bite at a time!" With every great challenge in life, we must learn the fundamental law of "one step at a time". No building is erected in a day, no mountain is climbed in one leap, and no strong family is made strong by one single effort. We *can* change and improve—but only one step at a time. One family said, "When we started a

'Family Improvement Program' we chose for our motto 'A day at a time you can do it. Don't see the mountain ahead of you. Just go as far as you can each day.' We've really tried to follow this philosophy and it has made progress possible!"

Many people have suggested that the place to *start* when you desire to really make creative changes in your life is with: 1. daily physical exercise 2. scripture reading 3. prayer. The sense of "being in control" that comes as we discipline ourselves to do these things regularly; plus our increased physical and spiritual well-being, can "spill over" into every area of our lives and give us the strength and confidence to initiate the needed changes. There is great power in consistency; and if we can do something regularly, day after day (even if it is only for five-minute periods) we build strength and self-discipline. This is of vital importance because a degree of self-discipline is essential to every step of progress!

One caution to remember whenever beginning any daily program: almost everyone finds it necessary to start over and over. So don't be discouraged if you suddenly realize you have missed a day or a week. Just start again! This is the point where Satan would like to convince you it's of no use. But if you start again, you will be headed in the right direction once more. (And direction is more important than velocity!) Other possible steps for moving forward in the right direction are:

1. Accept and "try on" total free agency.
2. "Put off" procrastination.
3. Pinpoint the need to change.
4. Be willing to pay the price.
5. Get the point of perspective.
6. "See" a new self.

We will discuss each of these in turn.

'Try On' Free Agency

When was the last time you heard someone say, "Sure I'm a big grouch until 10:00 a.m. But I'm a night person—that's just the way I am. I can't be cheerful early in the morning and my family will just have to accept that." Many of us excuse ourselves for our natural tendencies. But although every individual has definite tendencies which he may express in a positive or a negative way, any negative expression is part of the natural man and can be put off at will as we choose to put the spirit in control.

Wherefore, men are free according to the flesh;...And they are free to choose liberty and eternal life...or to choose captivity and death...

(2 Nephi 2:27)

"The most exciting, and at the same time the most uncomfortable feeling I've ever had was to reach the point where I accepted my own total free-agency," said one father. "I found I could no longer blame conditions, relatives, or the government for the flaws in my character, my problems, or my unhappiness. I was left without excuses and could no longer find a comfortable easy chair of rationalization and settle down to play the 'Poor Me' game. I finally had to admit that if I wasn't happy—it was *me* that needed to change—and I *could* change because I had my free agency."

By accepting our power to change our lives by changing ourselves, we begin to sense what freedom really means. We no longer feel "pushed around" by circumstances. It was Ben Franklin's philosophy that the world will start getting better when we make ourselves better and that we can change our own little world at will, because our positive influence spreads like ripples on a pond. It is important to remember that at any point in our lives we *can* choose to change. There is always hope. In fact, all that is best in us constantly urges us to reach up and grow and change. Because we have free agency, we have the power to change!

'Put Off' Procrastination

Procrastination is the greatest enemy to change; yet it is simply a habit which can be broken by *action.* One authority said that a sense of being overwhelmed is common to procrastinators because they constantly see a mountain of work before them and believe that all of it has equal priority. Some may see the changes they need to make in their homes as a whole army martialled against them, instead of single soldiers they can triumph over one at a time. But this sense of being overwhelmed can quickly be changed to a sense of progress by starting *now* where they are and doing one thing at a time to improve. We can form a new habit of starting a task as soon as we think of it (or whenever we've planned to do it); then we won't waste time worrying about the other things we need to do and whether one of them may be "More important". Some of us may need to try and "trick" ourselves into getting started by giving ourselves the

option of stopping in five minutes. But our most common difficulty is overcoming the inertia to start. Once we have started, we
usually feel a desire to continue and complete the job. The more
we do, the more we feel like doing.

Any positive action gives us a sense of progress and can
also cut a task down to size. (Another common trait of procrastinators is thinking a job is bigger and harder than it really is!)
One mother said, "One spring I procrastinated for weeks clearing
a flower bed of dead tiger lily stems thinking it would be a difficult, time-consuming job. When I finally tackled it, the stems
fell off to the touch and the entire job took only five minutes!
Similarly, I had an idea for a toothbrushing chart for the children,
complete with jingle bells to put on the toothbrushes and a little
rhyme to make it more fun. But for weeks I put off doing it, feeling I 'didn't have the time'. When I finally did it, it only took about
ten minutes!"

"DO IT NOW!" This motto can be one of our greatest helps
in overcoming procrastination and putting our plans into action.

Pinpoint the Need to Change

Claudia Black keeps a "crisis list" on her refrigerator. After
any kind of crisis or upset where she would like to avoid repeat
performances, she briefly notes the nature of the crisis, who
was involved, and what led up to it. At the end of the day, she
reviews the list and evaluates the cause of the problem and what
may need to be changed in order to keep it from happening again.
Claudia said that by focusing on, and identifying the need to
change, and looking for positive solutions, she has noticed real
progress. (Previously the same problem might happen over and
over and everyone would just feel frustrated about it.)

Another person said, "When I have a problem where I see
the need to change, I try to analyze what has happened and consciously decide how I will do better in similar situations in the
future; I 'see' myself acting in the better way. I think many times
we don't change because we don't know what else to do or don't
recognize the whole cycle that leads up to or triggers our bad
behavior. Once we can see this we can stop the cycle before
it begins!"

If we aren't aware of where a change is needed, we aren't
likely to make it! For this reason, keeping track of things can
be a real key to helping us improve our families. We begin to
have a sense of progress just by plotting and planning changes.

One mother we will call Pat, began feeling the need for some changes in her life. She wasn't feeling much satisfaction at the end of the day, so she knew she needed to take time for more of the things that really mattered to her. However, she had only a vague idea of where to start. She decided to make a list of all the things she felt would make her feel content and happy. These things she made into a check-list which she could quickly mark each night! The chart looked like this:

Time Priorities	Enjoyment	Progress in Self Mastery
____ God before all else (Prayer)	____ Sang at work	____ Exercise
____ Husband next	____ Sang with children	____ Scripture reading
____ Children—1 to 1 time	____ Played the piano	____ Journal entry
____ Human needs before other	____ Read uplifting things	____ Controlled anger
Thought of others:	____ Enjoyed nature's beauty	____ Morning routine
____ Thank-you's	____ Shared same with children	____ Noon routine
____ Birthday, occasion	____ Listened to music tapes	____ Evening routine
____ Phone calls	____ Read to children	____ Soft answers
____ Letters	____ Took a walk	____ Worked on file
____ Gifts	____ Explained something of worth	____ Other home improvements

By analyzing her check-list, she began to get a picture of the specific ways she needed to change her schedule. She began to plan time slots in her day to accomplish these extra things that made her feel alive and progressive; and her attitude toward her family and her life improved greatly!

One man said that the best way he ever found to pinpoint the ways he needed to change was to write his own epitaph and think of all the things he would like said about him—then compare those things with what he was really doing!

Be Willing to Pay the Price

"The key to perfection is taking one step at a time," Elwood Peterson said in a B.Y.U. Education Week class. "We can't grit our teeth and suddenly be something we're not. It takes time and lots of effort to change." He told the story of a boy who came to him for counseling and after he gave him some suggestions, the boy said, "Oh, I don't want to do all that. I just want you to tell me something so I will be different." Many times we would like the benefits without putting forth the effort required to get them! John A. Widtsoe said, "Decide what you want to be, pay the price, and be what you want to be." Paying the price is an eternal principle:

> There is a law, irrevocably decreed in heaven before the foundations of this world, upon which all blessings are predicated—
> And when we obtain any blessing from God, it is by obedience to that law upon which it is predicated.
>
> (D&C 130:20,21)

When we are working for improvements in our lives and our families, we need to be realistic about the price and our present ability to pay it. If we "discount" the price and make unrealistic commitments to ourselves, we will break them and feel discouraged. For example, if we are trying to avoid the problem of negative thinking, to say, "From this day on, I will never think another negative thought," is highly unrealistic and we would be committed to paying a price we are not capable of paying. But if we say, "Whenever I catch myself thinking some negative thought, I will immediately trade that thought for the words of a hymn," then we have made a realistic commitment that can be a great help in making the desired improvement.

Also, without recognizing it, we may rationalize to avoid the effort of changing. Have you ever been involved in a conversation that went something like this:

"Martha, I'm having such a hard time with my pre-schoolers during the day. I just can't seem to get anything done because of their messes, and their fights. Do you have any suggestions?

"Well, the thing that has helped me most is to show my children what I *do* want them to do and try to keep them busy with things that are constructive.

"Oh, yes I know, but, when I give David creative materials, he just eats them or messes them up, and Benji is just too little for that sort of thing.

"Well, let's see. Have you tried keeping most of their toys out of sight and just putting certain ones down each day so that they seem new to them?

"Yes, but I can't remember to rotate them. Anything I stick up in the closet just stays there and we get no good out of it. Oh, what am I going to do? I really am about at my wit's end!"

Many times, without realizing it, we can fall into the pattern of saying "yes, but" and making excuses in order to spare ourselves the effort of paying the price a solution might require! If we catch ourselves finding logical reasons why *not* to try new ideas or possible solutions, we should ask ourselves if they *are* reasons or only excuses.

Get the Point of Perspective

Change may be compared to rowing upstream. The rewards for the effort may be great, but they are not all immediate. On the other hand, drifting downstream requires no effort, and often delivers immediate pleasures and rewards; we can relax, quit trying so hard, and enjoy drifting with the tide. Sometimes the full realization of the consequence of drifting doesn't come until we reach a destination where we didn't want to go at all! So, striking out for a better goal upstream requires *perspective* in order to keep in mind where we are going and why it it worth the constant effort of all that rowing.

To help keep this perspective, we might make a list of all the possible benefits we could receive by making a change. If we focus on them, think how we would feel if we had already achieved them, and see ourselves living in the better way, the possible rewards will seem more real.

It is also effective to list the prices we pay by *not* changing. We might list things like lack of progress, poor self-esteem, damaged relationships, and miserable feelings of frustration and guilt. If we really *feel* how much we are hurting ourselves and others and remember we have the power to choose between the rewards of our first list or the pains of the second, we will be highly motivated to change.

Keeping goals clearly in mind also gives us courage to live with the realities and imperfections of the present. It's like putting up with an unfinished and poorly decorated kitchen during the time it takes to make it the way we want it. If we keep a clear picture in our minds of what it will be like when it is finished, that vision can keep us moving toward the goal!

'See' a New Self

"Now close your eyes and think back to the first time you can remember doing your self-defeating behavior," Dr. Jonathan Chamberlain was saying in a class on Eliminating Self-Defeating

Behavior. "Keep going back and back until you can't go back in your memory anymore." (Earlier Dr. Chamberlain, a counseling psychologist at B.Y.U., had told the class to pick one behavior they knew was not helping them in their lives, which they would like to rid themselves of.) One class member relates this experience: "I had picked my weakness of being 'quick-tempered'. Now, as I went back in my mind, it suddenly came to my awareness that the first time I could remember losing my temper was when I was fifteen years old! Not only that, but from then until I had several children I could only think of one or two other times when I had lost my temper. As I realized that for a good half of my life I had lost my temper only a few times, a feeling of great relief swept over me. I had been thinking of myself as a 'quick-tempered' person, and the label was a constant drain on my self-esteem. As I gained a new picture of myself as someone who had 'learned' an undesirable behavior, I had new hope. If I had 'learned' it, I could 'unlearn' it! Through this simple exercise, I was no longer chained to the false conclusion that I was 'that kind' of a person." She further explained, "Along with a new self-concept, Dr. Chamberlain also gave the class a positive direction by suggesting that we find a new 'label' for ourselves, to replace the old one we were discarding. Instead of 'quick-tempered', I began to think of myself as 'patient' and 'not easily provoked'. Each time in the following weeks when I was in a stressful situation, I would remind myself that I was a 'patient person' and that I didn't need to act the way I formerly had. I began to see immediate improvement in my own behavior, and my self-esteem rose in proportion.

"Dr. Chamberlain teaches that the labels we give ourselves, although they are just words, *do* make a difference, and that when we change what we tell ourselves (and repeat the new, positive labels often) in only about ten days the new and better seeds will take root and result in improvement in behavior."

One counselor suggests a similar technique he calls "Affirmations", another author calls this process "auto-suggestion". (Both explained in Chapter 12.) Each program is based on the same premise: our actions are influenced greatly by what we think of ourselves. If we can improve our self-concept, we will invariably improve our actions and our lives!

Set the Pattern

"My parents taught by example the importance of constant change and improvement," said Linda Garner. "They would never pretend to be perfect, but we knew they were trying to live the gospel in every way they could. When they became aware of something that needed to be changed, they discussed it with us, and we would all make a decision to work on it together. For example, our family used to be more casual in Sabbath Day observance than we are now. But at different times over the years, Dad called us together and said something like, 'Your mother and I have talked it over and we have decided it might be better if we made it a practice never to buy anything at all on Sundays. How do you children feel about this?' We discussed it, Dad explained the reasons, and we all decided to go along with it. In the same way we decided to quit watching T.V. and quit studying on Sundays. These changes I saw in our family helped me get the concept of progress and repentance. I began to understand that when you are doing something that is not the best (even though you've been doing it for years) when you recognize a better way, you don't continue the old pattern; you change! My respect for my parents was really increased as I saw them do this."

An exciting thing to remember during the family improvement process is that even negative situations and reverting back to old ways *can* be learning experiences. One mother told of a morning when they forgot scripture reading and prayer (everyone was grouchy and everything seemed to go wrong). By pointing out their forgetfulness and "starting the morning over right", the children were impressed with the difference scripture reading and prayer made in their day. As children see efforts to change and do better, a helpful concept of the growth process will be formed in their minds.

Give Creative Motivations!

For parents and children alike, *knowing* what you *should* do may be quite unrelated to being able to *do* it. It is only through being motivated to practice and experience new ways of behaving that children can generally change. Many parents told us of exciting ideas that have worked in their homes to motivate children to change and reach goals. The suggestions all have one thing in common: they are positive in nature. This is especially appropriate because the positive approach is stressed throughout this book.

Royce and Melba Flandro have found a fun and novel way to initiate needed changes. Every once in a while they have a

"Best Foot Forward Dinner." Melba makes a lot of "footprints" out of colored construction paper. She chooses one for each family member, and types their name on them along with a list of things she thinks they are doing very well, plus one thing she wants them to improve in. These footprints are placed at each person's place at the table. Melba says the children have responded very favorably to this approach, and it is a way of bringing about necessary changes and helping children reach their goals without causing bad feelings between parents and children.

When Linda Garner was in college, she and her roommates decided to have a weekly "Project Perfection". They hung a picture of a baby in a prominent place in their apartment, and underneath, posted the words, "I am a Child of God." Each week they chose a goal such as "Avoid all gossiping", or "Encourage instead of criticizing." They tried to focus on that goal during the week and evaluated their progress at the end of the week.

After Linda had little ones of her own, she decided that this would be a worthwhile project for their family. So whenever she notices an area of special need where she would really like to see some change or improvement, she initiates "Project Perfection" week with her children. They put the picture of the baby up and talk about what it means to be a child of God and how we should try to be like Him. Then she tells them the special goal she would like them to work on during the week, such as minding better, sharing, or not quarreling. She tells them that every time they look at the picture she wants them to remember what they are working on that week, and that the reason they are doing it is to become better children of God and more like Him.

Chart Their Progress!

Margaret Johansen uses a chart system to give her children goals and motivate them to improve. (It also gives her special incentive to notice and encourage progress!) If Trina (five) is quarrelling with her brother, Margaret might put on Trina's chart "Didn't quarrel with my little brother." Then each evening, she talks to Trina and analyzes how she has done. If she has improved, she gets to put a colored dot on her chart for that day. (She also gets lots of praise from mother.) Margaret also includes Trina's work responsibilities and little character-building things on the chart (such as "Do something special for a friend"). In addition to the praise and attention they get from the charts, they also get rewards.

Darla started an improvement program with her boys which she called their "Sure I Will" project. When her requests for help were met with reluctance she said, "Boys, whenever I ask you to do something and you say, 'Sure, Mom!' and do it quickly and cheerfully, we'll put a mark on your "Sure I Will" chart. Whenever you get one hundred marks, I'll take you to lunch, and you can decide where to go and order anything you'd like!" They were enthusiastic, and with a lot of attention for good efforts along the way, the boys made it to their goal in about a month—and repeated their success the next month. In the meantime, they formed a good habit of more positive responses to Mom's requests!

Arlene made posting charts which she called "self-image charts" and hung them in her dining room. Then she wrote favorable comments about each family member and posted them on the charts. She made a point to write one when someone did well in an area she wanted to encourage them to improve in. The children loved reading the comments about them, and when Arlene's college-age daughter, Loree came home, she joined in the fun and began adding her positive observations about her family.

Plans such as these can keep us one step ahead of the children, and usually result in more positive actions!

Principles, Patience and Progress

Since change is a step-by-step process, not an overnight transformation, we need to learn to be patient and compassionate with ourselves along the way and avoid comparing ourselves with others. Many people take new ideas and insights and use them as a measuring rod to make themselves look bad by comparison. (Oh, I feel so inadequate. I hate to hear about all those things I'm not doing. It makes me feel like a terrible person!)

New ideas and the good example of others can give us a vision of the *possible,* and can be the first step toward our own progress, if we realize that everyone faces his own challenges, and that the success we see in others was likely won through hard effort and lots of stumbling and climbing. If someone else has been able to do it—so can we!! We need to learn to enjoy the challenges of the change process; to smile and laugh at our mistakes and the inept way we might handle things when we are trying to do something new. We need to remember that the Lord understands. He is long-suffering and patient, and He *knows* we can grow out of our problems and fulfill our potential. Being patient with ourselves can help us keep perspective, and maintain a truth-seeking attitude. It can give us the courage to be actively honest in heart—to say "I want to know more truth so I can try to apply it." In reality, recognizing our weaknesses *can* lead us to our greatest source of strength.

> I give unto men weakness that they may be humble; and my grace is sufficient for all men that humble themselves before me; for if they humble themselves before me, and have faith in me, then will I make weak things become strong unto them.
>
> (Ether 12:27)

Anyone who has sensed his own weakness and tried to improve his life has probably experienced the frustration of trying to change by "will power" alone. A certain amount of progress is possible that way, but when our goals are celestial, we must realize that the changes we need to make to reach them are only possible through the Savior. He said, "I am the way, the truth, and the life; no man comes to the Father, but by me." Through his atonement, and his help, nothing is impossible. Paul said, "I can do all things through Christ which strengtheneth me." (Philippians 4:13) The gospel is a gospel of power to change man's nature, to replace bad habits with divine ones. This is the great gospel principle of being "Born again of the spirit." As we sense our need, ask for help and learn to rely on the Holy Ghost, he will lead us and strengthen us on a moment-to-moment basis. Through this process we *can* overcome the tendencies of the natural man through the power of Christ. As we develop a relationship with the Lord, we will feel His arms around us, and feel Him change our lives—then we will reach the goals the Lord wants us to reach!

Ten Things to Try

1. Post mottos such as "A day at a time you can do it. Don't see the mountain ahead of you. Just go as far as you can each day," and "Do it Now!"

2. Keep a "crisis list" on your refrigerator to help you evaluate changes you need to initiate in your family.

3. Make a check-list of all the daily activities that would give you the most satisfaction. After checking the list each night for a week, evaluate what changes you need to make in your schedule in order to include more of them.

4. Write your own epitaph, and include all the things you would like to have said about yourself; then work to close the gap between where you are and where you want to be.

5. Make realistic commitments to change—one step at a time!

6. Analyze the "yes, but" rationalization pattern. Give yourself a reward when you avoid it.

7. Make a list of all the benefits you might receive by making a desired change. To motivate progress, compare this list with an analysis of the prices you pay by not changing.

8. Try charts (such as "Sure I Will", "Self-Image" or Goal charts) to motivate children to improve, and to keep track of the progress.

9. Have a "Best Foot Forward" dinner for your family.

10. Start a "Project Perfection" week to help each family member progress toward a worthwhile goal.

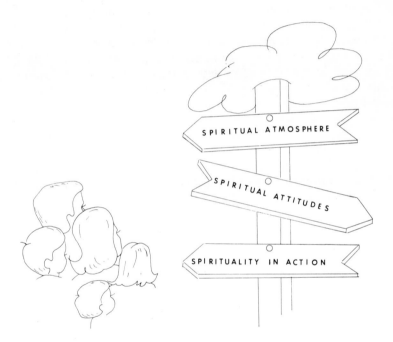

21

Spiritual Signposts

The Savior said, "Come Follow Me." Every effort we make to improve ourselves or our families helps us keep that commandment more fully. The Savior has given us guidance to know how to follow him in every area of our lives through his total church organization. We are counseled to make the gospel part of everything we do, and this approach was evident in the homes we visited.

Sharlene Tyler said, "Teaching the gospel to our children is more our whole approach to life than it is a set of techniques. I believe in giving my children reasons for living the gospel, but I also want to 'show them' by the way I live what the gospel is. I want them to know that the gospel is worth living and that we are choosing to live it—not doing it because we have to. I try to involve my children in my church callings and help them feel that those callings are a special part of our life. I let my little girl help make and deliver invitations to stake meetings, and I practice my lessons and stories by giving them to her. This way I teach her, and she doesn't even suspect she is being taught! I make my visual aids out of pellon, so that she can play with them (then I 'borrow' them for my stake meeting). I also try hard to be organized so that if the children are staying home with Daddy or a babysitter while I go to a meeting, I can have time to make a small treat or surprise to put under their pillows, or record a story in my own voice for them to listen to while I am gone. You don't need to have everything else done to take time for the thoughtful things. But I think they make a difference to a child's attitude about the gospel."

Helping our children feel good about the gospel is part of helping them gain a testimony, and is, as Sharlene said, accomplished by our whole approach to life. There seems to be three A's involved in this accomplishment—atmosphere, attitude, and action! As we try to follow the example of Jesus, the greatest leader, these three A's can give us some spiritual signposts along the way.

Signpost Number One: Create a Spiritual Atmosphere

1. Create a Spiritual Atmosphere in a Tangible Way: The first thing we noticed as we entered John and Carol Davis' home were the picture arrangements. On one wall there is a beautiful framed picture of Jesus. On another wall is an arrangement including a family picture, and on the third wall is a picture of President Spencer W. Kimball. In the attractive china closet there is a specially bound large white Bible. Carol says, "Our children know that this room is special, and that these are special people and objects. We have talked about it once or twice, but I don't think you have to say much. These are visual reminders of the values of our family. It is all part of an atmosphere we are working to create in our home."

Margaret and Trent Johansen said, "We have had some of our most spiritual home evenings in an atmosphere created with about twenty small decoupaged plaques of the Savior and His words. The lovely pictures of Jesus, and the spirit they give have been very impressive to the children. Whenever we have a lesson about the Savior, or any highly spiritual topic, we meet here where we can be influenced by the atmosphere created by these pictures."

2. *Create a Spiritual Atmosphere in an Intangible Way:* When President Christiansen married David and Rachel Mc-Omber in the Logan Temple, he gave them some suggestions which Rachel says have been great guidelines for creating a spiritual atmosphere in their home. She says, "After thirty years of marriage, I can see that the spirit we maintain in a home makes a difference in the attitude of the children toward their family and toward the gospel. Three guidelines President Christiansen gave us (plus scripture reading), invite a certain spirit into a home which can come no other way. They are:

1. Come back to the temple often.

2. Never forget prayer in your home and your lives.

3. Do not allow quarreling between yourselves or your children. (This is Satan's tool. When we have encountered this in other homes, we sense an unhappy feeling exists in the home.")

A spiritual atmosphere is quickly destroyed by criticism and contention in a home. Therefore, many parents felt this was a major issue to learn to deal with effectively. Janice Nisson said, "One practice which I feel especially helped our family was that my husband and I never allowed our children to fight and quarrel with each other. As a result, our home was usually quiet, peaceful, and harmonious."

Most parents find this idea a most difficult challenge, but have found various ways to work on the problem in order to improve the spirit in their homes. One family uses hot pepper on the tongue of any child who is guilty of "disturbing the peace" by name-calling or quarreling; other parents separate children who are bickering or arguing (sending each to a different bedroom to think of ways to solve their problem without quarreling). Still others have used the "standing in the corner" technique for any children who engage in verbal battles; others have deprived the child of privileges for disrupting the spirit of the home. Incentives and consequences can help parents achieve the goal of a harmonious atmosphere where the spirit of the Lord can stay.

3. Cleanliness and Orderliness. To create an atmosphere of peace in a home there must also be cleanliness and orderliness. A mother of a large family said she felt achieving the goal of an orderly house was a matter of attitude. She said, "With a large family I can either say, 'My house is a mess, but what can I expect with so many of us living here?' or I can say, 'I don't have any excuse for my house being a mess when there are so many of us to keep it straight.' " Regardless of the size of the family, we can have the attitude that "I don't have time (or energy, or know-how) to keep a clean house; or we can say, "I will learn how to manage my time (or use my energy, or learn what I need to know) to keep my house lovely so that it will be an appropriate setting for gospel living."

4. With Learning: Creating an atmosphere where learning is a natural part of life is another way to further family progress in gospel living. Learning is part of change and growth. Throughout this book there are many specific examples of what parents can do to encourage this atmosphere, but the single most effective method is to set the example of continuous interest in new ideas. Marilyn McOmber Skousen said, "We've noticed that our mother is always striving to learn. She is always reading and taking notes on what she has read. I think it is because of these new ideas she gets from her constant studying that our family has never been dull, and I'm sure this attitude has encouraged us to want to learn and improve, too."

Signpost Number Two: Maintain a Spiritual Attitude

1. Children are Blessings: "In my husband's patriarchal blessing he was told there were many choice spirits waiting to come to him who would be his companions," said Carol Jeanne Ehlers, "and the other day I came across some verses in the scriptures that really verified the fact that children are blessings, gifts from your Father in Heaven, (such as Psalm 128:3,4). Yet many people have expressed sympathy to us because we have twelve children. It reminds me of the prophecies which say the day will come when the world will say 'Blessed are the barren' (Luke 23:29) and because of the next verse we know this is definitely a sign of the last days. So I feel that to have a spiritual attitude in our home, we must begin by having the attitude that our children are blessings to us."

2. Children are Spirit Children of God who have Great Potential. Another attitude which has great spiritual implications is one of respect for our children because we sense who they are, and their potential as children of God. One family said, "We taught our children they were special sons and daughters of God, and so they live that way." Rex Stallings said, "When we recognize that our children are full-grown spirits who are merely in small bodies, we try to show them the respect they deserve. I believe we gain a better perspective of who they are by making a practice of looking into their eyes. As it says in the play *Saturday's Warrior,* 'There is endless promise in their eyes.' We very seldom look deeply into children's eyes, but I think that this helps a parent see who his child really is, and what he is capable of." Marion and Deanna Bentley also expressed this philosophy explaining further that they believe even though we knew this child in the spirit world, we are now going to have to become reacquainted with him not only by his actions; but by recognizing who he is as we look into his eyes (which are the windows to his spirit). When this recognition occurs, we can reflect our knowledge to him, and he in turn perceives who he is more fully because of what we see. The parent has a tremendous role to help the child discover the way to develop the potential we recognize. Deanna adds, "This involves goal-setting based on who they really are. If we all have a mission in this world, (and I believe that we do), then we should be seeking to know who we really are so we will be able to fulfill that mission, and be able to help our children fulfill their mission in life."

A father with many years of experience said, "A spiritual tone in the home all starts with the parent's attitude. The stronger your faith in the Lord, and in yourself, the more you have to offer your children. The more secure you are in your own world the better prepared you are to help them gain good feelings about their world, and then finally about the gospel."

3. The "Attitude of Gratitude" is one of the basic attitudes parents must teach to encourage gospel living in the home. If children are taught to be grateful, they will be more unselfish, more loving, and kind; and will be more willing to sacrifice for others. If we encourage children to show gratitude for their blessings, perhaps they can learn that happiness does not depend on having what they want, but rather on appreciating what they have. One mother exclaimed, "I want my children to learn that the scriptures tell us that we should always be 'returning thanks unto God for whatsoever things ye do receive' (Alma 7:23). I try to express gratitude not only in my prayers, but whenever I notice any small thing that makes life easier or more pleasant or which has helped me learn a lesson. I encourage my children to express their gratitude by asking them things like, 'Aren't we grateful (or happy, or glad) that Heavenly Father has given us noses, so that we can smell the delicious smell of food cooking? And aren't we glad he gave us the food!' "

Many parents mentioned that they felt children should work for the things they needed and wanted, and that this helps them to appreciate the things of this world. Giving a child too much without effort on his part seems to foster ingratitude.

Signpost Number Three: Put Spirituality into Action

1. Spiritual Goal-Setting: Goal-setting is the first step to action. The gospel gives us our long-range goals, but it takes daily action to reach them. Goal-setting can motivate action and can fill an important function in helping children grow to their potential. Some parents have used the conference talks to help them select family and personal goals (seeing them as the Lord's list of things they should be concentrating on). Patriarchal blessings and the temple endowments are other ways the Lord tells us what we should be doing and reveals our potential. Through them the Lord tells us our possibilities, and what we can become if we choose to set and reach the goals he has for us.

After each of their older children have received their patriarchal blessing, the Leo Giffords talk to them about what a great asset these blessings are. They help the children set goals using the blessings as a guide. They often review the patriarchal blessing with the child and talk about what he can do to bring his own promises about. The specific things he decides become important goals in his life. Leo and Katherine have told their children how their own blessings have helped them to set goals and make important decisions in their lives. When the family received the opportunity to go to Samoa to help with the church school system, there was no doubt about accepting because one of their blessings had mentioned they would be able to do much good in foreign lands. They welcomed this opportunity to achieve this goal.

Another young man (who just left on a mission) used his patriarchal blessing as a guide when he was searching for answers to his own questions of "Who am I?" and "What should I do with my life?" As a result, he is convinced that he is now doing exactly what the Lord wants him to do. He is leaving a sweetheart behind whom he realizes may not still be waiting when he returns. But he says, "As long as I know my goals are right, I can leave with complete peace of mind. Neither she nor I could be happy if I didn't carry out the goals the Lord has for me." He feels his patriarchal blessing will continue to be a guide for him as he makes other important decisions in his life.

2. *Service:* Jesus said, "Inasmuch as ye have done it unto one of the least of these my brethren, ye have done it unto me", (Matthew 25:40) and "Love thy neighbour as thyself". (Mark 12:31) These and many other scriptures tell us that service is "the gospel in capsule form". If this is true, perhaps we should give more attention to the priority we give to service.

It has been said that two of the sources of real joy in life are creating something and giving unselfish service. Because creating and serving are godly attributes, when we combine the two to do something worthwhile for someone else, perhaps the joy is greatest of all.

LaDawn Jacob believes that children should be taught that talents are given to us in order to help us serve others and make them happy. Whenever her children don't want to practice their music, she reminds them that it is a great privilege to have a talent and be able to develop it. They often talk together about the ways our talents can bless others.

"My mother had the attitude that the home is the place to learn the joy of service," said Joye Billings. "I was one of fifteen children, and I was taught the joy of giving and the joy of service in my home. When I became very ill, I believed for a time that I might have to leave my four children without a mother. I decided the thing that was most valuable in my life and that I most wanted to teach them was the joy of serving and helping others. So we began all sorts of fun projects that we have continued. We take baked goods to retired and elderly people in our area, and sing to them as we visit them. In the summer we share vegetables and flowers from our garden, and fruit from our trees. We also deliver uplifting or complimentary notes. We have worked together on many special service projects such as keeping one elderly widow supplied with firewood. I also teach my children that they are giving service when they give up some of my time and attention when I am needed by someone else."

A stake leader said, "The real essence of spiritual discipline is service which requires sacrifice of our time, convenience, and means." It is a law of this life that when we sacrifice for a person or cause we will learn to love them more.

3. *Priorities:* "What is lived by our parents is what we will live, what is condoned by our parents is what we will condone," said Mary Stewart. "We have to decide what is important to us, because if we say something is important, but we don't really feel it, that will come across to our children."

Deciding what is important to us sometimes gives us trouble. We may beleive that something is important and yet give it no priority in our lives. This is called doublemindedness, and this lack of integrity between our beliefs and actions causes conflict in our minds and hearts and lives. In order to make sure our values determine our time priorities, we must thoughtfully evaluate, plan, and choose. When we have learned to thoughtfully choose how we spend our time, we will begin to find time for the eternally important things. Picking priorities is like picking the first peaches of the season. We can either pick randomly and haphazardly without giving attention to the quality of the fruit, or we can pick carefully and find the most beautiful, well-shaped, unblemished fruit that will give the greatest satisfaction and value.

4. *Time to Teach and to Show Love:* "I think it is very important that parents spend time with their children," said Rachelle Safsten, college-age daughter of Robert and Mary Safsten. "My parents are everything to me. If they thought the church was true, then I felt it must have something for me to look into. If they did something, like going to church or paying tithing, and said, 'This is right for us, and this is right for you, too' I believed them because I trusted them. This trust developed during the time they spent with me. Even though I am one of eleven children, they found time for each of us. My mother is my very best friend. She didn't work, and she was always there when I needed her."

5. *Put Principles into Practice:* Our children do look to us and develop most of their values from the way that we live. Are we living the principles that we want our children to learn? Even though we may attend our meetings, keep the word of wisdom, pay our tithing, etc., if we fail to live the higher laws of love, kindness, compassion, or service, our children may not see the gospel as something which brings joy. If we are missing the joy ourselves, it is time to do some re-evaluating of our lives. A church leader recently said, "If you are not happier than you were a year ago, you are not keeping the commandments better

than you were a year ago. If you are keeping the commandments, you will be happy." When we set an example of happiness, we paint a true picture of gospel living for our children.

6. *Follow Jesus' Example:* Helen Sharp said, "The main thing I want to teach my children (and it sounds simple, but is a real challenge) is to treat each other the way the Savior would treat us. If they learn this in our home, when they have families of their own they will be able to treat them that same way. When I get upset, I think, 'Now, Helen, what would Jesus do if he were here?' and that is one of the main motivating forces in my life. I think how we treat each other in our home is so important because we are teaching our children what the gospel is. We can teach the principles of love (accepting people for what they are) and forgiveness or we can teach the opposite by our actions." Darlene Hurst said, "If we say to our children when they are being unkind, 'If the Savior were in your place right now, what do you think he would do?' It really makes them think, and improves the feeling tone immediately. I'm sure it affects the way I treat them, also."

Summary Findings

After analyzing the findings from nearly one-hundred interviews with Latter-day Saint families, we were able to observe a very noticeable pattern emerging. Since this might indeed indicate a "success pattern", we have organized our findings into some "signposts" which are worth noting.

Signpost #1: *Gospel-Centered Traditions:* It is significant to us that 100% of the families we visited held regular home evenings, family prayer at least once a day, went to church meetings together as a family, and were regular scripture readers. It appeared that the mother supported and encouraged the father in his leadership role, but the mother in nearly every case organized and carried through special projects and ideas.

Signpost #2: *Family Togetherness:* These families without exception believed in teaching their children to work, and most of them planned and set goals together and worked to carry out the goals as family projects. All were progress-oriented and were frequently looking for new ideas. Family togetherness (trips, outings, projects, picnics, activites) was stressed and valued as important.

Signpost #3: *Time Alone with One:* An outstanding trait of every family was their belief that each child deserved some individual time with Mother and Father. They arranged for this time in many different ways in order to help each child to feel loved and important regardless of the size of the family.

Each of these signposts is especially significant because they either lead us to the Savior or help us, as families, to follow His example. Following the Greatest Leader is, in our opinion, the only true measure of a successful family, and the goal which each Latter-day Saint family should seek.

Index

A

Accomplishment Chart, 248
Action
  goal-setting motivates, 330
Activities
  "Idea Bank" for, 164
  provide positive, for children,
  164, 165
Affirmations, 178, 318
Allen, Dantzelle Lewis, 29, 171, 235
Andersen, Dwayne, 211
Andersen, Peggy, 211, 225
Andersen, Shirley, 41, 74, 146, 301
Andersen, Verlan, 301
Ashton, Marvin J., 57
Approval
  as a part of discipline, 239
Atmosphere
  creating a spiritual, 326-328
Attitude
  creating a spiritual, 328-330
  of gratitude, 329

B

Barnes, Arlene, 88, 103, 197
Bedtime Routine, 298
Bentley, Deanna, 329
Bentley, Marian, 329
Best-Foot Forward Dinner, 320
Birthday Traditions, 120-121
Billings, Joye, 51, 52, 71, 85, 102, 111,
  121, 126, 197, 258, 303, 331
Billings, Terah, 71, 126, 303
Black, Claudia, 68, 128, 159, 160, 191,
  252, 253, 314
Black, Dean, 128, 160, 191, 252, 253
Black Family Buck Plan, 253
Blackburn, Clyda, 163
Book of Remembrance, 74, 175, 177
Bosch, Margaret, 172, 173
Bowen, Walter, 190
Bradshaw, Lillian, 256, 260
Brimhall, Greg, 204
Brimhall, Lynnette, 204, 262, 263
Brimhall, Willis, 204, 262, 263
Buck, Deanna, 170, 194, 195
Buck, George, 170, 194
Burgoyne, Charles, 96

Burgoyne, Mary Lou, 89, 96
Burton, Alma, 28, 29, 111
Burton, Clea, 19, 28, 29, 111, 118
Burton, Janice, 38, 53, 95, 141, 142,
  145, 238, 256, 260
Burton, Robert C., 95

C

Capener, Annette, 96, 269
Chamberlain, Jonathan, 317, 318
Change
  recognizing need to, 314-317
  in family patterns, 310
  overcoming obstacles to, 311
  place to start, 312, 321
  confidence to, 312
  accept power to, 312, 313
  focus on benefits of, 317
  motivation to, 317, 319-321
  step-by-step, 311-321
  to overcome discouragement, 181
  check list for, 315
  possible through the Savior, 322
  contract for mutual, in
  marriage, 285-287
  acceptance helps others to, 287-288
  can only, self, 288
Charts
  miscellaneous, 315, 320
  crisis list, 314
  "Sure I Will", 321
  self-image, 62-63, 321
  time-use, 141, 142
  accomplishment, 248
  job, 254, 255
Chastity
  plan for teaching, 211-225
  script for special, book, 217, 225
Choices
  time-investment, 300
  in time-use, 139, 140
  in jobs, 259, 260
  rewards and consequences of,
  242, 243
  responsibility for, 241
Chores and children, 247-263
Christiansen, Elaine, 79, 119, 170, 259
Christiansen, Elvin, 19, 52, 119,
  170, 267

Christmas traditions, 128-135
Circumstances
  controlling, 139, 140, 223-225, 313
Clock
  timing jobs with, 140, 141
  look at, with satisfaction, 140
  "Beat the," home evening, 151, 152
  "Be Kind to the" week, 152
  "Who's Afraid of the Big Bad, " 152
Communication
  love, skills, 48-50
  in marriage, 289-291, 294
  in problem-solving, 270-272
Conflict
  solving, between children, 274-277
  solving, in marriage, 285-287
Consistency, 312
  new definition of, 236
Contention
  spiritual atmosphere destroyed
  by, 327
Countdown to Christmas, 135-137
Covey, Stephen, 45, 55, 83, 150
Covey, Sandra, 112
Criticism
  negative effect of, 26, 285, 327
  cure for, 27
  praise more effective than, 27
  covers up love, 47
  expression of inner dissatisfaction, 57
  in marriage, 285, 287

D

"Daddy Days", 23
Davies, Bill, 27
Davis, Carol, 39, 64, 103, 255, 326
Davis, John, 103, 326
Deadlines, 148, 149
Delegation, 144, 145
Despain, Deanne, 99, 105, 112,
  304, 305
Despain, Roy, 94, 99, 105, 112,
  304, 305
Discipline
  definition of, 228
  respect in, 228, 229
  positive reinforcement in, 238, 239
  and relationships, 243, 244
Discouragement
  overcoming, 177-184, 312

dangers of, 176, 177
"Do It Now", 314
Dunn, Paul H., 18
Dunnigan, Rehan, 230

E

Eddington, Delbert, 24, 97, 123, 301
Eddington, Vera, 97, 101, 105, 131,
  247, 248
Edison, Thomas A., 192
Edwards, Kay, 149
Ehlers, Carol Jeanne, 34, 37, 39, 72,
  82, 148, 157, 174, 328
Ehlers, John, 174
Ellsworth, Betty, 82, 83, 114, 119, 120,
  160, 179, 182, 188, 254, 259
Ellsworth, Richard, 114, 119, 120, 160
"Enabling experiences", 69-71
Evans, Charles, 19, 28, 102, 103,
  106, 130
Evans, Connie, 101, 102, 103, 130, 171
Evans, Helena, 39, 43, 77, 120, 228,
  232, 241, 250, 259, 269, 275
Evans, Oman, 120, 122, 131
Evaluate
  plans, 306
  need to change, 314, 315
  time-use, 141
Example
  of the Savior, 188, 326, 333, 334
  of others, 321
  of parents, 146, 151, 197-198, 241,
  318-319
  of our Heavenly Parent, 228
  of church leaders and teachers, 191
  of living relatives, 196-197
  of ancestors, 194-196
Excellence
  encouraging children to seek,
  187-199
Exercise, 205, 312
Expectations
  Lords, of us, 229
  clear, 229, 230, 234, 235

F

Facts of life
  plan to teach, 211-225
Faith
  building children's, 170-175

exemplified by children, 169-170
share your, 172, 173
how to activate, 180
Family
    "Emergency Plan", 65
    goal-setting, 300-304, 310
    outing day, 306
    putting, first 21, 39, 42
    prayers, 112, 207, 310
    success pattern, 333
    success principles, 298
    togetherness, 333
    vacations, 117-119
    training sessions, 158
Family Councils, 301, 302
    for problem-solving 277-279
    democratic approach to, 280
    patriarchal approach to, 280
Family Home Evening, 28, 73, 99-100,
    106, 113-117, 123, 129, 193, 194, 205,
    206, 209, 251, 253, 301, 305, 333
    "Beat the Clock", 151
    traditions, 112-117
Fathers, 17-31
    as spiritual leaders, 28
    blessings, 28, 29
    influence of personal life of, 30,
    197, 198
    programs honoring, 41-42
Flandro, Melba, 118, 123, 126, 256,
    319, 320
Flandro, Royce, 319
Franklin, Benjamin, 193, 313
    character developing plan of, 193
Free-Agency, 312-313
    in time-use, 140, 152
    in work, 259-260
    to make mistakes, 239-242

G

Garner, Linda, 29, 42, 53, 56, 64, 97,
    105, 111, 118, 166, 173, 192, 233,
    235, 236, 248, 249, 318, 320
Garner, Marshall, 29, 64, 105, 111,
    166, 236
Gifford, Leo, 26, 51, 112, 115, 129,
    302, 330
Gifford, Katherine, 51, 112, 115, 129,
    258, 302, 330
Goals
    five steps to reach, 299

helping children set, 303-305
for missionary service, 202-203
Goal-Setting, 297-307
    as a family, 300-304
    for the new year, 303
    for summer activities, 303-304
    to overcome discouragement, 180
    spiritual, 330
    approach to interviews, 24
    motivates, wise time-use, 298
Gospel Teaching
    as a whole approach to life, 325-326
Greatness, 187-199
    in living relatives, 196-198
    of church leaders, 191
    of ancestors, 194-196
    motivating children to, 187-199
    stories to motivate, 191-196
Gregersen, Darlene, 51, 276
Griffin, Glen, 23
Griffiths, Kenneth A., 234, 235

H

Habit, 311
    aid to reaching goals, 311
    overcoming bad, patterns, 311
    of procrastination, 313
    building the responsibility, 248-263
Happiness insurance policy, 157
Heiner, Calvin, 95, 102, 273
Heiner, Ruth, 54, 95
Hendry, Gil & Kathy, 132
Hilton, Wanda, 211, 212
Holiday Traditions
    Labor Day, 125
    4th of July, 126
    Easter, 126
    Halloween, 126
    Thanksgiving, 126-128
    food as a, 128
    Christmas, 128-137
Holy Ghost, 57, 85, 176, 177
    help of, 57
    seek and recognize promptings of,
    85-87
    companionship and guidance of, 89
    rely on, 322
Home Evening-see Family
    Home Evening
Hoole, Daryl, 67, 147, 150
Hougaard, Lucene, 55, 67, 72, 266

Housekeeping
  tips for efficient, 37-39
Hurst, Darlene, 204, 333
Hurst, Linden, 28, 79, 175, 240

I

Incentives
  to work, 255-259
Interviews, 24
  questions to ask in, 25, 65-66
  goal-setting approach to, 24
  as follow-through for
  goal-setting, 303

J

Jacob, Jim, 42
Jacob, LaDawn, 41, 43, 63, 103, 150,
  159, 275, 280, 331
Jardine, Winnifred C., 49
Jesus
  as example of greatness, 263
  follow example of, 325, 333-334
Jobs
  timing, 140
  high priority, 147-148
  organize, according to
  importance, 148
  let children choose their
  own, 259-260
Job-Card System, 252
Johansen, Margaret, 22, 98, 128,
  320, 327
Johansen, Trent, 22, 128, 327
Johnson, Lucille, 46-48, 55, 309, 310
Jones, Thelma, 25, 51, 116, 170,
  172, 269
Jones, Veldon, 25, 116

K

Keller, Helen, 194
Kimball, Spencer W., 190, 326
Krzymowski, Kent, 158, 160, 254
Krzymowski, Marlene, 160, 254

L

Larsen, Arland, 30, 234
Larsen, Fern, 234

Larsen, Bob& Carolyn, 65-66,
  277, 306
Larsen, Bob & Mina, 132
Leadership
  spiritual, 28, 291-292
  financial, 292
Learning
  creating an atmosphere of, 328
  experiences, 159-162
Lee, Betty Lou, 150
Lewis, Malin, 29, 98, 118, 122, 251-252
Lewis, Myreel, 22, 98, 122, 251-252
Limits
  setting, for children's behavior,
  232-233
Love
  must be expressed, 46
  ways to express, 48-54
  ways to increase ability to, 57-58
  communicate, by giving time, 51, 66

M

Mackay, Floy Dawn, 261-262
Mackay, Ian, 261-262
Mackay, Rosemary, 203
Marriage, 283-295
  takes work, 285
  looking for good in, partner, 288, 290
  removing areas of friction in, 286-287
  acceptance attitude in, 287
  communication in, 289-290, 294
  differences in needs in, 289-290
  spiritual submission of wife in, 291
  husbands spiritual leadership in, 291
  husbands financial leadership in,
  292-293
Marshall, Barbara, 26, 83, 194
Marshall, Don, 26, 83, 194
Maughan, Connie, 270
McFarland, Faye, 80, 266, 272
McOmber, David, 30, 327
McOmber, Rachel, 71, 79, 81, 84, 114,
  302, 327
Minutes
  double-duty, 145-146
  making, count 146-147
Mishap Margin, 149
Mission Preparation
  encouraging, 201-202
  financial, 204
  physical, 204-205

social, 205-206
spiritual, 206-207
scriptural, 207-208
miscellaneous tips for, 208-210
Money
for chores, 260-263
teaching children to manage,
260-263
Moore, Julia, 67, 159, 174, 180, 272
Moore, Walter, 67, 159, 174, 327
Morality
teaching, to children, 211-225
Moss, Audra Call, 69-70
Motherhood
many poorly prepared for, 34
rewards of, 42-43
Motivations
to change, 304-305, 317-321
Mottos, 178, 312, 314

N

Nelson, Beverly, 54
New Years Goal-Setting, 303
Nisson, Bob, 297
Nisson, Janice, 327
Norton, Velma, 64

O

One-to-One time, 22-25, 65-69, 145,
332, 333
questions to ask during, 65-66, 77-78
Organization, 144, 302
planning calendar, notebook, 302
time, 139-153
job, 147-148
Orgill, Jean, 22, 230, 239

P

Pace, Diane, 175
Pace, George, 80, 89, 181, 280
Parcell, EvaDean, 197
Patriarchal Blessings, 180
as a guide to goal-setting, 330
as a guide to decision-making, 330
Patience
with ourselves, 143, 321
with children, 247-255
Paying the Price, 315
to be a good father, 20-21

to be a good mother, 35-36
is eternal principle, 316
be realistic about, 316
for blessings desire, 181-182
Payne, Jaynann Morgan, 36
Pearson, Carol Lynn, 166
Perspective, 298, 306, 317
in time-use, 143
Petersen, Mark E., 301
Peterson, Elwood, 239, 315
Pinegar, Colleen, 43, 68, 122, 305, 234
Pinegar, James, 122, 305
Plain, Carolyn, 172, 184, 279
Planning, 303
calendar, notebook, 302
time-use, 143, 147-151
Plans
revamp, 143
time, 143, 147-151
children's, 151
evaluate, 306
Porcaro, Jean, 65-66, 73, 113-114,
130, 234, 254, 303
Porcaro, Robert, 65-66, 73, 113-114,
130, 234, 259, 303
Positive activites for children, 164-165
Positive approach to parenthood,
155-168
defined, 156
power of, 157
Positive approach to change, 319
Positive approach to discipline,
238-239
Praise
re-inforces good behavior, 27
more effective than criticism, 27
Prayer, 35, 77-91, 250
family, 83-84, 112, 310
to increase ability to love, 58
understand power of, 77-78
questions to direct child's, 79
scripture to teach, 80
sharing, experiences, 80
helping our children through, 82-83
to solve problems, 279-280
Principles
for success, 298, 333
Priorities, 332
time, 36-37, 140-144, 147, 150
Problem-solving, 265-281
what would you do if? method
of, 272

by listening, 267-269
by communicating, 270-272
pointers, 272-274
by humor, 274, 286
as husband and wife, 277
as a family, 277-279
Procrastination, 313
habit broken by action, 313-314
with a plan, 144
Programs
honoring father, 41-42
Progress, 298, 313-315
spiritual price of, 35
first step of, 312, 321
"Project Perfection", 320
Promptings of Holy Ghost
how to identify, 86
as warnings, 88-89
"Punch Card" job assignment
plan, 253

Q

Quarreling
discouraging, in the home,
274-277, 327
Satan's tool, 327

R

Reilley, Frank, 277, 304
Reilley, Karen, 52-53, 73, 80, 171, 192,
250, 251, 256, 266, 271, 277, 304
Relationships
discipline and, 243-244
Respect
in discipline, 228, 237
for developmental stage, 231
for feelings, 237-243
Responsibility
to increase self-esteem, 72
teaching, 247-263
sharing, 250
Richins, Judy, 20, 55, 83, 95, 190, 197
Richins, Ross, 20, 23, 29, 46, 55, 83,
86, 95, 190, 242
Riley, Herb, 117, 131
Riley, Virginia, 117, 131, 177
Rosen, Marlene, 147
Routine
importance of, 235
Rules

in teaching time management, 151
clear, and expectations, 229-233

S

Sabbath-Day
traditions, 111-112
projects, 112
training for church meetings, 166
observance, 319
Safsten, Mary, 117, 163, 254-255, 332
Safsten, Rachelle, 111, 117, 332
Safsten, Robert G., 117, 332
Schedules
secret to make, work, 143
Scoresby, Lynn, 72, 162, 239, 249,
276-277
Scripture games, 105-106
Scripture tapes and records, 104, 145
Scripture of the week, 102
Scriptures
to build faith, 175
to teach greatness, 188
to prepare children for missions,
207-208
Scripture-Reading, 35, 57, 151, 312
should begin at home, 94
special family, times, 94-107
creative approach to, 99-104
Self-Defeating behavior
eliminating, 317-318
Self Discipline, 312
in time-use, 144, 148, 150
help children gain, 150, 152
Self-esteem
positive labels help, 62-63, 317-318
attention & approval raises, 64-65
one-to-one time builds, 65-68
share skills to increase, 69
service develops, 71-73
self-mastery increases, 73
building righteousness builds, 74
related to time-use, 145
Self-image
charts, 62-63, 321
positive experiences helps, 69-71
Service, 331
as an aid to self-esteem, 71-72
as an antidote for depression, 180
Sharp, Helen, 46, 79, 81, 84, 87, 111,
129, 179, 229, 275, 280, 333
Sill, Sterling, 249

Skousen, Marilyn McOmber, 30, 115,
  238, 240, 328
Smith, Joseph, 189, 194
Smith, Joseph F., 240
Snow, Eliza R., 190
Sorenson, Mollie H., 57
"Special-Time Box", 81
Stallings, Barbara, 243, 274, 310
Stallings, Rex, 24, 30, 240, 243, 265,
  273-274, 329
Stewart, Doug, 65
Stewart, Mary, 332
Success pattern for family, 333-334
Successful living, 150-151
Sunday-see Sabbath-Day

                 T

Teaching Moments
  building faith during, 170-172
  to inspire greatness, 192
Television, 144
  homework before, 151
  family, code, 278
  on Sundays, 319
Thanksgiving, 126-128
Time
  one-to-one, 22-25, 65-69, 332-333
  balancing demands on, 36-37, 142
  priorities, 36-37, 143-144, 149
  for individual interests, 37, 41, 145
  give children your, 51, 332
  as an asset, 139
  using snatches of, 146-147
  cushion, 149
  learning to be on, 149
Time Limits
  for jobs, 148-149
  for children's work, 151
  for goals, 299
Time-Management, 139-153
  first step of, 140
  tips, 147-150
  teaching, to children 151-152
Time-use
  keeping a record of, 141-142
  keys, 142-145
  double-duty, 145-146
To-do List, 147-148
Traditions
  definition of, 110
  value of, 110

Sunday, 111-112
  family home evening, 112-117
  family vacation, 117-119
  Green Thumb party, 119
  Last Fling picnic, 119
  Saturday outing, 119
  morning, hymn, 120
  birthday, 120-121
  of weekly family newsletter, 122
  of yearly family testimony
    meeting, 122
  with married children, 122-123
  holiday, 125-138
  of teaching chastity, 211-225
  gospel-centered, 333
Tyler, Sharlene, 33, 177, 326

                 U

Ursenbach, Bernice, 81, 171, 176,
  234, 268-270
Ursenbach, Wayne, 121, 125, 130

                 V

Vacations, 117-119
  planning, 118

                 W

Whiting, Gayle, 164
"Whose Turn Wheel", 66
Widtsoe, John A., 90, 316
Wise, Gayla, 68, 87-88, 198, 257
Wise, Joe, 280
Wolfgramm, Joella, 71, 170, 275, 303
Wolfgramm, Louie, 303
Woodford, Narda, 164-165, 250
Work
  before play, 151
  as discipline, 233
  importance of, 248-250
  incentives & motivations to, 252-259
  making, fun, 253-254
  rewards of, 256-257
Wright, Mary, 43, 72, 140, 173,
  197, 280

                 Y

Young, Brigham, 189
Young, S. Dilworth, 97